FIREFIGHT

FIREFIGHT

THE CENTURY-LONG BATTLE TO
INTEGRATE NEW YORK'S BRAVEST

GINGER ADAMS OTIS

palgrave
macmillan

In memory of John Ruffins,
1923–2015,
an FDNY Captain, proud Vulcan member,
loving father and husband,
skilled historian, generous mentor to many,
and a dedicated public servant.

FIREFIGHT
Copyright © Ginger Adams Otis, 2015.

First published in 2015 by PALGRAVE MACMILLAN® TRADE
in the United States—a division of St. Martin's Press LLC, 175 Fifth
Avenue, New York, NY 10010.

Palgrave® and Macmillan® are registered trademarks in the United
States, the United Kingdom, Europe and other countries.

ISBN: 978-1-137-28001-5

Library of Congress Cataloging-in-Publication Data

Otis, Ginger Adams.
   Firefight : the century-long battle to integrate New York's Bravest /
Ginger Adams Otis.
 pages cm
   1. African American fire fighters—New York (State)—New York—
History. 2. Fire departments—New York (State)—New York—
History. 3. Discrimination in employment—New York (State)—New
York—History. 4. New York (N.Y.)—Race relations. I. Title.
TH9505.N5O85 2015
363.37089'0097471—dc23
                                              2014041818

Design by Letra Libre, Inc.

First edition: May 2015

10 9 8 7 6 5 4 3 2 1

Printed in the United States of America.

CONTENTS

PROLOGUE

ALL FIRED UP

East Harlem
February 2012

FDNY CAPTAIN PAUL WASHINGTON JERKED HIS MINIVAN TO A HALT ON EAST 123rd Street near Second Avenue to find a line of impatient students waiting for him. There was just enough light in the settling dusk for him to see annoyed expressions on the 30 or so faces that stared his way as he jumped out. It was 7:45 p.m., and he was late to set up for his own class. He should have been in East Harlem about 30 minutes ago, but traffic from his Brooklyn firehouse delayed him. Washington pushed his rimless glasses a little higher on his nose and turned to the black firefighter who drove in with him from Engine 234.

"Can you find a place to park? I'm going to grab this stuff and head downstairs," Washington said, hefting a couple of boxes full of tutorial workbooks. Inside the Taino Towers, a huge housing complex in the center of Spanish Harlem, colloquially called El Barrio, six more firefighters waited for him. Like him, they were all members of the Vulcan Society, the official fraternal organization for blacks who made it into the FDNY. He hurried everyone a flight below into the basement room the Vulcans had rented for the night. Something about the line of students outside nagged at him. In the few seconds he'd been able to look them over, Washington caught a glimpse of a cluster of whites in the back. That alone wasn't unusual. A few always showed up at the Vulcan classes, even though everyone knew the tutorials were primarily meant for black kids studying to become firefighters. But tonight that brief glance wedged itself into his head, probably because of the e-mail he received earlier warning him that some whites were planning to crash his classes. It had come from a fellow FDNY officer, one of the heads of the Uniformed Fire Officers Association, the union that represented the rank of lieutenant and above. The officer wasn't a supporter of the Vulcans' cause, but he felt honor-bound to let Washington know something was brewing.

"I don't like to see anyone blindsided," the officer wrote.

Washington wondered what the night might bring. He motioned to the Vulcans with him to set up the check-in point while he got busy unfolding chairs. By the look of it, they'd need at least 200. If some white guys wanted to attend his class, let them come, he decided. His tall, narrow frame moved in a relaxed rhythm as he worked. A buzz of anticipation fueled him. In his nearly 25 years in the FDNY, he'd tutored hundreds, if not thousands, of black and brown kids who wanted to become firefighters—all on his own time. He'd lectured, heckled, encouraged and drilled them on the best way to gain entry to the fire department and start a career that everyone—in the FDNY at least—agreed was the best job in the world. The key to joining the select fraternity—and it was a fraternity, even with a handful of women in the ranks—was to score well on the FDNY's written entrance exam. Given only once every four years on average, that written test was the first hurdle to overcome to get a coveted firefighting job.

"It's not enough to just pass," Washington would drill into his students' heads. "You have to score in the top 10 percent to have a real chance."

The competition was fierce—and Washington fully understood why. Aside from the honor and prestige that came with being a member of the city's beloved FDNY, the average firefighter stood to earn more than $100,000 within five years of joining the agency. And that was just the first step on the pay ladder. By the time firefighters climbed a few rungs up the promotional chain, they could pull down at least $140,000—not including overtime, and there was plenty of that. Then there was the unlimited paid sick leave, the five weeks of paid vacation, the very generous retirement pension and—the ultimate public employee benefit—the tax-free, three-quarters pay, disability pension awarded to Bravest who got hurt on the job. And, to top it all, firefighters only worked two 24-hour shifts every eight days. It was a career filled with daunting, exhausting challenges, often enduring killer heat and haze, sometimes rescuing people in car crashes, helping heart attack victims, people trapped in elevators, or responding to stabbings or shootings. Fires could mean exploring filthy basements or hallways on hands and knees in pitch black smoke, slogging up seemingly endless flights of stairs in the increasingly vertical city, with as much as 70 pounds of gear on your back—and always with the possibility that the job could take a firefighter's life. But nobody could deny the city rewarded its firefighters handsomely.

Given all that, there were usually at least 20,000 applicants every time the FDNY cycled into a hiring phase—vying for 2,500 spots at most. It was easier to get a gig with Google than the FDNY. Washington and the Vulcans did everything they could to prepare their students, and still, time and time again, the FDNY exam results rolled in with just a smattering of blacks in real contention. For the entirety of Washington's career, there'd only been about 300 blacks on a force of about 11,000. That was roughly 3 percent. It was pitiful for a city of 8.2 million, where blacks made up approximately 26 percent of the population.

And for the entire 150-year history of the FDNY, there had never been more than about 650 blacks on the job at once—about 7 percent. That brief pinnacle came in the late 1970s, thanks to a court order that forced the FDNY to hire one black or Latino firefighter for every three whites. That order lasted for four years. The minute it expired, the city went back to pulling applicants in ranked order from its list of candidates. The number of black firefighters once again drifted downward.

But this class was about changing that. These students, blacks and Latinos, were intended to be part of the first class to enter the FDNY since the Vulcan Society filed a discrimination lawsuit against the department in 2007. And by the end of 2013, another 300 or so minority candidates would get to take the FDNY exam. Some of them would be well past the usual cutoff age of 29—a few might even be over 40. Washington called them his second-chance candidates, blacks and Latinos who'd taken the FDNY tests in 1999 and 2002 and didn't get hired. Some started the process but were knocked out by background checks or other FDNY criteria. Some scored above the cutoff mark of 70 but were too far out of the upper percentile to ever have a chance. Soon they'd all have a shot at trying again, thanks to the controversial ruling by a Brooklyn judge in favor of the Vulcan Society's lawsuit.

The Vulcans had forced a reluctant city and the FDNY to overhaul hiring procedures, some of which were over a century old. It had been a bitter, brutal, decade-long battle, but Washington and the Vulcans had prevailed—in the courthouse, at least, Washington reminded himself. He hadn't won many hearts and minds in the firehouses to his cause. He knew he was persona non grata among the majority of white firefighters and among many of the high-ranking chiefs at FDNY headquarters too.

Washington signaled to a black firefighter to open the door. The room filled up, mostly with young men, but Washington also counted about eight women. He took that as a good sign. Maybe word about his lawsuit and the FDNY hiring changes was starting to spread, he thought. Many of his students came to class straight from a day job. He saw FedEx and UPS uniforms, greasy mechanic jackets, dust-covered work boots and tool belts carried straight from construction sites, even a Starbucks shirt as people straggled in. Without a doubt, some would be asleep before the two-hour class ended.

Outside, one flight above Washington's head, FDNY Deputy Chief Paul Mannix cut through busy Third Avenue and wheeled his black Saturn into an empty parking spot in front of one of the ugliest firehouses in the city—a short, squat, cement building called Heaven in Harlem. It hardly seemed celestial, at least from the outside. Two stories high and nearly an entire block long, it presented a strip of uninterrupted brown cement. Aside from the traditional bright red doors, the firehouse that held Engine 35 and Ladder 14 was as unappealing as the corner it sat on.

The name would have seemed like a joke to anyone outside the FDNY, but most of the Bravest working that area knew it had come from late Battalion Chief Fred Scheffold. Scheffold had loved his command at Engine 35/Ladder 14, headquarters of the 12th Battalion. He'd answered the phones with a cheery "Heaven in Harlem" and made sure that was the message recorded on the firehouse answering machines. Scheffold and his fellow Battalion Chief Joseph

Marchbanks had died directing civilians out of Tower Two on 9/11. As Mannix got out of his car in the darkening light, the names of both men were just visible on the street signs above him bracketing the firehouse.

This visit to the neighborhood was a little bit like a homecoming for Mannix. He'd fallen hard for historic Harlem, gritty and enticing in equal parts, when he was a young cop assigned to the 28th Precinct in 1985. He'd only had two years on the force then and he could still remember the first time he'd stood on Lenox Avenue at the corner of 116th Street, staring straight into the bright green foliage of Central Park six blocks to the south. The street was so broad and beautifully structured it almost looked like a boulevard in Paris, if you ignored the junkies and drunks and the trash littering the sidewalks back then.

Three decades later, brownstones he remembered as burnedout hellholes were going for upward of $2 million. Even the most notorious section of Harlem along 116th Street and Frederick Douglass Boulevard, the former epicenter of Harlem's heroin trade, was cleaned up and almost pristine.

125th Street and Third Avenue—close to the Harlem River, which separates the working-class neighborhood of East Harlem from the Bronx—didn't have all that going for it yet. This section of East Harlem, a mostly Puerto Rican and Mexican enclave, still had the rough flavor he remembered from his days as a rookie cop. He'd walked a beat that was noisy and chaotic, just like they'd said it would be in the police academy.

He counted himself lucky to have gotten a partner he knew well, a kid who'd grown up alongside him in an Irish-Italian section of Queens. The two white cops patrolled together, keeping an eye on the johns and drug dealers while trying to create some rapport with local businesses and home owners. Mannix had liked the energy and movement that section of the city had, the warmth and working-class camaraderie that clung to a few street corners even after the drugs moved in. He had missed it after he left the NYPD to become a firefighter. Many cops, like Mannix, sat for both the NYPD and FDNY exams. They'd start out policing and switch to firefighting when the opportunity came, and at that time the city let them bring their accrued pension with them when they moved. Mannix might have stayed a cop, but the agency—struggling with its own diversity challenge from black cops—started messing with the exam he'd taken to become sergeant. Promotions were delayed, and then delayed again. Mannix took the FDNY entrance exam in the early 1980s, passing both the written and physical tests with high scores. By the time his hiring number came up at the fire department in 1988, he was ready to move on.

The FDNY had brought him up to the Bronx, and he'd been happy there. Life had been easier, in a lot of ways. He'd been much closer to the Long Island home he eventually bought with his wife, and firefighting was different than policing. Just as dangerous, and just as demanding, but at least he wasn't tangling—most of the time—with the local drunks.

He felt some of the long-ago liveliness from his NYPD days stirring around him as he took in the mostly commercial street near Heaven in Harlem. He raised his hand and knocked on the small side door to the firehouse.

"OK to park here?" he asked, tilting his head toward one of the officers who'd come toward the door. He recognized a couple of the guys at the house and he greeted them with handshakes.

"How long you think you'll be, Chief? We got some guys coming in later who will need a spot," the officer asked, as he rolled up the bright red doors to the firehouse's main bay. He snapped on the overhead fluorescent lights, and the two polished fire engines gleamed like angry dragons. The gigantic tower ladder had been donated to the firehouse by residents of Tennessee following 9/11.

"Not long. I'm just going down the street to go to a Vulcan tutoring class. I have a relative who wants to get on the job. So I thought I'd go see what their tutoring class is like. It's a free country," Mannix said. He was already familiar with the Vulcans' training materials. For the last two FDNY hiring cycles, their tutorial classes had been far better than any of the others he'd heard about.

A couple of firefighters nodded. They knew Mannix headed up Merit Matters, a group of firefighters who saw no need for the Vulcan Society's discrimination lawsuit. Mannix liked to remind everyone that Merit Matters was not the white guys group. He had black, Latino, Asian and female members too. It was also not an antidiversity group, he insisted, but rather an organization dedicated to preserving the city's civil service hiring system and promoting equal treatment—not special treatment. Merit Matters liked to hand out dark blue T-shirts with a paragraph from the FDNY's equal employment opportunity office emblazoned across the back: "The Fire Department is firmly committed to fair employment practices for its employees and applicants and ensuring that employment decisions are made without regard to . . . color . . . gender . . . race . . . religion . . ."

Some other firefighters, mainly Latino and Asian, who opposed the Vulcan Society's efforts had their own shirts too. Their logo was MADD—Minorities Against Dumbing Down.

Mannix stepped beyond the firehouse and made his way down Third Avenue, ignoring the occasional curious look thrown his way. Some other white applicants were pulling up in front of the firehouse in their cars, also headed to the Vulcans' training, he knew. He didn't hang around to wait for them. He wanted to make sure he got inside to claim a seat. A short block away, his destination dominated the darkening sky.

Down the street, the black firefighter who drove into East Harlem with Paul Washington from their Brooklyn firehouse was still circling Taino Towers, battling rush hour traffic in the hunt for parking. As the clock ticked closer to 8 p.m., he gave up. Somewhere nearby was a firehouse, he knew, called Heaven in Harlem. He would try there. It was part of the firefighting code to allow a fellow member the courtesy of empty parking spaces, even if they didn't work at that particular house. He edged the minivan northward.

"What the hell is this?" he said. A group of about 20 young men, all white, were milling around in front of the firehouse. The firefighter put his foot on the brake as he rolled past. He considered lowering the window to wave over one of the firefighters standing by the door, observing all the activity. But as his eyes swept the small lot, he saw every vacant spot at the firehouse was taken. He let the van drift along the street, watching in the rearview mirror as the group gradually turned and went south. They were walking calmly in a single file down Third Avenue to 123rd Street. They were headed toward Taino Towers, he realized.

I wonder if Paul knows they're coming, he thought.

Inside the basement, Washington was just about ready for the candidates who had been filtering in, their voices rising to fill the low-ceilinged room. His mind wandered as he set up the computer, flickering to the memories of black firefighters he'd met when he came on the job in the 1980s. Most were already retired, and soon he would be too. Hopefully he was about to meet the next wave, those who could step up and replace the black legends like Kirk Coy, who lived a few blocks away from Taino Towers. Coy had enjoyed an almost storybook career, the type any firefighter would be blessed to have. The burly smoke eater had joined the FDNY in 1982 on his own initiative. Nobody had ever encouraged the young Brooklynite to be a firefighter. But after he'd graduated from high school and started looking around for serious employment, he'd somehow known it was the ideal life for him. He'd scored in the top 5 percent of test takers in 1982, which put him at number 1,774 on the FDNY's hiring list. It took nearly six years for him to get selected, but the excitement started the minute he walked into his new assignment, Engine 5 in the grungy underworld known as Alphabet City. His company covered the forgotten and abandoned avenues along the dangerous fringe of Manhattan's East Village. The men he joined in Engine 5 had an intimate knowledge of all the abandoned, rotting shells inhabited by squatters in a five-block radius, frequent targets of police raids and late-night fires. Coy was the only black man in the tight-knit company of 30 guys, but he solidified his reputation early on as a hard worker, even before he got any action in a fire. If there were dishes in the sink, Coy was the first one there. When it was time for committee work, the daily tasks of cleaning and preparing the firehouse, Coy did double the chores of everyone else, as every good junior man was expected to do. He established himself so well in his first few weeks that when he screwed up his schedule and missed a day of work, the whole company held its breath out of fear his punishment would be harsh. He was only a few months into his first year, which meant he was still a probie.

Coy feared he'd be fired, so much so his mouth felt dry as he walked into the small firehouse the day after his missed shift. Everyone was waiting for Engine 5's commanding officer to lower the boom. Captain Jack Boyle, round, squat and bald with a cigar forever in his mouth, had joined the fire department the year Coy was born. He liked to remind his young probie that he had 28 years of experience to Coy's none. Boyle was so old school he refused to use most of the new equipment the FDNY shipped in, including the air tanks and breathing apparatus that helped keep firefighters alive.

"Any man who wears a mask is half a man," Boyle was fond of telling his crew. He went in with nothing, like the smoke eaters of decades past. Privately, Coy thought of him as a cross between W. C. Fields and Archie Bunker, both for his looks and his old-fashioned attitudes. But there was no denying Boyle lived for the job, and he loved his crew with the same devoted protectiveness he likely would have given his children, if he'd had any. Boyle and Coy hadn't had any problems in the probie's first few months on the job, but now that Coy had messed up, he was on tenterhooks to find out if the captain would can him.

He didn't have to wait long. Boyle's voice crackled through the firehouse PA system, ordering Coy to his office. As he took the stairs to the second floor, Coy heard the firefighters rushing to the kitchen. The acoustics in there were best for eavesdropping on the captain's snug lair. Coy knew they would hear every word that was said.

Boyle was waiting for him, his round face screwed into angry disapproval, chewing furiously at his cigar. Coy lowered himself into the chair in front of his desk. The captain waved a hand, inviting him to speak.

"Captain, I just messed up. I thought it was my day off. I misread the schedule," the nervous probie said. Boyle pulled his cigar out of his mouth.

"You know you owe a day to the man who covered for you," he snapped. Coy nodded.

"And I'm going to dock your pay," the captain added. The probie said he understood. He took a breath as relief washed over him. He wasn't going to be fired. But Boyle wasn't done with him yet.

"You know, I got a lotta assholes in this house, but I never considered you one," Boyle said, leaning forward to glare at him. Coy nodded again.

"This is a good job for a white man, but a great job for a black man. It's better than picking cotton," the captain said. Distantly, down in the kitchen, Coy heard the other men explode.

"Did he just say that?" one firefighter exclaimed.

Boyle dismissed him. Coy ran down the stairs to join the other men.

"Are you gonna report that?" one of the firefighters demanded. "You don't have to take that. You should call headquarters, or the Vulcan Society. If you don't do it, I will."

That was the last thing Coy wanted. He'd understood what Boyle had been trying to say. It was no secret to him that a black man had to work twice as hard to get ahead. He didn't have a problem with plain talk as long as he was treated with respect.

"No man, please. Let's drop this. I don't want to drag it out and honestly, I'm just glad I still have my job," he said. The men grumbled, unhappy about it for the rest of the day. Coy was touched by their reactions. He took it as a sign he'd been accepted into the all-white crew.

Not long after, he got his first fire. The back of a tenement building near Tompkins Square Park had blown up, and the whole first floor was in flames. Engine 5 roared up, and an officer from the nearby ladder company who'd popped into the inferno just as quickly popped back out.

"Captain, the entire first floor is fully engaged. Are you sure you want your probie on this?" the officer asked, looking to where Coy stood, gripping the hose in his fists. He'd been waiting months for a chance to be the lead on the hose, the nozzle man, and take his crew into a fire.

Boyle threw him a dismissive glance. "Take the knob," he said to an older firefighter next to Coy, gesturing toward the metal hose tip. Instead, the firefighter turned to the probie.

"You want this?" he asked.

"Hell yeah," Coy said.

"Then let's go."

Boyle studied the men for an instant and then let Coy charge ahead. He followed right behind in a tight huddle as the leading officer, giving Coy instructions as needed. For 20 minutes, the company fought their way through the burning rooms. Coy had never seen a fire like that, eating up the walls and the ceiling until he was gasping in a cavern of flame. The adrenaline rush was so intense he didn't even realize he singed his ears beneath the flaps of his helmet until much later when the fire was extinguished. The men hauled him out that night for some "Atta Boy" drinks, and it had taken Coy longer to recover from the hangover than any of the residual effects of the fire. It was a great start to a dedicated career that only ended

Firefighter Kirk Coy after he saved the life of a man hit by a cab, East Village, New York, 1992. Copyright © NY Daily News.

when an injury sidelined him in 2007. Now retired, Coy was still a Vulcan, committed to bringing more black firefighters on the job.

Caught up in his own thoughts, Washington was startled when one of his Vulcans leaned over to whisper in his ear.

"Captain, we have company," he heard. Washington's eyes widened at the long line of men stretching up the staircase, all the way to the front door. There were no longer just a few white kids signing in for his class. There were dozens. And standing in line with them was one man Washington never expected to see in a New York City housing project unless it was in flames: FDNY Deputy Chief Paul Mannix. The firefighter recruits on the stairs fell into an awkward quiet. At the door, Washington's black firefighters continued to check people in, taking their names one at a time and ticking them off their attendance lists. If Mannix felt any discomfort as Washington looked him up and down, he gave no sign of it.

Washington's mouth drew into a grim line. He knew his views were considered radical—incendiary even—by many firefighters. He'd fought ire and scorn from just about everybody in the fire department. Even a few black firefighters had approached him to express their disagreement with his discrimination lawsuit. But nobody had ever dogged him with the intensity of Mannix.

In 20 years, the two men had only spoken a few times. They didn't meet in person until around 2005, when Mannix walked up to Washington in a Queens firehouse and introduced himself. They already knew each other by name—they'd been trading opinions in the press about firehouse diversity for years. Washington shook Mannix's hand, and then turned away to talk to another firefighter. The nonchalant snub had taken some time to register. Mannix stood a few seconds before he took the hint and walked away. After that, they ran into each other at a departmental meeting on diversity. They'd also bumped into each other at a hospital, where they had both gone to visit two injured firefighters, one of whom happened to be Washington's older brother. The two men disliked each other but in many ways were mirror images of each other—although neither one would acknowledge it.

Mannix liked to say that he grew up on "Irish welfare," an old-school expression for Irish Americans who'd worked their way into the middle class off solid public-sector jobs. All four of his grandparents came from Ireland, and one grandfather had been determined to get in the FDNY. Mannix's father was a cop and his mother a teacher, and he'd never for a second considered anything but a blue-collar union job for himself.

Washington was a second-generation firefighter whose father was one of a small group of black World War II vets who'd leveraged their way into the FDNY off their military service. Like Mannix's family, Washington's father had been keen to capitalize on the generous benefits and salary that firefighting offered. With that job, he'd solidified his hold on a secure middle-class life on Staten Island for his family.

Both Mannix and Washington were strong and fit at 48. Washington didn't have Mannix's weight lifter's solid build, but his wiry frame had its own power, developed over a decade of martial-arts training. When he was a probie, he'd won some challenges against firefighters who dared him to haul himself up the firehouse pole using just his hands.

Each man was intractable when he believed he was right—and that's where their similarities ended. For Washington, that meant doing whatever was necessary to force the FDNY to remove the barriers that kept blacks from joining the department in significant numbers. It started with the written exam, which the Vulcans argued had been unfairly keeping out qualified blacks for generations. It wasn't because the test questions were biased, or the subject matter too difficult. The problem was the way the city hired based on the scores. Only those with the very highest results got the job—yet there was no indication a higher grade translated into a better firefighter out in the field, and plenty of blacks were left out of contention. Then there were the blacks who got past the test, only to run into the tightly woven friends-and-family network that dominated the rest of the department. That network helped determine who got the best assignments, whose minor transgressions got overlooked, even who got which position on firehouse tours. Try as they might, blacks couldn't penetrate it.

For Mannix, doing what was right meant no exceptions for anyone based on gender or race, and no court-imposed quotas that dictated FDNY hiring. Washington stared across the auditorium at the ruddy-haired deputy chief and felt a hot flush of fury. He was sick of Mannix's constant harping about special treatment, and his regular diatribes about the dangers of allowing unqualified candidates on the job. His complaining hadn't done anything to derail Washington's lawsuit, but he'd made life immeasurably harder for lots of blacks trying to get along in all-white firehouses.

"I can't believe that motherfucker is here," Washington snapped.

The deputy chief outranked him and outweighed him, but Washington no longer cared. He took a few long strides to plant himself right in front of Mannix, even as a small part of his brain registered that a FDNY captain really shouldn't get into a physical altercation with a deputy chief—especially with an audience of about 200 potential recruits looking on. If he lost his cool, he'd be fired and likely lose his benefits, not to mention the civil service pension he was hoping to enjoy one day. Too many people would be happy to see both him and Mannix go—probably even Mayor Michael Bloomberg. Washington brushed the distracting thought aside as he came face-to-face with the other officer. Mannix met his direct stare with one of his own.

"You can't be here," Washington said in his raspy voice.

"You can't kick me out. I have every right to be here," Mannix answered.

"No, you don't. This is private property and we rented it for the night," said Washington. "You gotta go."

"This is a class about FDNY business, and it's an extension of the workplace. You can't tell me to leave, I have a right to be here," Mannix insisted, not backing down. His relaxed pose was gone.

"This is a class for people who want to become firefighters, not for people who are already on the job," Washington said, and he took a small step closer to Mannix. They stared directly at each other, with a shared contempt.

"I can tell you to leave, and I am telling you to leave. You gotta go," Washington repeated. There was a moment of thick silence when neither man moved.

"Alright, fine. I'll leave," Mannix said, to Washington's surprise. The deputy chief turned away, already going over in his head the wording of the complaint against the Vulcans he might file with the fire department.

Washington watched Mannix march stiffly up the stairs, brushing past the line of students still waiting to get in. He was surprised the deputy chief had shown up, but even more so that he left. Whatever Mannix came there for, he didn't get it. But ultimately, Mannix and his protests didn't matter to Washington. The Vulcans had taken on City Hall and the FDNY and won. The courts had spoken, and it was in their favor. Black and Latino firefighters were going to come on the FDNY in record numbers starting as early as 2013, and there was nothing anybody could do to stop it.

Similar things had happened in other cities, like Baltimore, Boston, Chicago and Philadelphia. The federal Department of Justice had sued Chicago in the 1970s because its fire department was less than 5 percent black in a city where African Americans made up 33 percent of the population. Two decades later, the Chicago Fire Department was nearly 45 percent black and the NAACP was on the cusp of a major victory in *Lewis v. Chicago*—its long-running discrimination challenge to an entry-level firefighter exam in 1995. In Baltimore, black firefighters had just petitioned the Justice Department to step in on their behalf, claiming widespread racial discrimination in hiring and promotion practices for officer positions. Boston was notorious for its diversity challenges in the 1970s, when minorities made up 1 percent of its fire department. At the time, in a city of roughly 640,000, blacks were 16 percent of the population. Thirty years later, blacks held 30 percent of the firefighting jobs in Boston, even though challenges remained in getting blacks into high-ranking spots. In Philadelphia, courts imposed a 12 percent quota on black hires in the 1970s—a time when blacks were only 3 percent of the department but 34 percent of the population. The quota was effective despite white opposition; blacks reached 24 percent a few decades later, while Latinos and women hovered at 4 and 1.3 percent, respectively.

The only holdout to the march of progress so far had been the FDNY. The second-largest firefighter force in the world next to Tokyo, the FDNY considered itself a forerunner in everything, except, as its detractors pointed out, in diversity.

Washington turned back to his classroom. He'd always known the legal victory was just one part of the war. Now the real battles would begin inside the firehouses. Life would never be the same for the tight-knit world that for more than 150 years had been almost exclusively white and male. Black firefighters had faced bigger odds and won, he reminded himself. There was a time when there had been just one black man on the entire force. Whatever exile Washington faced today, it was nothing compared to what New York's Bravest had done a century ago to the black firefighters who came before him.

CHAPTER 1

INTO THE FLAMES

818 East 223rd Street, Bronx, New York
January 10, 1919

"WHEN WILL YOU BE ABLE TO COME HOME AGAIN?"

His wife's question floated over Wesley Williams's broad back as he bent down to tie his thick black work boots. He yanked hard on the laces, pulling them through their holes with unusual vigor. He wanted them neat and flat against the soft tongue, the leather a snug clasp around his ankles. Straightening up, he shook out his pants. The rough navy cloth was baggy around his thick legs, making him look even stockier. His soft cotton shirt, a plain dark blue, hugged his barrel chest. He hoped the cheap material didn't rip when he got busy in the firehouse—and he anticipated a lot of strenuous work on his first day. At five feet nine and packed with 180 pounds of compact muscle on a bulky frame, he didn't exactly fit the standard-issue size. The fire department mandated that all new recruits show up in a work uniform made of specific material and in a precise style, but the men had to pay for it themselves. The only contribution the fire department made was to send a list of tailors who were authorized to do the work. Williams's tailor had thrown up his hands when he saw the young man's beefy proportions—a direct contrast to the meagerness of his purse. At least the pants were nice and loose, Williams observed. They fell in crisp lines from his waist, where a pair of new suspenders traveled in white vertical lines over his shoulders, then crisscrossed down his back.

He had not an ounce of fat on him for all his girth. He swam daily laps at the colored YMCA and greeted each morning with enthusiastic calisthenics. Williams turned to Peggy, who stood wrapped in a faded bathrobe next to the door. She'd already straightened their bed, hiding the threadbare sheets under a hand-made coverlet. It gave the plain room a homey feel, along with the creaking of the old steam radiator that insulated their boxy Bronx apartment from the bitter January cold.

Once he stepped out his front door, Williams would be virtu-ally unreachable at his firehouse downtown. Nobody knew what awaited him there, and he could see concern etched on his young wife's face. Peggy had stayed up half the night making sure the pleats in his pants were sharp as could be and his shirt didn't have one wayward wrinkle. He'd heard her clanking the stove in the kitchen of their two-bedroom railroad flat to heat the iron wedge she used to smooth out his uniform.

"Peggy, love, we talked about this," Williams said. "I won't be able to get back for at least 15 days. But I'll be all right. Let's go see the boys."

He took her hand as they moved through the predawn darkness of the apartment, down the narrow hallway that separated their bedroom from that of their two boys. James was almost three, and Charles was nearly two. If the history of his short marriage was any guide, it wouldn't be long before pretty Peggy, barely past 20, gave him another child. A spasm of worry gripped Williams as he stepped through the half-open door to stare down at his sons. They lay tumbled across the small bed they shared. He smoothed their warm foreheads, bending to press a kiss to each.

"I'll be back soon," he whispered.

Giving Peggy a final hug good-bye, Williams shrugged on his heavy wool coat and muffler. It was almost 6 a.m., and he had to step lively to make it to the nearby subway stop and get all the way downtown for 8 a.m. roll call in his firehouse. It was only a few blocks to the 225th Street station where he could catch the White Plains Road subway line that ran on an elevated track through the Bronx and into Manhattan, but Williams was leaving noth-ing to chance. He hurried down his building's narrow staircase to the front door, carrying a small satchel stuffed with clothes and the assignment papers that told him when and where to report for duty: Engine 55, 363 Broome Street, the heart of Little Italy. A probationary firefighter—especially one with so many eyes on him— could not afford to be late, ever.

Williams rounded the corner and heard the rattle of the approaching subway. Bounding up the steps, ticket already stashed in the pocket of his greatcoat, he claimed one of the wicker seats by the window. He'd timed the trip down to Broome Street in Little Italy twice in the past week, and knew he had nothing to do for the next 45 minutes while the train shimmied its way into Manhattan.

A million things raced through his mind, but uppermost was his concern for his family. One part of him hated that he was embarking on a dicey new career with two small kids and a wife dependent on him. If he got hurt or killed, his boys and Peggy, a nervous, anxious woman, would be left on their own. Just the thought of it made him squirm in his seat. But if he could survive, well . . . all things were possible, even a new apartment in Harlem, right in the thick of the striving black class in New York. The job of firefighter held the allure of glory, but Williams was happy to settle for a steady paycheck that was better than anything he'd ever earned before. At 21, he was already a seasoned worker who had been supporting his wife since they married at 16. He and Peggy were native New Yorkers, and they'd come of age in a flourishing and expanding city. Shaking off the economic doldrums that had ended the Gilded Age in the 1890s, New York was roaring back. Williams grew up amid a time of unparalleled growth in urban projects and planning, all of which required labor—preferably cheap. New York's black population was exploding as well, buoyed by the Great Migration that carried poor laborers into northeastern cities like Boston, Chicago, Philadelphia and Baltimore. In the early days of the twentieth century, more blacks were looking for work in New York than at any time in the city's history, and their eyes fell on the opportunities created by government projects. From his earliest days as a young schoolboy in Harlem, Williams's teachers exalted the benefits of getting a good city job.

"You must never get arrested," his teacher had drilled into his head during his six years of grammar school, which was all the formal education he got. She'd chattered at him for many tedious hours after school, and her favorite topic was the importance of staying out of trouble with the law so he could get a civil service job. As a lefty, he was kept behind almost daily to force his cramping right hand to carefully copy the essays she set out for him. It was a vain attempt to change his natural left-handedness. But Williams heeded her instructions well, and while some of his friends wound up in more dangerous enterprises, as soon as he completed his basic education he signed up to work as a Sandhog digging subway tunnels. He might have stayed in the job, forever working in underground passages darker than night, returning home exhausted and grimy, except for two things: his father demanded he quit every time there was a dynamite-induced collapse, and they weren't infrequent; and a black man, Sam Battle, had somehow managed to join the New York City Police Department when Williams was 13 years old.

"Big Sam," a six-foot-three black man from North Carolina, was sworn into the NYPD on March 6, 1911, and it was a day Williams never forgot. The news spread far and wide through the black newspapers that a "race man" cracked the mostly Irish police ranks. Sam J. Battle, 28 years old, had turned into an overnight folk hero. It didn't matter to anyone in Williams's world that Battle was immediately assigned to patrol the blacks in San Juan Hill, known today as Lincoln Center. Back then it was still the heart of black Manhattan, although a shift northward into Harlem was slowly occurring. Williams read all about Battle's historic breakthrough in the black papers, and he heard his teachers sing Battle's praises, and he knew Battle, a close family friend. And at the San Juan Hill YMCA, Williams listened to all kinds of tales about Big Sam and his exploits on the job. Williams had always pegged himself for a city worker, like the black laborers who were the ditch diggers for subways, the blasters for tunnels, the men who built railways, and the porters who staffed them. But Battle had broken the mold and survived. There was nothing like the misery of digging ditches to make Williams look at the city's uniformed positions—higher-paid and, in the eyes of many, more prestigious—and wonder why he couldn't break through too.

It wasn't until after the FDNY selected him that Williams discovered he wasn't the first Negro to join the fire department—even though all the black newspapers declared him so. The news came in the form of a letter sent to his Bronx home. His name and address were clearly written out in block capitals, with the return address in the upper corner: John H. Woodson, PO Box 145, Jamaica, New York. Williams didn't know anybody named Woodson, but he dutifully opened it. He'd had all kinds of well-wishers writing him since his appointment. News had traveled fast, and he'd been reported on in black newspapers in Chicago, Boston, Philadelphia and even on the West Coast. Many of the friends and family and strangers who wrote to congratulate him included clippings of the newspaper and magazine articles that heralded his accomplishment.

Woodson's note, however, contained a surprise. It informed Williams that at least one other black man had come before him—and it was John H. Woodson himself. In fact, Woodson was still an active-duty firefighter in Queens. As he careened downtown on his train, Woodson's words jumped through his mind.

"You'll find quite a lot of jealous and narrow minded men," the unknown black smoke eater had written.

The life of a "race man" who had to sleep and eat alongside white firemen in the firehouse was not an easy one, Woodson said. He wrote that he decided to reach out after he heard of Williams's appointment in the *Weekly Defender,* the most widely read black newspaper in the country. Published in Chicago, the *Weekly Defender* excoriated the Jim Crow racism of the South and urged blacks to head northward. The paper offered tantalizing descriptions of a better life amid the factories and dance halls and theaters of the northern cities. It ignored the darker underbelly of exploited workers and strains of racism that existed there too—topics Woodson hinted at in his unsolicited words of advice.

"Do your work and do it as near perfect as you can, [and] do everything the commanding officers tell you to do, no matter what it might be, do it. Don't force your friendship on anybody and if there is an argument don't join them; just say 'I'm neutral.' If they speak of our race before you, in your presence, as niggers, pay no attention—go and do something or take a newspaper and read," Woodson wrote.

He concluded with optimistic "best wishes" for his fellow race man, but the letter had left Williams with a touch of anxiety. In 1919, the fire department was one of the most celebrated city agencies in New York. Its members were ordinary men who became larger than life when they were tearing through neighborhoods and hurling themselves inside raging infernos to haul out helpless citizens. They rode chugging engines, a few of which were still pulled by horses, with perpetual soot streaks across their beat-up faces and often with a dog at their feet. They commanded respect in most parts of the fire-prone city. Certainly, for the black population, they were a more welcome sight than their brothers in blue, the NYPD.

The police department had yet to be forgiven for its role in the 1900 Tenderloin Riots—not even the appointment of Sam Battle eased the bitter memories of most old-timers. For three days in August, in the middle of a sticky, miserable heat wave, the mostly Irish cops declared war on the black neighborhood. The disaster started when a plainclothes cop wrongly accused a black woman of soliciting on a popular corner of the seedy entertainment district—known today as Chelsea. When her boyfriend showed up, he saw a white man harassing his girlfriend. Not knowing the man was a cop, a fight broke out. The cop was knifed twice and died the next day, setting off a wave of brutality that stretched across the city. Whites attacked blacks, the black population armed themselves and fought back, and the cops stood back and did nothing, or used the fights as a pretext to engage in their own violent street assaults. Innocent black store owners and barkeeps were hauled into jail. When the smoke cleared three days later, scores of blacks had been beaten and arrested on trumped-up charges. Progressive groups clamored for a full investigation. When the results came six months later, the city found the NYPD guilty of no wrongdoing, and black resentment ran deep.

Yet to say race relations were better with the fire department was not to say they were good—or that the city was ready to welcome a black man into the ranks of its heroes. In 1903, not long after the Tenderloin Riots, New York was gripped by the Darktown Brigade sensation. For days the city talked of little else, and the incident—a mixture of humorous and horrific to New York whites—made the *New York Times*. It all started with a fire in a Paterson, New Jersey restaurant that was very in vogue with well-heeled diners. The small blaze that broke out inside W. F. Garnar's that hot September night was hardly noteworthy in itself. It was the group of black men who rushed in to extinguish it that caused the uproar.

"Black Firemen Cause Panic: Women Faint and Men Prepare for Defense," wrote the *Times,* describing pandemonium when "patrons . . . saw a crowd of black men come rushing in with axes and pikes and other apparatus of firemen." Female diners, decked out in their finest attire, threw screaming fits and fell into terrified swoons as the men tore through the room in a frantic effort to tamp out the flames. The male diners, spurred to chivalry as their women dropped like flies, shouted and yelled, brandishing the delicate dining knives from their tables and thrusting their chairs to push back what they saw as a gang of marauding Negroes.

The chaos only abated when the black firefighters, grown hot and sweaty from their exertions, began to wipe their faces— revealing white skin. The screaming patrons finally realized they'd been rescued by a group of off-duty Irish firefighters who dubbed themselves the Darktown Brigade. Decked out in blackface, the white firefighters had been performing a minstrel show at a popular carnival when the flames broke out. Without pausing to consider the effect of their costumes, they sprang into action—and the ensuing panic eventually gave way to even greater hilarity. All of white New York laughed at the spontaneous trick played on W. F. Garnar's wealthy patrons, and probably even some of the city's blacks were amused by it. But it underscored a larger reality that wasn't lost on the young black men constantly prowling the city looking for work: the idea of a Negro firefighter was both laughable and terrifying. Fifteen years later, Williams could only hope things had changed.

He stood as his train neared Grand Central Terminal, a place as familiar to him as his Bronx apartment. He'd spent countless hours there since the Vanderbilt family had it built in 1913, watching his father work inside the cavernous structure whose ornate facade loomed over a teeming intersection of commuter and railway lines.

His father, James Williams, was already at work. His dad was the king of the Red Caps, the baggage handlers who supervised the transfer of luggage in and around bustling Grand Central Terminal and also at Penn Station. From underneath the serene, sky-blue domed ceiling, studded with twinkling constellations, his father was the fixed point for all the scampering porters. The hum of a thousand voices bounced off the high walls, pierced by the shouts of announcers as trains pulled in and pulled out.

To most hurried commuters, James Williams was just another bag handler, a personable, hardworking older black man who'd reached the top of a humble profession. But to the black community in Harlem, where he lived, the older Williams was a commanding, sought-after figure. He doled out summer jobs to the right sort of young men—the ones that hungered for a chance to work and thrive, and maybe even go to college. He'd even given a job to a young Sam Battle. His square-jawed face, dominated by wide brown eyes and a generous, easy smile, was often the last thing the city's elite saw when they chugged out of New York, and the first thing to greet them when they returned. It was understood that Williams would personally escort the Rockefellers, the Vanderbilts, the Goulds and the Morgans when they arrived at the station. His august figure was also a welcome sight to the likes of Mayor John F. Hylan, known as "Honest John," as well as four-time Democratic governor of New York Al Smith, and even the archbishop of the Catholic archdiocese. Theodore Roosevelt, a frequent train traveler, bellowed out a hearty "Jim!" anytime he arrived at Grand Central Terminal and embraced the dignified Red Cap. Social climbing families vied to be seen traversing the slick marble floors accompanied by Williams, who never lifted bags himself, but oversaw their transfer with old-fashioned gentility.

His father would be anxious for news on how his first day went, Wesley Williams thought as the train slid into the busy 42nd Street station for a moment, and then with a clang of closing doors continued downtown. If James Williams got any information from his son over the next few days he would be able to carry it home to Peggy, couching it in some appropriately optimistic way. It would be a relief to Williams to let his worried wife know he was doing all right, but it was unlikely he'd have a chance to leave the confines of Little Italy anytime soon. Firefighters worked 151 hours a week— a round-the-clock schedule that meant they slept, ate and labored alongside each other continuously. Most of the men got assigned to a firehouse near their families, so they could go home for three hours a day, or take an hourlong break to go home for each meal. Williams, stationed so far away from his Bronx apartment, didn't have many choices on where to go. He hoped to find time to get to

Grand Central to visit his father, but that would have to wait until he found out what life was like inside Engine 55. It wasn't an ideal situation for a man with two young boys at home, but Williams would have sacrificed a lot more to get the $1,500 yearly salary, the average take-home pay among the city's 2.5 million employed workers in 1919.[1] Government salaries averaged about 49 cents an hour, and in Williams's world that amounted to a pretty princely sum.

Williams stood up as his train car approached Union Square at 14th Street in Manhattan. The subways were still in their infancy, but the city was slowly being ribboned by them underground. He'd helped dig out and blast the space for the line running down the west side of Manhattan from Harlem to Brooklyn. He'd seen two cave-ins during his career, enough to spur him to get out while he could. He'd applied for every type of civil service job available, including New York City firefighter in 1918, but it was the United States Post Office that called him up first. He half-expected that he would never hear from the fire department again, even though the published lists showed he'd scored 100 percent on the physical exam and nearly 100 on the written. He was the only man in his class to get a perfect 100 on the physical, and only the second to do so in the FDNY's history. He was ranked number 13 out of 2,700 candidates—the top percentile. But months passed and nothing came of it, so when the post office rang, Williams took a job driving a mail truck. At least, he reasoned, he was getting a useful skill by learning how to master the newfangled automobiles.

Finally, the letter that Williams never actually believed he would receive arrived in the mail: addressed to Probationary Firefighter Williams, it told him to report for duty January 10, 1919, at 8 a.m. at Engine 55 in Little Italy.

And now that day was here. Bounding off the train and into the gray morning sky, Williams moved through the throngs of street vendors and housewives hurrying with baskets until he turned onto Broome Street. A block later, his feet brought him right up to the vivid red door under a wide marble arch. Stenciled above it he saw his new firehouse's name, Engine 55. Williams paused for just a second to take a calming breath, then lifted his hand to twist the knob on the small side door that was the firemen's entrance. He knew he was ready for whatever came next. He just hoped his soon-to-be firefighting brothers were too.

CHAPTER 2

UN-CIVIL SERVICE

THE INSULAR, ALL-MALE, ALL-WHITE WORLD THAT WAITED FOR WESLEY
Williams in Little Italy in January 1919 was essentially the same
one inhabited by Captain Paul Washington nearly a century later.

In 1919, New York was a rapidly growing city with a burgeoning black migratory population layering over the constantly lapping
waves of Irish, German, Italian and eastern European immigrants.
In a city of 5.6 million, there were 152,467 blacks—roughly 3 percent. The rest of the city—all 97 percent—was white. Two statistically insignificant groups filled the gaps: 149 people identified as
"other," or "mixed," and 8,000 Asians, fairly new arrivals, contributed .14 percent to the melting pot.[1]

Blacks were in the uneasy position of transitioning from a free
but subservient class to one that was seeking a higher rung on the
economic ladder. Their numbers had more than doubled from
60,000 a decade earlier. The indisputable growth of their population increased the existing racial tensions as they competed more
fiercely than ever, and mainly with the poorest Irish immigrants,
for cheap housing and menial laborer jobs. The economic pressures
were exacerbated at the end of World War I with the return of
thousands of soldiers, white and black, looking for work. The initial joyous postwar celebrations gave no hint of brewing trouble,
and black New Yorkers in particular had reason to feel jubilant.
They were eager to give a champion's welcome to their homegrown

soldiers from the 369th Regiment, dubbed "Harlem's Hellfight-ers." The all-black troops acquitted themselves so bravely on the European battlefields that Germany's enlisted men admitted to fearing nothing so much as fighting America's "smoked soldiers." On February 17, 1919, just one month after Wesley Williams's first day at his firehouse, Harlem's Hellfighters came home to a hero's welcome. As many as 1 million New Yorkers turned out to cheer and clap as the black soldiers marched north from midtown Man-hattan through the all-white neighborhoods along Fifth Avenue. But the exultation reached its highest pitch when the men, near-ing the end of their trek, turned left onto 110th Street and then right onto Lenox Avenue, officially entering Harlem. As many as 100,000 spectators roared their approval. "Fifth Avenue was but a whisper" compared to the overwhelming enthusiasm that greeted the black soldiers as they double-stepped their way into the new heart of black Manhattan, one newspaper wrote. Years later, histo-rians would mark that date as the official beginning of the Harlem Renaissance, a burst of cultural and creative energy that produced some of America's finest literature and music.

The good feelings did not last. Within six months, white mobs across America had begun launching attacks on blacks, with some of the violence related to job competition. Between April and No-vember in 1919, a period known as the Red Summer, there were dozens of lynchings across the Northeast and parts of the rural south. Nearly 100 blacks were killed and countless others injured when hordes of white mobs attacked African Americans. New York City avoided the violence, but Chicago, Baltimore, Philadel-phia and Washington, D.C. saw the biggest clashes outside of the Deep South. The worst outbreaks of mob viciousness ended in the fall of 1919; the bubbling resentment and anger did not. In the increasingly urbanized and mechanized workplace of the twenti-eth century, the question of who got access to jobs—especially the better-paying ones—was a driving concern in black and white com-munities, and would remain so in the decades to come.

Wesley Williams, in the thick of the post–World War I employ-ment angst, was insulated from the worst of the desperation thanks to his city job. A person's color, creed or ethnicity held no sway in the merit-based civil service system, at least according to its propo-nents. New York City was expanding at lightning speed in 1919, and the demand for public services—clean streets, water, housing, green spaces—meant an expansion in municipal jobs. City positions were awarded through a system of written and sometimes physical exams, depending on the agency. Applicants' test results were tallied and placed in order of score on a hiring list. Each agency picked as many employees as it needed, starting with top of the candidate rankings and working down. It was touted as a straightforward system free from the smothering effects of racial discrimination. But it ignored the cruel realities of segregation and the dehumanizing effects of Jim Crow. It left many blacks hamstrung by hiring tests written for and designed by the white majority.

NEARLY 100 YEARS after Williams joined the FDNY, the system is still in place. It's used to award hundreds of thousands of city positions. Civil service jobs have kept pace with the explosion in the city's population, which soared to 8 million by 2012. Whites were still the largest demographic group but no longer the majority. They accounted for 44 percent of the city's residents, according to that year's census. African Americans and blacks—whether from the Caribbean, Africa or elsewhere—composed 26 percent of the population, roughly 2.1 million. There were newcomers too. Latinos, nonexistent at the turn of the twentieth century, had in the decades since the 1950s outpaced the black population, reaching 2.3 million, or nearly 28 percent. Asian immigration had also increased to more than 1 million, or 12 percent, with a particularly huge and recent influx from South Korea. More than 37 percent of the city was foreign-born.[2]

For the most part, that new reality was reflected in the city's workforce throughout the 1900s and into the twenty-first century. By 2012, blacks and Latinos, through the civil service hiring system, were the dominant groups in nearly all city agencies but one: the FDNY. Ninety-three years after Williams joined the force of about 5,000 men, the FDNY's ranks had doubled to approximately 11,000. Yet the number of blacks hovered around 300, roughly 3 percent. Every other uniformed agency in the city—the Department of Sanitation, the Department of Correction, the NYPD, even the fire department's own Emergency Medical Services—had a higher representation of minorities, if not an outright majority.[3] But the

FDNY remained stubbornly—and some said defiantly—white. The reasons for its aberrant status had created decades of contentious debate, multiple discrimination lawsuits and an unfortunate schism along color lines inside many firehouses. But there was no denying that 150 years after the formal creation of the FDNY, the much-ballyhooed egalitarian effects of civil service hadn't penetrated its parochial walls. Was it a failing of the department, a flaw in the so-called merit system itself or—as Captain Paul Washington and the Vulcans argued—was it both?

Some of the answers can be found in the determined arc of Wesley Williams's career. He and many of the earliest black firefighters who fought the worst of the Jim Crow battles in the firehouses left an indelible mark upon the FDNY. Williams's life, in turn, was shaped by many forces, but in particular the dynamism of three specific men. In their unique ways, each one was emblematic of the larger elements imposing their will upon the city, molding it into modern New York. Two of them loom large in history books; the third remains forever nameless and faceless, just another poor black out of the millions who came to New York in search of a better life.

That man was Wesley Williams's grandfather, John Williams. Family lore has it he was born a slave in 1852 on a Virginia plantation. He was the mixed-race child of the slave owner's son, who impregnated a female slave with West African roots named Sarah Powell. As a boy, young John was taken into the woods by his father to receive clandestine reading lessons, because it was against the law in the slave-holding South to educate blacks. As soon as he was old enough, John ran away, heading north via the Underground Railroad. Although he lived to a ripe old age, little is known of his home life beyond the fact that he made it to New York, got married and raised a well-educated family. Pictures from the early 1900s reveal him as a slender, courtly figure endowed with a generous white mustache.

By 1890, John's son James was living in Manhattan, on the fringe of the Tenderloin District. As a young man James Williams worked in a flower shop on Fifth Avenue. His employer was Charles Thorley, a self-made man who dabbled in politics and progressive ideas. It was in that shop, in the early 1890s, that James Williams took a flower order from a vivacious and dashing young lady named Lucy Metrash. It was a tremendous stroke of good fortune for James: not only did he fall head over heels for the hazel-eyed beauty, but she happened to hail from one of the oldest and most respected African American families in Connecticut. Before long, the two were married and living in Harlem. But during their short courtship, James Williams had ample opportunity to learn the ins and outs of railroad travel on weekend visits to Lucy's home. There was a sense of urgency and excitement around railroad travel that got James Williams's heart pumping, even when he was just taking a ho-hum commuter train for an hour to Connecticut. The railroad industry had a lot more going for it than working in a flower shop, he decided. Before long, he'd said goodbye to Mr. Thorley and signed up to be a baggage porter at busy Grand Central Depot (later to become Grand Central Terminal). He started in the lowliest of positions, confident that soon he'd work his way to something better.

A young man with a new job and a new wife soon finds himself with a new family, or at least that's how it happened in the late 1800s. The couple's first son, Wesley, arrived August 27, 1897, in Harlem. By then, the family had a firm toehold in the city and high expectations for the second generation born out of bondage. The flight of Williams's grandfather along the Underground Railroad presaged the influx of southern blacks who slowly came north after 1865—many from Virginia, which was a day away by boat. They sought relief from the oppressive, violent Jim Crow south in the decades that followed the Civil War. Wesley Williams grew up in a city and a neighborhood that struggled to absorb these undulations of black movement, especially after the floodgates opened with the Great Migration. He and the newcomers shared the same hungry ambition to do more than drudge through the days in economic misery—but Williams had advantages. He was literate, he knew the city, and his family had managed to put down roots and forge connections—many of them more powerful than they immediately understood. Williams was uniquely positioned to capitalize on the increasing attention paid to the plight of the Negro by northern white progressives. Before 1910, blacks were left largely to fend for themselves. Trying to survive in an indifferent city that often turned downright hostile, African Americans and black immigrants formed their own social clubs, relief halls, churches and philanthropic and charitable groups. Their efforts to help other blacks were largely unrecognized and functioned on a grassroots level, with no direct city or governmental support. With the exception of the Quakers, most white philanthropy was directed toward European immigrant groups, which shut homegrown Negroes out. But with the increasing industrialization of city life and the need for cheap labor, urban planners and social workers began to focus on black poverty in cities like Philadelphia, Chicago, Boston and New York. Between 1909 and 1911 the first two national organizations dedicated to the defense and the improvement of black life sprang up, both in New York City: the NAACP and the National League on Urban Conditions Among Negroes.[4] Between the Civil War and the 1890s, there was only one group—the Colored Mission—in Manhattan dedicated to helping destitute blacks. By 1915, more than a dozen such groups were concerned about Negro welfare.[5] As black life in New York expanded, so did the city's need for color-driven boundaries. Harlem became Manhattan's de facto black neighborhood. Some white churches that had previously catered to mixed congregations closed their doors to blacks. With so many all-black institutions popping up in the city, colored congregants could move on, the churches decided.[6]

Around the same time that Wesley Williams's grandfather was saving himself from a lifetime of ill-use in the Virginia cotton fields, another striving young man was doing the same 600 miles away in the festering Manhattan slum known as Five Points. William M. Tweed, son of a Scots-Irish furniture carver, was born April 3, 1823, on a tiny street inside a filthy, crime- and vermin-ridden urban ghetto. Five Points was dominated by gang activity, and nimble-footed Tweed, taken out of school at age 11 to learn his father's trade, flourished there. In the early 1820s, the FDNY technically didn't exist—but the city did have a firefighting force. It was made up mainly of volunteers, about 1,200 men on 46 engine companies.[7] The city paid for the equipment and the firehouse upkeep—the men worked for free. The rough-and-tumble firefighters had only just given up the bucket brigade system of getting water onto flames. Still, the volunteers, immediately identifiable from their vivid red shirts, black caps and dark trousers held up by suspenders of all colors, were a vast improvement from the early days of Manhattan.[8] In its infant colonial era, when straw- and thatched-roof cottages were stacked tightly along narrow cobblestone streets,

Four generations of the Williams family, starting with Red Cap chief James Williams, his father John Williams (escaped slave) and James' son Wesley Williams, shown here with his firstborn son, in Harlem circa 1920s. Photo Credit: Charles Williams, Family Collection, Schomburg Center.

any type of accidental blaze had calamitous potential. Every able-bodied citizen, including women and children—and the slaves a household owned—was expected to turn out to help avert disaster.

As the city grew and its mercantile interests expanded, it became prudent to have a corps of eager, young, civic-minded men to rush out at the first sign of fire. By the time young Tweed came along in the 1840s, the city boasted 50 firehouses placed in its densely packed wards, or neighborhoods. The firefighters usually volunteered in the firehouse closest to where they lived, and even though all they got for risking their life was glory, the competition to wear a red shirt was fierce.[9] In the cramped, diseased tenements below 42nd Street, the firefighters were the heroes of the neighborhood. The firehouses were popular hangouts and social clubs, and, before long, hotbeds of political intrigue. At any given moment, when a fire alarm sounded, all the men present would drop what they were doing and rush out, followed by hordes of children and yapping dogs.

In gang-infested Five Points and other slums, the firehouses were also rife with tribal allegiances. It wasn't unusual for fights to break out between enemy engine companies as the men raced with their hand-pulled pumpers to be the first to get water on a fire.[10] Sometimes they even sent fast-moving scouts ahead to hide fire hydrants under buckets, just to make sure a combatant gang didn't get there first.[11] Local politicians treated firehouses like their own private fiefdoms, taking great pride in turning out a big bloc vote for elections.[12] Among the many volunteers in Five Points, only a few hoisted their firefighting tools with the thunderous dexterity of Bill Tweed, who stood six feet tall and 270 pounds by his twenty-first birthday. A hardened street fighter who'd taken his licks defending his Cherry Hillers gang against the Hill Street gang, Tweed was right at home in the fire department of the 1840s, an eclectic, motley crew of street ruffians who reflected the violence of the city at large. Firehouses teemed with members of the Bowery B'hoys, the Pug Uglies, the Dead Rabbits and numerous other neighborhood tribes running amok in the fetid slums.[13]

Most if not all of these firehouses were under the sway of Tammany Hall, a political club that was incorporated in 1789. The politicization and nepotism within the volunteer ranks of the city's firefighters was so entrenched that by 1840 elected officials were meeting to discuss a radical idea: do away with the volunteers and establish a paid force. City planners hoped to make firefighters more loyal to their paycheck than to their fraternal bonds and ward bosses—but the idea fizzled and died. Yet change, creeping along at a snail's pace, was afoot in the fire department—specifically in the ethnic makeup of its members. In the 1830s, the fire department was only about 7 percent Irish. The majority, nearly 60 percent, were of British or Nordic descent.[14] Those Irish present were likely Scots-Irish, like Tweed himself. Which is to say, English-speaking and Protestant. But then the terrible Irish Potato Famine of 1845 sparked a massive diaspora from the Emerald Isle to America. Nearly half a million impoverished Irish were evicted from their cottages by unscrupulous landlords, and most found themselves packed into unseaworthy "coffin ships" and then dumped penniless onto America's shores. In many ways it was very similar to the Great Migration of blacks to northern cities that would occur decades later, plunging Irish and blacks into direct competition and conflict. As it was, the percentage of Irish in the fire department rose to nearly 40 percent during the Potato Famine.[15] These Irish were poor, uneducated, often only spoke Gaelic and—most distressing of all to the city's upper echelon—were Catholic. But to the ward leaders at Tammany Hall, these huddled masses were a boon. Desperate, homesick and anxious, they cleaved to the one political group that seemed to pay attention to their needs, the Democratic Party, vis-à-vis Tammany Hall. By then Tweed, a foreman at a fire company he had helped form, Americus Engine Co. 6, otherwise known as "Big Six," had started to edge his way into politics by running for a seat on the City Council. Fittingly, he made the mascot of his new engine company a roaring tiger. It was an apt image for Tweed himself, who usually ran ahead of the Big Six fire engine shouting commands to his men through a brass trumpet. Tweed's exploits in the fire department were legendary and numerous, but as he gained ascension in Tammany Hall, he showed no mercy in plundering the agency he loved. Any part of the city budget was fair game in Tweed's eyes. He became the Tammany puppet master, coordinating extraordinary pilfering of the city's fledgling municipal budgets from his shadowy position on the board of supervisors. Savvy Boss Tweed was a true believer in the patronage system of politics, which rewarded loyal henchmen with government jobs and the accompanying perks and benefits. In the internecine world of late-nineteenth-century New York City, where a ward handler knew down to the single digit who lived on his block and where, Tammany Hall gained an unbreakable hold on city government by leveraging support from the latest wave of Irish arrivals.

The fire department might have continued its colorful, character-driven, volunteer ways indefinitely if not for a dark and terrible tragedy that arose in 1863: New York City's Draft Riots. The nearly weeklong explosion of violent murder and mayhem was prompted by President Abraham Lincoln's demand for fresh troops for the bloody Civil War—but the riot had been simmering for a long while. In New York City, Lincoln's Republican Party had quietly supported the call for emancipation, and within its ranks a strong antislavery movement had taken hold. Meanwhile, the white proslavery supporters in the Democratic Party had been warning its German and Irish loyalists to be ready when emancipation came: blacks would fly north by the thousands, they said, and steal all the jobs and marry their daughters.[16] One of the most prolific producers of vicious, antiblack editorials was James Gordon Bennett, a Scots-born newspaper baron often touted as the father of modern journalism. Bennett, who wrote many a proslavery diatribe, was so grateful when fire department members extinguished a fire in his opulent townhouse that he endowed a special medal to be given in his name. The James Gordon Bennett medal remains the highest honor handed out by the FDNY today. The fear and loathing inspired by his and other editorials was particularly virulent among some Irish, and it wasn't limited to New York— communities in Philadelphia, Boston and Chicago felt the same way. The zealous proslavery reaction among many Irish Americans was an ugly surprise, given Ireland's pride in its own history of fighting oppression. It was a common boast in Ireland that in "seven centuries, no slave had set foot on Irish soil," thanks to a prohibition on the trade made in 1177 at the Council of Armagh.[17] So great was the disdain in Ireland for America's "peculiar institution" that its most revered leader, Daniel O'Connell—known as the "Liberator" for his tireless efforts to restore Irish home rule and be free of the British Parliament—stated publicly that he refused to visit the United States until slavery was abolished. Hoping to silence him, a member of the West Indian Trade Company offered a deal. O'Connell was promised the support of the company's 27 members of British Parliament on "Irish issues" if he stopped his antislavery speeches.

"Gentlemen, God knows I speak for the saddest people the sun sees; but may my right hand forget its cunning, and my tongue cleave to the roof of my mouth, if to save Ireland, even Ireland, I forget the Negro one single hour!" the Liberator replied defiantly.[18] His roiling words worried and angered proslavery interests in the South, who quickly saw a way to capitalize on the all-consuming passion of the Irish for their own home rule. Wealthy plantation owners poured money and support into the Irish American effort to raise cash for what was known as the Repeal, the fight to get Ireland free from British parliamentary rule. In exchange, the landowners expected the unqualified proslavery support of Irish Americans in the United States. It was a cruel kink of fate to make the Irish— a group renowned for their fierce fight for self-determination—an agent of oppression in America.

Such was the attitude and atmosphere in New York City in the spring of 1863 when the word came out that male citizens between 20 and 35 and all unmarried men between 35 and 45 were subject to military duty. New York City firemen, long held exempt from wartime service due to their volunteerism, were furious to learn they were eligible for this draft. Adding to their rage, the wealthy could buy their way out of the obligatory service by paying the government $300—or bribing some poor soul to take their place. Perhaps most galling of all to the white laborers was the fact that blacks, who were not allowed to be citizens, couldn't be drafted. That alone would have been enough to inflame the masses, but months of proslavery newspaper editorials from Bennett and others about the "nigger war" had dredged up seething antagonism. The city tensely waited for the first draft picks on Saturday, July 11, 1863. Twelve hundred names were called out at the provost marshal's office on Third Avenue and 46th Street.[19] Several volunteer firefighters from Engine Co. 33, known as the Black Joke company, were among those whose names were called. Black Joke was the firehouse first associated with Boss Tweed before he went on to form Big Six. Twenty-four hours after the first round, a group of antidraft protestors carrying signs picketed outside the provost's office as the second draft got under way. It was peaceful, until the red shirts from the Black Joke company burst on the scene, hurling rocks and stones and setting fire to a nearby building.[20]

Soon, mobs were rampaging across the city, some with Black Joke firemen embedded in them. By four in the afternoon, the infuriated pack had zeroed in on the Colored Orphan Asylum on Fifth Avenue. Some 233 Negro children were hiding inside when several thousand men and some women burst through the doors. Within minutes, the frenzied mob had stripped the orphanage of as much furniture, bedding, clothing and food as could be carried away and set it aflame. Only the valiant efforts of the fire department—which was battling mightily to contain the destruction started by its own members—prevented the children from being killed.

The 1863 Draft Riots had begun, and over the next five days racially motivated attacks, murders and hangings would kill at least 100 blacks. The city was left smoldering and shell-shocked. So many blacks fled that the Negro population plummeted to below 10,000, the lowest since 1820.[21] The actions of the Black Joke company were universally condemned, but the firefighters overall acquitted themselves well. The fire department and its volunteers were lauded for their bravery and courage in battling both the mob and its numerous acts of arson. Nonetheless, the Draft Riots spelled the end of the firefighters' freewheeling volunteer lifestyle. It was time to bring in paid professionals.

On August 1, 1865, the new Metropolitan Fire Department took over and the red-shirted volunteers surrendered their firehouses resentfully.[22] The governor now had the power to appoint four commissioners to oversee the fire department, all its tools and implements, and the 600 firemen the commissioners envisioned hiring. The total budget for the Metropolitan Fire Department was $564,000 for the year, including salaries and equipment costs.[23] Firefighting was now a paying job—but a lot of the fun had gone out of it. Racing to fires was prohibited, as was drinking, gambling and swearing. The red shirts were gone, replaced with sober blue flannel. The fire department's deeply partisan nature was also a thing of the past—on paper at least. Firemen were not allowed to be "a member of any political or partisan nominating convention."[24] Firehouse roll came at 8 a.m., and firemen were to have cleaned the bunk rooms and fed the horses by then. Firemen lived and slept in their quarters, and got one 24-hour period off three times a month. Those who lived close enough could go home for meals—but they had to be staggered so the firehouse was never empty. The bright red front doors—so often invitingly rolled up in the earlier days—were to be closed as much as possible to prevent visitors from wandering in, the department decreed.

Yet with all that, and its paltry pay of $700 a year, the Metropolitan Fire Department was overcome with applicants. Nearly 2,300—on top of the existing volunteers who tried to rejoin—vied for the 600 spots. For Boss Tweed, now the leader, or "Grand Sachem," of Tammany Hall, the professionalization of the fire department was like manna from heaven. The growth in public-sector agencies and jobs just gave him more opportunity for corruption and graft—and positions to fill with deserving Tammany backers. All Tweed needed was an Albany governor to return the fire department—and the police department and other city agencies— to local control. He got his man in John T. Hoffman, elected in 1868. Within two years, thanks to extensive bribing, Tweed had the power he wanted. The Tweed Charter was passed, creating the Fire Department of New York City—otherwise known as the FDNY. It encompassed Brooklyn and Manhattan, and it answered to the machine-controlled mayor, not Albany.

The Tweed Charter turned out to be one of Boss Tweed's last acts before the pesky reform movement caught up with him. His greed had gotten too big to ignore, and when the worst of his excesses became known—money laundering city funds to the tune of $200 million—not even his well-oiled Tammany machine could save him. He died in 1878 in jail, but the nuts and bolts of his political empire remained in place. The legacy of Tweed's venality was twofold: it wove Irish Americans so deeply into city government and politics that to pick apart the Irish heritage from the various agency traditions was next to impossible, particularly in the fire department and the police department. And it created a dogged and persistent desire among well-born Republican politicians— including a young Theodore Roosevelt—to break the spoils system that created such unswerving Democratic loyalty among immigrants. It both irritated and terrified Republicans to realize the Irish accounted for more than 35 percent of city voters. In 1881 Roosevelt, a fledgling reformer, had a firm grip on the cudgel of upper-class Protestant morality, and he was determined to wield it to smash political patronage to smithereens.

Nobody would have guessed that Theodore "Teddy" Roosevelt, born in 1858 in an elegant brownstone home a block from Gramercy Park, was going to make it to the White House—or that he would come to champion the civil service system that decades later would lift so many free blacks into the middle class. Roosevelt was a walking, talking example of white privilege at its finest. His father was a generous philanthropist and a firm practitioner of the principle of noblesse oblige, but his charitable acts didn't extend to hands-on examinations of the lower-class lifestyle. Teddy Roosevelt eschewed such distant benevolence. He was a new breed: the urban reformer. He befriended Jacob Riis, the journalist whose photographs of city slums shocked America's conscience. He toured the cigar-rolling factories that existed inside Lower East Side tenements; he bridled at the Tammany factionalism that held back progress in street-cleaning and general sanitation. Roosevelt, firmly declaring himself an "anti-machine" candidate, threw his hat in the ring for state assemblyman and embarked on a 40-year political career that was characterized by an unswerving hatred for the spoils system.

By 1881, Roosevelt's Republican Party had already taken aim at the patronage system on the federal level, instituting a National Civil Service Reform League. In Congress, Ohio Senator George Pendleton drafted a bill to create a three-man commission to oversee a system of competitive exams for federal office seekers. Modeled after the British Civil Service system, the Pendleton Law only covered a small number of the 100,000 federal jobs at the time, but it showcased the Republicans' determination to do away with the era of machine-made voter loyalty and the accompanying corruption. It was aimed squarely at New York's Customs House, a nerve center of Tammany graft.[25] A few states passed similar laws, and New York created a civil service commission in 1883 to depoliticize government hiring—or try to, at least. Roosevelt became an advocate not for "a government that tried to create equality, [but] government's responsibility in creating equality of opportunity."[26] Later historians would note the element of prejudice in some of the reformers. Opposition to machine politics increased significantly as Irish Catholics became the ones bootstrapping themselves into a better life through Tammany's doling out of city jobs. The FDNY, dominated by the newly politically powerful Irish, would soon erect its own barriers to keep out another burgeoning and dispossessed group: blacks.

Much to Roosevelt and other reformers' chagrin, it didn't matter how many federal, state or even city civil service laws were passed. Tammany's muddied waters flowed right around whatever obstacles were hurled in its way. The fire department was no exception. The FDNY in 1879 stipulated certain physical characteristics for its applicants: no older than 30, at least five feet seven inches tall, and height and weight were tied to specific measurements. The department was not looking to hire weaklings; a man who stood five feet ten had to weigh at least 150 pounds with a chest diameter of at least 35.5 inches.[27] Not long after, in 1883, the FDNY started a School of Instruction too. Headquartered on the third floor of Engine Co. 47 on Amsterdam Avenue, newbies spent ten days, unpaid, learning the ropes—or in this case, hoses—of firefighting 101. Anyone with an oafish lack of aptitude could be sent packing at the discretion of the instructor.[28] Soon the training school was moved to a bigger space on East 67th Street in Manhattan, the FDNY's new headquarters. By 1894, New York City was giving civil service tests as a gateway to employment.[29] The FDNY and NYPD were the city's biggest agencies: 65 percent of all municipal jobs were in those two departments.[30] Now the fire department had specific hiring guidelines it could point to when accused of nepotism or political favoritism: any candidate who scored high on the exam, met the physical requirements, was deemed sound mentally and physically by a doctor, and who proved himself an apt trainee could get hired. It all looked above board, for the FDNY as well as the NYPD. But if that were the case, it's unlikely that Teddy Roosevelt would have stormed back to the city from his position in D.C. to become police commissioner—giving up his spot on a civil service committee created to root out patronage on the federal level. Later historians would note that "the firemen . . . served under the direction of superior officers, who in turn were under the direction of Tammany Hall."[31]

In 1895, when Roosevelt took over as police commissioner, the bulk of his job consisted of sitting on an oversight committee to make sure that hiring, firing and promotions were made through the merit system, not personal connections. The NYPD had a worse reputation for nepotism than any other agency outside of the Customs House; it was common knowledge that any cop could buy an appointment for $300. One captain actually confessed he'd paid $15,000 for his promotion. The hustle to get into the NYPD was based on the nearly limitless opportunity for graft once on the job: police got $500 from businessmen who wanted to open a brothel, then $25 to $50 a month to protect it once its doors opened.[32] Just about every citizen, from the corner fruit vendor on up, paid some kind of police extortion. Roosevelt spent two years in the city try-ing to clean up the sewer ethics of the NYPD, with only partial suc-cess. During that time, he never trained his eagle eye on the FDNY. It was not accused of the same excessive corruption. Yet it didn't escape notice that two of the highest positions in the fire depart-ment were at that time held by Irish Americans from Five Points who'd ridden the Tammany system to the top. While they were men whose moral fiber was considered above reproach, it was hard to eschew the Tammany mantra of looking out for one's own—an ideal that's still deeply ingrained in firehouse culture. New York imposed its statewide civil service law in 1883. Five years later, an FDNY survey showed that 284 of its 1,000 firemen were Irish-born. Add in those born in America to Irish parents, and 75 percent of the department was Irish.[33] The merit-based system championed by Roosevelt in response to Tammany Hall may have succeeded, over time, in depoliticizing city hiring and firing, but it never fully eradicated the tradition of looking out for family and friends—as black firefighters soon found out.

CHAPTER 3

WE SHALL OVERCOME

J.H.S. 72 Catherine & Count Basie Middle School,
Jamaica, Queens
February 29, 2012

A FEW DAYS AFTER THE NEAR DEBACLE IN EAST HARLEM, ANGRY WHITE applicants gathered forces and tried again, with help from Merit Matters. This time it was at a Vulcan Society tutoring session at a school in Queens. Paul Washington wasn't able to attend, but after what had happened in Harlem he knew some last-minute instructions were necessary for the Vulcans who were going to oversee things.

"We know there's likely going to be some mischief," he said in phone calls to FDNY lieutenant Andrew Brown and firefighter Rannie Battle. "Stick to the list of names I gave you. Anybody who is trying to get in but whose name is not on the list has to step aside and wait until we see if there's room."

Washington felt a little uncomfortable. His instructions had the effect of preemptively divvying up the class by race, but there wasn't really any other way to go about it. The Vulcans worked off the list of black applicants that their lawyers got from the city. Every one of the potential black candidates had gotten an e-mail from the Vulcans telling them about upcoming tutoring classes. Given the number of whites who'd started appearing in big groups, the Vulcans had to assume Merit Matters, or someone else, had gotten a copy of one of those e-mails and been busy forwarding it around. Some of the white applicants who started appearing at classes seemed genuinely perplexed about why they weren't immediately allowed in. The Vulcans pegged them for candidates who were sincerely interested in the job. Others seemed fully clued in to a different agenda. They came to agitate for entry, even though they could care less about the actual class. The active-duty Vulcans even recognized a few of them and knew they were already firefighters. Washington was sure the white turnout was going to be even bigger in Queens than it had been in Harlem the other night, given that Jamaica bordered Long Island—home base for what seemed like three-fourths of the entire department and the bulk of its future candidates.

It promised to be a rowdy event. Washington wished he could be there—or better yet, he and Michael Marshall, a longtime Vulcan Society member known for his cool head. The current president of the Vulcan Society, John Coombs, was going to show up later, and there was no doubt he could hold his own if anyone tried to make trouble. He had a hard edge to him. Coombs, 46, grew up in Brooklyn. He became a plumber while still in high school, then worked his way through college doing temp jobs in banks and doubling as a security guard. He graduated with a marketing and communications degree, but made his money fixing pipes. Before long, he was a certified member of the Local 1 plumbers' union. By the time he was 25, he was married with the first of four kids on the way. He only sidestepped into the FDNY thanks to a fortunate run-in with two Vulcan members in Brooklyn, who convinced him to take the test. He'd come on the job in 1999, and if anything, Coombs was even more outspoken than Washington. In tense situations where someone like Michael Marshall might try to smooth things over, Washington and Coombs were just as likely to throw a little more fuel on the fire.

As it happened, the NYPD got called to the Queens classroom at almost the same time Coombs arrived that night. White class takers started arriving early, about 100 of them. The Vulcan members hadn't even gotten through the front doors to set up the lobby check-in spot when the school security guards were on them.

"You can't be blocking the front entrance like this. All these people have got to wait outside in an orderly line," one adamant guard insisted. The Vulcans rushed to set up their check-in stations and then open the doors, but they quickly lost control of the impatient crowd. Black candidates arrived and moved to the front of the line, where their names were checked off the Vulcans' list. They passed into the classroom, while those stuck in the lobby got restless. Amid the flood of young students coming out of evening activities and parents trying to pick up kids, the disorganization threatened to spiral out of control.

"Are you with the FDNY? Are you a firefighter?" one of the white class takers said to a Vulcan who was trying to keep some peace among the angry group. "What company are you with?"

"Sir, please stand to the side over there. Your name is not on the list, but if there's room once we've checked in all those who did sign up, we'll let you in," the firefighter answered.

"I did sign up and I got a confirmation, see?" the man responded, waving a slip of paper. "We all signed up and were told it was okay," he said. "Why won't you let us in? You're letting in everyone else, why not us?"

"Sir, I don't know where your confirmation e-mail is from, but it's not from our group. You didn't sign up with the Vulcans and we're the ones running this class tonight, so as I said, you can wait and we'll see if there's space after everyone from our list is checked in," the firefighter responded.

An angry din broke out as the Vulcans started shouting out the names of blacks on the list. The shoving mass of pissed-off men around the check-in table—more of a blockade than a line—linked arms, making it all but impossible for those called to get up front. Several parents and their kids, trying to get out the front door, got caught up in the tussle.

"This is a disaster," the black firefighter thought to himself, just as the group of whites broke into a loud, off-key rendition of "We Shall Overcome."

"I'm black Irish!" one of the white men shouted as the song petered out after a few rounds of the chorus. Another one yelled out that he would don "black face" if that would get him in the door.

When six school security guards came out to quell the noise, the crowd threw taunts at them.

"You're too fat to be real cops," one of the angry men jeered. Lieutenant Brown and firefighter Battle exchanged glances. This was getting too hot for them to handle. It was time to call the police to help disperse the men. Brown and Battle recognized several of the faces in the furious crowd. These were full-time firefighters, already on the job.

John Coombs, observing from the classroom, emerged in time to catch the white crowd shouting, "No justice, no peace!"

One of them, spying Coombs, shouldered his way to him.

"I got a right to go inside. I was told to come here," the candidate declared.

"Oh, yeah? Who sent you? Who? I know it can't be Merit Matters," Coombs shot back. "That organization says we're cheaters, that we can't do anything the right way and have to look for special treatment, so I know that group can't be sending you here to take a tutorial run by the Vulcans—that wouldn't make sense, would it?" he snapped. "So who invited you here? Because it wasn't us."

Out on the street, red and blue lights flashed, and two NYPD patrol cars pulled up. They were followed by several TV vans, which immediately disgorged reporters and camera crews who switched on bright lights to record all the action. Only those students already in the classroom were allowed to stay. Everyone else was hustled out.

The next day, the newspapers and local media were full of reports from white firefighter candidates who claimed they'd been shut out of the Vulcan classes because of their race. The Vulcans had called only the names of black candidates but refused to let anyone else in, the group said.

"My dad [a firefighter] was killed on 9/11. I always wanted to be FDNY," said a contender named Rob, 21, who was quoted by the *New York Post*.[1]

"What would Martin Luther King do?" another man, described as an "agitated applicant," told the news cameras.[2] A complaint was filed with the FDNY, asking the agency to investigate the legalities of the Vulcans' actions. Two of the men who signed up online to take the Vulcan tutorial that night would later file complaints with the city's human rights commission, alleging the white candidates were victims of reverse discrimination. They were represented by Merit Matters's pro bono lawyers. School officials, frightened by what had happened and distressed to see their school in the press, told the Vulcans they were not welcome on the premises again.

Out in Utah on a ski trip, Michael Marshall struggled to hold his temper. It was unlike him to lose control of his emotions, especially anger. But as call after call came in from reporters looking for a little inside intel on what had gone down in Queens, he gained a better understanding of the picture that was being painted of the Vulcans, and his voice got heated.

"I wasn't there, I'm on vacation. But I can tell you that whatever happened is a bunch of nonsense," Marshall said for the umpteenth time, as a reporter from the popular news channel NY1 called him for comment. "We have never kept whites out of our classes, we don't do that. That's not what we are about. We're here to help people, and in probably every class we've ever given some white candidates have showed up and we have let them in. This is just a stunt, a cheap, nonsense stunt," he railed.

Marshall was no newcomer to the media game, having dealt with the New York press for more than ten years, but he had to tip his hat to Mannix for the canny way Merit Matters had set its narrative up—and how voraciously reporters were chasing it. It was quite a trick to make the black firefighters—with their paltry FDNY numbers—look like they were the ones causing a racial divide. Nobody in the Vulcan Society would deny that the organization's main purpose was to get more blacks on the job—that was essentially why it was founded in 1941. But that unapologetic goal didn't mean they also actively worked to keep other groups out of the FDNY—in fact, the opposite was true. The Vulcan Society had worked with the FDNY's Hispanic Society in 1973 to file a legal challenge to the city's written firefighter exam. The shared goal had been to get more Latinos and blacks into the ranks.

A federal judge agreed that the test was unfairly weeding out candidates of color and imposed a hiring quota on the city for four years. Between 1973 and 1977, for every three white firefighters hired, the FDNY had to pick one minority. That test became known as the 1-and-3 list because of it.

Not long after, in 1978, the FDNY opened its firefighter testing to women for the first time in its 117-year history. As far as the FDNY knew, its last female smoke eater had been a slave named Molly Williams. She'd belonged to a New York City merchant named Benjamin Aymar in 1818. The wealthy businessman liked to dabble as a volunteer firefighter at Oceanus Engine Co. 11 in

Lower Manhattan, not far from where Zuccotti Park is today. Some say Williams also doubled as the firehouse cook, perhaps lent to the Engine Co. as Aymar's chattel. Either way, Williams stepped up when a blizzard hit the city and an influenza bout wiped out most of the male volunteers. A fire alarm came in and she was the only one fit to respond. The sturdy slave, in her calico dress and checked apron, hauled the firehouse pumper through the swirling snow with as much strength and speed as any man, and thereafter became known as Volunteer No. 11, according to lore. After her, the FDNY wouldn't see another woman firefighter for more than 150 years.

Confronted by a group of women determined to take the test in 1978, the FDNY changed its physical exam from a pass-fail to a scored one that an official later described as the toughest challenge the department had ever given. All 90 of the women who took it failed—exactly as the all-male department expected. Brenda Berkman, a young lawyer who wanted to join the FDNY, filed a historic lawsuit challenging the new test. She argued that the FDNY had chosen extremely difficult feats that had nothing to do with the actual job of firefighting—and the court agreed with her. A judge ruled that the FDNY violated federal law by creating a demanding physical test meant to keep women out of the firehouses. In 1982, Berkman and 41 other women joined the Bravest. But their ordeal wasn't over. Berkman and another woman were told they flunked the Fire Academy and had to do it all over again, ostensibly because they needed extra training. When they graduated a second time they were fired, prompting another lawsuit. In 1983, after the judge found "extraordinary evidence of intentional discrimination," they were reinstated. The fire commissioner at the time said that he dumped Berkman—who went on to serve for 25 years and retired in 2006 as a well-respected captain—because he was "convinced to a certainty" she could never control a pressurized hose line.[3] Not a single fraternal organization in the FDNY supported the women in their quest—except the Vulcans. While the Uniformed Firefighters Association—the union of the rank and file—openly opposed accepting women firefighters, the Vulcans set up a "Godfather Program" to help train the women ahead of the physical test, and to act as mentors once they got in the firehouses.

Out in Utah, Marshall broke off the conversation with the reporter and hung up the phone. He was usually quick to see the humor in most things, and if his luxurious mustache bristled at all, it was in laughter rather than rage. But after 30 years of banging his head against the closed minds of the FDNY, the bitter irony of black firefighters being labeled racist left him too dispirited to laugh. It was never a problem for white chiefs to do a little extra to get their nephews and sons on the job, put in a word to get them a plum assignment or clear up a paperwork problem, but let a black firefighter try to help other blacks improve their odds, and the entire department was flooded with cries about special treatment.

He was 52, with more than 30 years as a smoke eater, yet Marshall hadn't forgotten that he and most of his generation owed their FDNY careers to a lucky turn of fate—usually, a black firefighter already on the job who turned up at just the right time. Nobody from the FDNY was out recruiting back then, especially among minorities. He hadn't grown up in a firefighting family and nobody in his Flatbush, Brooklyn, neighborhood had either. He'd never seen a single black firefighter on the engines that wailed past him and his friends as they crowded his block to play skelly, handball and stoop ball. His family was the first—and for a long time only— black household on his street, but that hadn't affected his perception that he was living in a boyhood paradise. His mother, from Bermuda, was so light-skinned that she blended right into the all-white neighborhood. She stayed at home with the kids, while his African American dad made a decent living moving furniture. They owned no property and had no savings, but Marshall grew up with all the trappings of the middle class. A mischievous, high-spirited child—gifted with his mother's agreeable charm and his father's work ethic—he felt right at home among the Jewish, Italian and Irish kids who lived around him. It was the type of blue-collar, multicultural upbringing that many New Yorkers experienced, until the rapidly expanding highway system and white flight of the 1970s changed the landscape of the inner city and remapped the suburbs.

Marshall worked his way through junior high and parts of high school at the corner hardware store owned by a Jewish neighbor. He graduated from unloading trucks to waiting on customers and eventually to installing gates and locks. By the time he was 17, he had a steady gig as a locksmith on Flatbush Avenue. His reputation as a hard worker grew along with what would become his signature mustache, and by 18 he was a card-carrying member of

Local 1888, the Harlem construction union, otherwise known as the black local.

For a few years Marshall thought he was doing all right, but then a rough patch took hold. The regular ups and downs of seasonal construction work turned into an eight-month drought. A friend told him the city was preparing a round of civil service tests. Feeling a little desperate, Marshall vowed to sign up for them all. He took the firefighter exam in 1977, the same year as the department's first women firefighters. Even with the city wrung dry by its ongoing fiscal crisis, he saw long lines everywhere, for the NYPD and NY Transit cop tests, even the post office exam. If just one came through, he figured, he'd find his way into a better-paying and more stable job. With that, he had nothing to do but wait and hope, and watch his small pile of savings dry up. Then he got a much-needed phone call—not from the city, but from a construction buddy.

"Hey Mike, you working?" said the familiar voice of Frankie Abbondanza. Marshall met the older Italian guy on his first real construction job, building a pollution plant out on Wards Island. They'd remained close ever since.

"No, man, and I really need to. What you got?" Marshall said.

"Meet me on the corner of 31st Street and 31st Avenue in Astoria tomorrow morning, six o'clock," Abbondanza said. "Bring your tools."

By the early 1980s, Marshall was feeling flush. True to his name, Abbondanza steered him toward an abundance of work, and he'd been able to move out of his old apartment and find something roomier. At 26, Marshall was about to get married and start a family. He was earning decent pay now, but the worry of another long work lull with no income was always in his head. He found it odd that—four years later—he'd never heard back from any of the city jobs he applied for. One day, on a whim, he called a friend of his who had a regular 9-to-5 desk job, with access to a phone during business hours, and asked him to check with the city agencies to find out where he stood, starting with the fire department. The next day, he got some surprising news.

"Michael, the FDNY already passed your number," his friend said, when Marshall reached him at home that evening. "You were 3,024, and they're long past 3,000."

"What? How is that possible? I never got a phone call, or a letter. Nobody told me anything," Marshall said.

"Well, they're past your number on the list, so they said you better get down to the investigation office on Pier A and see if you can still get in," the friend said. Marshall hung up the phone, then picked it back up and called his construction boss to get the next day off.

On December 3, 1981, he hustled down to Pier A in Manhattan, and that's where Lady Luck stepped in. After explaining his situation to the young man at the front desk, the clerk disappeared into a backroom. When he came out a few minutes later, an older black man in a firefighter's uniform followed behind him, flipping through a manila folder.

"Michael Marshall, took the test in 1977, ranked number 3,024. Where you been? We've been looking for you. I sent you a letter six months ago," the man said, fixing a stern brown eye on Marshall's youthful face. Startled, Marshall tried to launch into an explanation of how he'd moved, but the man waved his words away.

"Don't worry, I'll take care of you," he said, introducing himself as Henry Blake, firefighter and member of the Vulcan Society. "I'm part of the association of black firefighters, and when you get on the job, you can join and be one of us."

In a development that must have helped many a young black candidate in the late 1970s, the fire department had appointed Blake as one of its background investigators. Many years later, with the advent of computers but also the uptick in attention to the racial disparity in FDNY hires, the department would bring in outside professionals to do its background checks. But for most of its history, firefighters carried out the task of looking into a candidate's background to see if they were fit for the job or not. The investigators looked for arrest histories, especially felonies, truancy problems at school, dishonorable discharges from the military—anything that might suggest a faulty moral character or a history of trouble with authority. Of course, with spotty record keeping, no computers and an institutional tradition of taking care of one's own, it was an easy matter for one candidate's paperwork to get lost while another's got pushed through. Or, in Marshall's case, for Henry Blake to make sure his application got a speedy and favorable review.

For the next three weeks, anytime Blake called him demanding a piece of paperwork—a high school diploma, a driver's license, even his birth certificate—Marshall took a day off to personally walk the papers down to Pier A and put them in Blake's hands. As 1981 drew to a close, Blake was still waiting for Marshall's fingerprint records to come back clean from the NYPD. The New Year came and went with no word, and Marshall resigned himself to more months of waiting. But just a week later, at 9:30 p.m. on January 8, Blake called him at home.

"Marshall, you need to show first thing tomorrow morning," Blake said in his firm way, snapping out a Manhattan address. "Do not be late."

"Did my fingerprints come back?" Marshall asked. There was silence on the other end of the phone.

"You let me handle that. Just be where I told you and on time," Blake said.

When Marshall showed up at the address Blake gave him, he gaped in confusion at the crowd of about 250 people around him. Everyone was dressed in suits and ties, and he felt an itch of discomfort in his casual pants and shirt. A black firefighter approached him.

"How come you're not dressed up?" he asked, introducing himself as John Tyson. His tone was friendly, but he wore a slight frown.

"I didn't know we were getting sworn in," Marshall protested, feeling abashed. He hadn't told his parents or his fiancée or anyone, he realized, as a cheer went around the auditorium. But it was too late to worry about that now. Within a few weeks he was taking his probie classes at Randall's Island, getting yelled at by red-faced fire officers and swearing back at them under his breath. He was one of just a few black firefighters training at the Rock, as Randall's Island was called, but he had no problem finding friends among the mix of Italians, Jews, Irish and Latinos that made up the majority of his class. In a way, it was just like his childhood all over again, he told himself, as he huffed and sweated his way through firefighting drills and calisthenics.

Six weeks later, as Probationary Firefighter Marshall, he was assigned to Engine 221 in Williamsburg. His first day on the job, he and his crew had to respond to a massive explosion. A tanker along the industrial waterline blew to bits, a victim of the combustible fuel in its belly. As baptisms went, it was a doozy, and in the first seconds after the explosion Marshall—hanging out of the firehouse window—stayed where he was, eyes bugging at the size of the greasy black smoke ball erupting in the sky.

He was unceremoniously hauled out by the more experienced firefighters, and before he knew it, he was part of a team pulling a two-and-a-half-inch hand line out onto the jetty. The firefighters got as close to the river's edge as they could and sprayed water everywhere, until the oil that oozed from the boat became a floating wall of flame headed right for them. Obeying orders, Marshall dropped the hand line and dove for the small space under the chain-link fence that kept out trespassers. It was the most expedient way out, and firefighters had cut a small hole through its bottom. They rolled under it one by one.

Marshall took to firefighting like any other young man with plenty of energy and a taste for adrenalin. He and the other rookie firefighters competed to see who could catch the most fire runs. Whenever he got a good one, he'd stand outside as the replacement shift rolled in and pantomime spraying a fire-hose nozzle.

"You caught one?" the other rookie would ask, a hint of envy in his voice. "What was it, tell me about it." And when one of them got a chance to experience a real hot fire, they'd do the same to Marshall when he returned to the house for his shift.

It didn't really matter to Marshall that he was the only black probie. For the most part, his new colleagues didn't seem to care too much about it. Whether by happy chance or Henry Blake's design, he'd gone to a company that had already housed at least seven black firefighters. The officers working with him had made the firehouse expectations clear: race didn't matter, but a firefighter's work ethic did. That was a motto Marshall could live by.

But the scarcity of blacks in general in the FDNY gnawed at him, and it was a frequent topic of conversation at the Vulcan meetings he now attended on a regular basis. True to his promise to Blake, he joined the fraternal organization as soon as he graduated from the Fire Academy, despite a few grumbles from some of the older white firefighters in his company. The lingering resentment from the Vulcans' 1970s lawsuit still permeated the department, and the black firefighters who got along best with their crews were the ones like Marshall who avoided discussing anything related to race, quotas or FDNY hiring. Even so, the challenge of getting more blacks on the job was something Marshall embraced wholeheartedly.

It didn't take long for him to learn that it wasn't going to be easy. It wasn't just one thing that kept blacks from joining the FDNY; there were many things, Marshall realized. The Vulcans had been trying through trial and error to bump up their numbers for nearly 60 years, and yet it remained a struggle to even get 500 blacks on the job at the same time. It wasn't just that black candidates didn't pass the entrance exam with high enough scores—it was that too few took it to begin with. And those who did get through often got washed out during the background check—the very place he nearly stumbled too. For every one black candidate who succeeded and got on the FDNY, there were several others, maybe even dozens, who could do the job but never even tried or got turned away by a technicality. The Vulcan system of having black firefighters do unofficial recruitment in the streets—approaching and talking to every young black male who looked reasonably fit—was like

FDNY lieutenant Michael Marshall (center), Vulcan Society vice president and FDNY diversity advocate, with Lieutenant Clarence Mclean (r) and Lieutenant Duane Dewitt (l), September 2014. Photo credit: Michel Friang.

dropping tears into the ocean. It was never going to add enough diversity to the department to even make a visual difference, let alone get them any real kind of firehouse parity.

Marshall needed someone in the Vulcans who would be willing to join with him to do whatever was necessary to force the FDNY toward real change—and that would require new blood. After a decade of firehouse bickering and battling over the court-imposed quota system in the 1970s, followed by a fresh wave of vitriol over the addition of women in the 1980s, few among the Vulcan leadership had the stomach for another protracted fight. The past 20 years had been exceptionally draining for everyone, fraught with racial and economic disasters and an acrimonious union strike in 1973. Called by the Uniformed Firefighters Association that represented the city's firefighters, the strike only lasted five and a half hours. But the damage it caused stayed around much longer. Many of the black firefighters refused to go along with the walkout, arguing that their inner-city neighborhoods were the ones most at risk. White firefighters also expressed disgust at the prospect of picketing outside their own firehouses, but many felt compelled to give at least a token show of compliance out of union solidarity. Some found a way to back the UFA, but also square their firefighting conscience: they manned the picket lines outside, but ran into the firehouse periodically to make sure they weren't missing any alarms. The union got lucky and no major disasters occurred to test their members' loyalty during the short work stoppage. Not long after the divisive strike, which the union president said his membership voted in favor of, it was discovered that he had falsified those results to force a walkout. The strike never should have happened. It was a hardball move devised by the union head to get a better contract for his members. His rash action imperiled public safety, poisoned the union's relationship with the city and added a bit more depth to the racial rifts already running through some firehouses.

The Vulcans needed to rebuild, financially and in other ways too. Marshall understood that at some point the group would be ready for more, and he would be as well. Six full and happy years later, he was an experienced hand at firefighting and the father of six-year-old twins, Michael Jr. and Melinda. He was also taking on a more active role as a Vulcan mentor to new black probies. That spring, the FDNY finished off its prior list with a final round of hiring and several more black candidates who made the cut got their chance to prove themselves in the Fire Academy. Marshall got the phone numbers of all the new black firefighters and he called them up to invite them to the annual African American Day Parade. The Vulcans had been marching in it for decades and, since 1971, usually accompanied by a charismatic young congressman from Harlem named Charles Rangel.

Marshall had met most of the new probies at Randall's Island already, so when he saw one tall young man, skinny as a pipe cleaner and wearing a spotless FDNY-issued blue work shirt, he recognized him right away. Paul Washington, probationary firefighter in the July class of 1988.

"Hey brother, good to see you. Glad you came out. You get your assignment yet?" he said, sticking out his hand. The younger man took it.

"Yeah, I'm headed to Engine 7, Manhattan," Washington replied, giving Marshall a hard shake in return. Neither knew it at the time, but it was the beginning of a revolutionary new partnership.

CHAPTER 4

NEW BEGINNINGS

New York City
1988–mid-1990s

IN 1988, WHEN MICHAEL MARSHALL AND PAUL WASHINGTON FIRST MET, New York City's Department of Personnel was on the cusp of administering another one of its highly competitive firefighter exams. This one was numbered 7022, although only the Department of Personnel understood the logic of its sequencing. When exam time came, the turnout in general was low: only 14,620 candidates took it. Blacks made up 10.85 percent, roughly 1,600 candidates. That year, both the physical and written tests were given ranked grades, with the two scores averaged into one final list number. The city set the passing score at 70 percent.[1]

But just passing the test wasn't going to do much for the applicants. To really have a shot at getting on the job within four years—at which point the city would scrap the 7022 hiring list and start the process over with a new exam—they had to get a score that ranked them in the top 5,000. And even that was no guarantee. On any given hiring cycle, the FDNY only absorbed as many firefighters as it needed. That usually averaged about 2,400 roughly every four years. In each cycle there were thousands of high-scoring, well-qualified candidates who never got called. And many would be eliminated by medical problems, background problems or other technicalities. The long, drawn-out and burdensome process of becoming a New York City firefighter didn't end with a high score. That just ranked everybody by their grade for a prolonged waiting game. For test 7022, there were 112 blacks in the top 5,000—about 2.24 percent. By 1995, when the city officially stopped hiring from that list, 2,256 firefighters had joined the ranks of the Bravest from exam 7022. Of those lucky few, 29 were black, less than 1.3 percent. It was a drastic drop from the 10.85 percent of blacks who started the process.[2]

Washington and Marshall were angry and dismayed by the dismal numbers. In 1990, blacks made up 29 percent of New York City's population, and unemployment was rampant after a decade of extreme financial and racial upheaval. The city had spent most of the 1980s trying to battle back from its abrupt and nearly complete financial collapse a decade earlier. Almost overnight, it seemed, the city changed from a hazy mix of middle- and working-class neighborhoods to a city of extreme wealth and extreme poverty, and it boiled with racial tension. The city's black and Latino communities were caught in a cycle of joblessness and hardship unlike any seen since the Great Depression. In the 1970s, 311,841 blacks lived below the poverty line; by the early 1980s it was 452,030 and growing. Compounding the situation, all but 14 percent of the city's black poor lived in what were known officially as "poverty areas."[3] In other words, the bulk of the city's poorest, marginalized blacks lived firmly in its urban ghettos, places like Harlem, the South Bronx, Bushwick, East New York, Crown Heights and Bedford-Stuyvesant.

From the mid-1960s into the late 1970s—the FDNY's infamous "War Years"—fire haunted the poorest sections, turning derelict old buildings into insurance payouts for avaricious landlords looking to cash out. The firehouses in these neighborhoods became the stuff of legends. Crews would turn out for two, three, even sometimes four fires a night. Some of them were arson, but others were just the byproduct of callous and calculated neglect: electrical fires from bad wiring, kitchen blazes from families who turned on the oven because they had no other heat, deadly conflagrations that grew from cigarettes that fell into mattresses, and even some fires that were deliberately set—not for money, but by bored, frustrated youth who had nothing better to do than watch something burn. The constant, frenetic pace had firefighters in affected areas jumping round the clock—making them the most sought-after fire-houses among pumped-up young smoke eaters eager for experience. Some of the same neighborhoods their parents or grandparents had fled from a few decades earlier became highly competitive places to work. The majority of firefighters commuted in for their shifts, and at the end of each tour they left the city—and its problems—behind. They returned to suburbia, usually Rockland, Westchester, Orange, Suffolk and Nassau counties, as well as Staten Island.

The adrenalin thrill of battling big fires—and saving lives—was the main lure that pulled the firefighters toward the busiest houses, but there were other, more practical benefits too. High-profile rescues earned praise and commendations from superior officers. Commendations and medals turned into extra points when it came time to take the civil service exams for officer positions. Lieutenant was the first rung on the fire department's long promotional ladder. Two steps above that was battalion chief, with a generous, eight-day-a-month schedule and six-figure salary. It was not a bad way to wind up a long and fruitful career—for those blessed enough to get through the hazards of the job. In the 1960s and '70s, with half the city going up in flames at any given time, it wasn't hard to land in a hustling firehouse. But as the worst of the crisis burned itself out, and property values started slowly rising along with improvements in fire prevention technology and regulations, those coveted spots became harder to get. Some firefighters waited years for the transfer they most desired. The only ones who seemed to go straight from probie school into the action were those who had a hook—the firefighting term for a high-ranking friend or relative who could pull the right strings.

Even in the late 1980s and early 1990s, the remnants of the prolonged inner-city blight were evident to any firefighter who worked outside the ring of Manhattan's upscale neighborhoods and commercial centers. It bothered Washington and Marshall and the Vulcans in general that in the poorest areas of the city, where steady employment was desperately needed, the communities rarely—if ever—saw a black face on the back of a fire engine.

"They all need jobs, good, solid, well-paying jobs. If we could get these kids better access to the tools they need to pass the test, they can get on the FDNY," Washington would say to Marshall when they met up. The two firefighters were part of a group of

Vulcans studying together to take the upcoming promotional exam for lieutenant in 1992. The city was also prepping for another entry-level firefighter test around that same time, and the Vulcans were doing what they could to help black hopefuls prepare.

"It's gonna take another a lawsuit," Michael Marshall would reply calmly. It was a frequent refrain from him. Six years Washington's senior, already a father and with more time on the job, he had his own idea of what it would take to bring more young blacks into firehouses. But for the moment he was content to let Washington test his mettle against the traditional ways of the fire department. Washington wasn't opposed to bringing a lawsuit against the city, but he wasn't convinced it was the best route for the Vulcans to take. It was going to cost a lot of money, for one thing.

"Let's see what we can do ourselves, by really trying to go out and recruit and help these kids all the way through the physical," Washington said. "I think we can get more blacks into the department, a lot more. It'll be like a wave."

"A wave, huh?" Marshall laughed. "Okay, let's give it a shot."

Nobody knew better than Washington the positive effect a civil service job could have on a family, for multiple generations. His dad, Cornelius Washington, was one of thousands of World War II vets who returned home after serving overseas determined to break the terrible grip of poverty that followed him and his ancestors out of slavery. He signed up for the firefighter civil service exam and found work as a bus driver until the FDNY called him up. When he walked through the door of his first assignment, Engine 69 in Harlem in 1956, his family was already on the path toward a comfortable, middle-class life. About a year later, he was transferred to Engine 154, a firehouse on Staten Island, where he and his family lived. Paul Washington grew up in a humble neighborhood known as Dog Patch, about ten miles away from Engine 154. On Staten Island, he was just one of thousands of cop and firefighter kids. Inside the boundaries of his neighborhood, his dad was one of two firefighters—the other one being Washington's Uncle Benny. Washington's family stood out not for its blackness but for its comparative affluence. His parents owned a beautiful house—built from the ground up by his dad and his uncles—and eventually two cars. His mother, Thelma, was a devout Catholic from Nassau, Bahamas, and raised him and his older siblings, Kevin and Lynn, in the faith.

The Washingtons were able to send their kids to a private Catholic school. Not all the families in his neighborhood could afford to do the same.

The Washingtons' little haven in Dog Patch, no more than eight blocks wide and six blocks long, was one of the few areas on the island where black and white families commingled. Outside that zone, the forgotten borough, as it was often called, had clear lines of segregation in the 1960s and '70s. Neighborhoods north of the expressway tended to be a mix of black and white families, while the south was mostly if not entirely white. Flares of racial animosity sometimes beset the island, which operated like a proud backwater town to the more sophisticated city that dominated its skyline. As a kid, when Paul and his friends rode their bikes beyond Dog Patch, they sometimes found themselves in areas that had been tagged with a warning graffiti sign, "NNL," for "no nigger land." They sometimes got chased out by adults, who would scream racial slurs at them and hurl soda cans. It wasn't anything new for the boys—Paul got the same treatment on his newspaper delivery route by passing cars. He grew hardened to it, but the steady barrage of racial animosity that he and his friends had to deal with left them wary and distrustful of whites.

He assumed his father was fighting some version of those same battles in his daily life at the all-white Engine 154. But he could only assume, because his father, known as Buddy, almost never spoke about his work. Paul visited the firehouse just one time, with his sister, and that was it. Cornelius Washington was the only black among Italians and Irish, and he busied himself as much as he could tending equipment a cordial distance from the kitchen hangout.

"Is that what firefighting is like, Dad?" Paul had asked once, transfixed by a made-for-TV movie, *Firehouse*. It featured a black man—actor Richard Roundtree, better known as the titular detective in *Shaft*—who had to survive among the white majority. His dad had looked up from his newspaper and glanced at the screen, where artistically sweaty and soot-streaked firefighters were able to carry on conversations in the thick heat.

"No, not at all," he'd said, burying his head back in his paper. Despite his reserve, the impact of Cornelius Washington's job on the family was profound. All the kids grew up with the sense that their father's work was something special. Not only did he race into buildings and save lives, he had plenty of time to work second jobs, which he always did. As they got older and more tuned into financial realities, they became aware that he was free from the burden of saving for retirement; he could provide for his family and he and his wife could get their kids to college. In his entire working life with the fire department, he never once worried that his paycheck wouldn't arrive. If Buddy nursed a hope that one of his children might follow in his footsteps, he kept it to himself and let them make their own choices. Thelma urged them to aim higher. She also fought fiercely to keep them from internalizing the racism around them. "You go back tomorrow and you tell them, 'I'm black and I'm proud,'" she told Paul after his first day of Catholic school, when one of his white classmates taunted him about his race. She wasn't afraid to stand up for herself, and she didn't want her kids to be either.

Cornelius "Buddy" Washington, FDNY firefighter, Engine 154, Staten Island. Courtesy of the Washington family. Copyright © Michel Friang.

"Why just a firefighter," she'd say to her son, when he started to show a serious interest in the job. It was a fairly common attitude among many black firefighter and cop families of the post–World War II generation. Having gotten the job that launched them into a higher socioeconomic status, they had aspirations of their children climbing even higher, becoming lawyers, doctors, even politicians. But Paul—along with his older brother Kevin and his two older cousins Gary and Mark, sons of his Uncle Allen—was hooked. Just like the thousands of white FDNY candidates before him who had followed a dad or an uncle into the firehouse, he simply couldn't imagine a job that would be any better.

That was the message he took to the streets with Michael Marshall as the duo began trolling Brooklyn and Queens in the 1990s. Armed with a card table, two wobbly chairs and a stack of specially printed index cards, they set up shop whenever and wherever they could on their days off, stopping any likely looking black youth and making their pitch to have them apply to the fire department. Other Vulcans would join them or go off to different corners in groups of two. At the end of each excursion, Washington entered any cards that had been filled out into a computerized database of prospective candidates. The Vulcans planned to follow up with each and every one—that was the only way to make sure the kids had really completed the application and made an effort to prepare for the upcoming test. For many inner-city kids, the way to pique their interest was through their wallets, Washington discovered.

"You see any firefighter on an engine, riding off to work, I guarantee you if he's five years on the job he's making nearly $50,000, with overtime," Washington would tell them. He liked to run through the medical benefits, the saving programs that helped grow families and put kids through college, even the generous retirement plan. By then, if the kid was still listening, he'd trot out the biggest perk of all: a firefighter's incredibly short working schedule.

"Guess how many days a month you'll have to work," he'd say. "Eight. No, no, no, I'm not kidding you. You will work eight 24-hour days a month. Anything after that is overtime."

If any of his firefighter brethren had happened to be near the Albee Square Mall on Fulton Street during the many times Washington and Marshall broadcast that news, they likely would have run over and clapped their hands over the Vulcans' mouths. There were many FDNY benefits that inspired envy among other city employees and regular workers—very few got the bountiful salaries, benefits and pensions of cops and firefighters. But probably none was lusted after as much as the eight-day work month. The firefighter practice of stacking shifts into 24-hour rotations—known as "mutuals" to the rank and file—had been around for decades. It allowed a standard 40-hour work week to be compressed into just a few days of round-the-clock service. The FDNY sometimes, as a disciplinary tactic, threatened to suspend the privilege. But mutuals had become so fundamental it wasn't clear if firehouses could function any other way. The unwritten rule among the Bravest was to avoid talking about their good fortune lest some city bean counter somewhere decided to mess with the tried-and-true system.

"You can spend time with your kids, go back to school, get a law degree, hell, you can open up your own business on the side," Washington would say, detailing just how many firefighters were also licensed carpenters, electricians, plumbers, even in some cases airline workers.

"Why do you think so many firefighters own bars?" Washington would joke. But it was true, many firefighters set up and ran clubs and bars, and used their off-duty brothers to sling drinks and double as bouncers.

"Think about this: you apply now, let's say you get on in the next five or so years. In the FDNY, you can retire after 20 years, so you'll be what, 42 by then? You'll be retired at 42 with a solid pension, and in the meantime you'll have earned good pay, built a family and gotten yourself educated and maybe even set up a second career," he'd say, using the patter he and Marshall had perfected. "It can't get any better than that."

It wasn't hard for Marshall and Washington to sell kids on the benefits. But they discovered it could be a bit more challenging to sell them on the lifestyle.

"What's it like in the firehouse? I don't wanna be in there with all those white guys," was a frequent question.

The answer was complicated.

In the early 1990s, the city remained in the grip of the prolonged and widespread racial and class divide. It was still suffering the fallout from a string of NYPD incidents that enraged the black and Latino communities, plus three high-profile deaths of young black men by white mobs, starting with Willie Turks. The 34-year-old transit worker was dragged from his car in Gravesend, Brooklyn, on June 22, 1982, and savagely beaten to death on Avenue X. He and two other black transit workers stopped there to buy bagels on their way home from work. In 1984, the same year a vigilante named Bernard Goetz shot four black men on the subway who he claimed were going to mug him, NYPD cops shot Eleanor Bumpurs twice with a 12-gauge shotgun. They were trying to remove the mentally ill grandmother from her city apartment for falling $98 behind in her rent. Two years later Michael Griffiths, a 23-year-old from Trinidad who lived in Bedford-Stuyvesant, was hit and killed by a car in Howard Beach, Queens, while trying to escape a white mob that had chased and beaten him and his two friends. It sparked a highly charged march in the mostly white and insular community a week later. Al Sharpton, then a little-known civil rights leader decades away from his improbable leap to national prominence, led a crowd of 1,200 mostly black demonstrators around the block while police held back the crowd of shouting, angry locals. It was just a few years after that, in 1989, that five young black and Latino youths were arrested and charged with brutally assaulting and raping a 27-year-old white female investment banker who was jogging in Central Park. The case inflamed an already unruly city and cemented the worst prejudices and suspicions on either side of the racial split. Screaming newspaper headlines said the suspects had been out "wilding."[4] The word was invented for this crime, and it meant the boys had been out tromping through the park looking for opportunities to terrorize and pillage. Within black and Latino communities, the initial shock gave way to outrage and accusations as details emerged of intimidation and trickery in soliciting confessions from the young teens, all under age 16 except one. Set against the backdrop of a racially charged mayoral election—three-termer Ed Koch running against black challenger David Dinkins in the Democratic primary—the case of the Central Park Five reached into every corner of the city and set the politicians chattering about the simmering problems of the new underclass. When a 16-year-old black boy, Yusef Hawkins, was shot to death by a white mob in the predominantly working-class Italian section of Bensonhurst on August 23,

1989, the city exploded. Hawkins had gone to the neighborhood with two friends to inquire about a 1982 Pontiac car for sale. The group was attacked by ten or so white youths armed with baseball bats and guns who were lying in wait for a black teen they suspected of dating a neighborhood girl. When the mob saw Hawkins and his friends, they jumped them. Hawkins was fatally shot twice in the chest. A month later, Koch was voted out by fed-up New Yorkers. They hoped Dinkins, who became the city's first black mayor, could do something to soothe the roiling hostility.

The bristling anger seeped into just about every aspect of city life, and that included its firehouses. Only an idiot would think that life behind those big red doors was untouched by the city's larger, more complicated realities. And the truth was, black firefighters never knew what they would face in the FDNY—and for that matter, no firefighter did. It was all luck of the draw.

Sometimes Washington would share a little bit about his days as a probie, when he endured that time-honored rite of passage of being hazed. His first year at Engine 7 in Lower Manhattan, his company decided it would be funny to turn the hose on him as he and a senior guy played basketball on the court outside. The crew roared with laughter while Washington took a silent soaking. It crossed his mind to give his grinning colleagues a lecture on the negative symbolism of hosing down the only black man on the court, but he swallowed the words. The joke wasn't motivated by anything racial; it was the typical firehouse stunt to bother the new guys. But one veteran firefighter, who didn't hide the fact that he didn't care much for Washington, was among those doing the spraying. He enjoyed it a little too much for Washington's taste. Even though Washington knew probies were supposed to take what was dished out and not complain, he didn't like the ill will lurking under the pretense of good-natured hazing—and he decided to push back with a joke of his own. Washington found his target sitting in the firehouse kitchen a few hours later, reading a newspaper. The probie quietly filled a bucket to the brim, after making sure the water was good and cold. Then he dumped it over the seated man's head. It made a huge splash, and the rest of the house screamed with laughter as they rushed to the kitchen and saw the older firefighter at the table, feigning indifference, thumbing through his wet newspaper.

The young probie was pleased with his revenge, but if he'd been wiser in the ways of the firehouse, he'd have known that some form of retribution was coming. The senior firefighters couldn't let an upstart turn the tables on one of their own—no matter how funny the result. A comeuppance was due. One night, not long after the bucket incident, Washington ran upstairs through the peaceful firehouse to go to sleep around 2 a.m. The night owl probie usually kept late hours. As was firehouse practice, he left the lights off as he entered the pitch-black bunk room so as not to wake up the rest of the sleeping crew. He lay on his bed and closed his eyes. Seconds later, a strange plopping sensation feathered over his face and chest. Something was falling on him. He jumped up and ran to the bathroom, stopping dead when he caught his reflection in the mirror in the dim light. He was covered in fluffy white dust. A powdery halo enshrouded his head and shoulders and coated his hair. Someone rigged a bag of flour over his bunk to spill on him when he lay down, he realized. Enraged, he stormed into the next room where he knew the older firefighter he'd dunked with water was sleeping. Washington was sure he was behind the late-night flour shower. He kicked the man's bed to wake him up.

"You think you got some kind of problem with me then why don't you get up and we'll deal with it!" Washington shouted, his chalky figure leaning over the blinking and bemused man. "Get up! I'll kick your ass," Washington said to the sleepy firefighter. He cursed and called him names when the man refused to move. The rest of the house was silent as Washington raged. He was so peeved he went down to the kitchen and scrawled a message on the blackboard, calling the firefighter a coward and a punk and challenging him to step forward and admit what he'd done. After leaving it where everyone would see it in the morning, Washington returned to the bunk room and showered off. It was only later that he learned the man he'd accused of the stunt hadn't been involved. But everyone else in the firehouse chortled under their blankets as Washington, white flour spattered across all six feet of him, stomped through the place on a shouting tear. When his sense of humor recovered, Washington laughed about it too.

What he didn't say to young kids he was recruiting was that sometimes the silly, childish pranks firefighters loved to play on each other—and particularly on probies—could go too far and take on a sharper, more offensive edge. He didn't tell them that some particularly cruel houses would appoint a firehouse goat. Life was hell for whoever the firefighters decided they didn't like, and the goal was to make the goat transfer out at the earliest opportunity. A goat couldn't let down his guard for a second, and usually broke under the pressure within a few weeks. He didn't say that sometimes the firefighters who would run into danger to save a black family without a moment's hesitation would later crack jokes or make derogatory comments about the inner-city communities they served, while some black firefighters—if there were any around—pretended not to hear.

If Washington had wanted to, he could have told his potential recruits about the time he'd been detailed to a firehouse not far from his regular assignment. When he sat down for the communal dinner, he was the lone black man at a table of 11 whites. He listened to the popular, jocular lieutenant in charge—a man everybody liked and respected—entertain the crew with a tale about his college-aged daughter and the time she came home for the weekend with a new set of friends, including a young black male. The joke centered on the officer's suspicion the two were dating, and his fumbling attempts over the weekend to figure out the true state of their relationship.

"I ain't got nothing against black people, but I certainly don't want my daughter to marry one," the lieutenant laughed as he delivered his punch line. The table roared, except for Washington, who sat without moving. His mind flashed the hundreds of black people living and working right outside the firehouse doors. Nearly a dozen white firefighters were there eating with him and none of them heard anything wrong in what the officer had just said.

"What specifically is it you wouldn't like about your daughter marrying a black man?" he asked the lieutenant, when the chuckles died down. "Is it that you'd have to sit down with in-laws who were black? Accept a black family into your family? What exactly is the problem?"

The room was silent for a second, then the table erupted as the men jumped in to defend the officer. Washington gladly took them on.

Washington didn't tell potential new hires that during his first challenging years on the job, when he was stuck at a slow house in Manhattan with only a few real fire calls, he made a hobby out of getting into long, intense racial discussions with the rest of his house. Firefighters had a general rule of not talking about politics, religion or another colleague's family—but truth be told, the third point was the only one any of them actually followed. The Vulcans always warned new recruits when going into firehouses to stay silent when firefighters teased each other about their ethnicities and cracked stereotypical jokes about Irish and Italians. Washington got that advice when he started too. A firefighter who laughed at someone else's joke about the Irish left himself open to the same kind of cutting humor when the focus turned on him. Washington never participated when those sorts of teasing taunts started to fly. But he wasn't willing to overlook a racist remark, whether it sprang from ignorance or a desire to be deliberately hateful. That's why, when he was again filling a vacancy in a Brooklyn firehouse, he jumped up and ran into the kitchen when he heard somebody joking about who was going to be the nigger that night.

"Excuse me?" he said to the three white firefighters who were trying to figure out who would be responsible for doing all the cleaning and scrubbing. He'd been sitting in the common room off to the side, about to turn on the TV, when the kitchen talk had reached his ears.

"Oh man, I'm sorry," said one of the firefighters, offering his hand to shake. "We forgot you were here." Washington ignored the hand, but zeroed in on the comment.

"So if I weren't here, what you just said would be okay?" he said. "It's okay for you to call the person who has to do all your grunt work the 'nigger'?" Before he knew it, the officer on duty and all the other firefighters were in the kitchen, arguing with him.

Later, he found out from another white firefighter who didn't especially enjoy the particular camaraderie of that crew that it was a regular ritual to appoint a "nigger" for every tour. It was one of a handful of times he heard that word thrown around in a firehouse when others didn't know he was in earshot. The offender always apologized when confronted. But it didn't take long for Washington to discover that his eagerness to delve into taboo topics was more than matched by many other firefighters, mostly whites but some Latinos too. He often found himself in the kitchen, debating fiercely with one or two or sometimes a half-dozen white firefighters, who were dying to get their feelings out. The talks got heated and could boil on for a whole day, ebbing and flowing around training drills and emergency calls. Sometimes, at Engine 7, his good friend Bobby Smith would join him in the kitchen. The two black men would stand together and take on everyone who wanted to voice an opinion. Not everyone in the firehouse liked these hot-tempered free-for-alls. Many times a white firefighter would enter the kitchen, hear the ruckus, and walk back out.

The arguments would range over a host of issues, sometimes related to the news events of the day, often centering on what many of the firefighters saw as the special treatment black candidates were getting from the Vulcans and Mayor Dinkins. And there was still bad blood about the 1973 lawsuit that forced a hiring quota on the city for four years. Yet no matter how hot the arguments got, the firefighters steered carefully away from slinging any slurs directly at Washington—although he suspected they had plenty to say about him when he was not around. There was only one time a firefighter dropped the n-word during an argument, and Washington immediately drew him up short.

"Let me hear you say that word one more time, see what happens to you," Washington said, as the man backtracked. But most of the time, there was no need for fists, or even the threat of them, and Washington much preferred fighting with his words anyway. He'd grown up on an island full of the sons and daughters of cops and firefighters. He never considered himself part of the glorified FDNY brotherhood, but he knew exactly how to zing them.

"Special treatment? You think black firefighters get special treatment? Those glasses you're wearing look pretty thick to me. How'd you get past the vision test? Maybe your daddy made a call down to headquarters for you?" he said to one visually challenged firefighter who joined the kitchen fray to complain about handouts to minority candidates. The man flushed red with rage. Washington relished the moment.

Another big complaint Washington heard was that blacks were lazy: specifically, the black firefighter candidates were so lazy the Vulcans had to fill their application forms out for them to get them into the fire department.

"Oh, okay, so you're saying you got all this because of your hard work, right?" Washington would reply. "Nobody ever reminded you to follow through on an opportunity? Your firefighter daddy or your uncle never filled out a piece of paperwork for you and carried it down to headquarters to hand in because you were busy that day?" Washington knew how the system worked, because that's what his firefighter dad had done for him. He was at Cheyney University in Pennsylvania studying geology when he came back to take his FDNY test. When he graduated with honors he headed out to the West Coast to work, including a stint in Alaska as an air traffic controller. His dad forwarded all the FDNY packets requiring signatures to him and reminded him of all the deadlines to submit his documentation.

But no matter how much Washington debated the other firefighters, they'd be right back in the kitchen the next day, flogging the same point. It didn't matter to Washington how many times they went down that endless road; he was more than happy to argue back.

It wasn't until 1992 that Washington got settled in Engine 234 in Crown Heights. His attempts to switch into a fast-paced firehouse had all failed until that year, when Bill Green, a black lieutenant, filed a suit against the FDNY, charging that he was being kept out of an elite rescue unit while whites with less experience got in. Once Green filed his claim, the FDNY cleared its backlog of black transfer requests, including Washington and firefighter Kirk Coy, who wanted out of the increasingly sleepy East Village and into action-packed Harlem. By a lucky stroke of fate, Washington's cousin Gary was also assigned to Engine 234. Not only were there many more fires, adding to the excitement and connection shared by all the firefighters, there were about four other blacks in the house. As was common in the FDNY, the firehouse was shared by two companies, known as a double house. Each company was assigned to specific tasks. Washington's engine company manned the rig that carried hoses and got water on the flames. The other half of the house was for the ladder company, whose chief job at a fire was to gain entry, vent the building to suck out the heat and smoke, and search for victims. Engine 234 also housed a battalion, which meant a battalion chief and an aide were stationed there, along with a bright red suburban that was used to ferry the top officer to and from emergencies. All told there were about 60 firefighters—all men—six lieutenants, two captains and four chiefs. There were none of the knock-down, drag-out verbal fights that had erupted in his past firehouses, in part because there were more blacks present and also because few of the white firefighters there had an appetite for that type of discussion. And beyond that, an officer who worked frequently with Washington, Lieutenant Bobby Boldi, didn't tolerate that type of infighting.

The captain of Engine 234 had sent Washington to chauffeur school so he could learn how to operate the company's big red rig. The young firefighter didn't mind filling in sometimes as company chauffeur, but he particularly enjoyed it when he got to work alongside Lieutenant Boldi. The two sat side by side as Washington roved the Brooklyn neighborhood of Crown Heights, with its unique mix of Caribbean, African American and Orthodox Jewish residents. Washington hadn't been stationed there when the Crown Heights riots popped off, three days in August 1991 of blacks and Orthodox Jews raging against each other. The violence started when a child of Guyanese immigrants was accidentally struck and killed by an automobile in the motorcade of Menachem Mendel Schneerson, the leader of a Jewish religious sect. The accident was like a powder keg to long-standing animosities and turf wars, and the riots played a major role in the 1993 mayoral elections. Dinkins was heavily criticized for an ineffectual police response.

In the chunks of time Boldi and Washington spent in the truck's front cab, while Engine 234's crew performed building inspections or checked out minor complaints, the two talked about anything and everything. In Boldi, who stood only about five feet eight but was built like a powerhouse, Washington discovered a rare kind of empathy, one that saw beyond color both inside and outside the firehouse. It wasn't a characteristic he'd found among his other white colleagues. The stocky, upbeat lieutenant, who always had a smile on his face and greeted everyone with respectful courtesy, almost never lost his temper. But when he did, the target of his ire was reduced to a quaking mess. Washington never witnessed Boldi exploding, but he heard tales from others. Boldi didn't gloss over the challenges that black firefighters faced. The unlikely pair sometimes even met up in the firehouse to chat in Boldi's office, talking frankly about race relations in the city, the obstacles for blacks to get on the job, the many ways in which they could feel isolated and alone even in the midst of a firehouse crowded with colleagues. There were one or two firefighters Washington liked in Engine 234, guys that he sometimes cracked jokes and talked sports with. But he didn't open up about race with anybody but Boldi, who was one of the few who seemed to get that people could be more than their circumstances. In their quiet moments together, the two men reached an affinity that created a firehouse bond Washington didn't have—and never expected—with other white firefighters.

Once, when Washington was detailed for a day to a nearby firehouse, he got into a brutal fight with a firefighter who had a reputation as a troublemaker. From the minute he walked in the door Washington recognized it was going to be a long shift. He'd encountered that particular smoke eater before, and they'd never mixed well. The man was huge, angry, and always eager to vent on someone. He enjoyed picking fights, and, like most firefighters, Washington found avoiding him the easiest way to deal with him. After a few hours on the temporary detail, when there was a break between runs, Washington went upstairs and stretched out on a bunk. He wasn't aware how much time had passed when suddenly the door flew open and the firefighter stood there, screaming his name.

"Where the fuck have you been? We're looking for you, asshole. There's a phone call for you and we're calling your name over the speaker and you're up here taking a fucking nap," the firefighter yelled. "I oughta kick your ass."

Washington leaped up from the bed.

"Yeah, go ahead. You think you're a bad man, go ahead and do it," he sneered back. That was all he got out before the hulking firefighter—who easily weighed over 230 pounds and had three inches on Washington—lunged forward. He wrapped his hands around Washington's neck, trying to choke the younger man. Washington twisted away, then spun the firefighter around and shoved his attacker backward on the bed. When he fell, Washington pounced. But even sitting on the firefighter's chest, it took every ounce of strength he had to keep the bigger man pinned. They grappled without saying a word, breathing heavily, as Washington struggled to hit him hard in the face. The firefighter beneath him dodged and blocked his punches with his beefy forearms. When the firefighter succeeded in shoving Washington from his chest, they jumped off the bed, still wrestling furiously. Everything happened in less than a minute, but they were both exhausted, trembling from the intensity of the fight. When the fire alarm went off, signaling a run, they stood glaring, gulping for air. As the bells continued to sound, the firefighter turned and walked away. Washington followed him down the stairs, still trying to catch his breath. A few seconds later Washington was on the truck, zooming away to respond to a fire. The other man, instead of going on the call, was relieved from his shift and went home.

By the time Washington got back to his own firehouse, word had already arrived. Gossip inside the FDNY ran faster than most flames, creating the often repeated joke, "Telegraph, telephone, tell-a-firefighter." Washington waved away the eager chatter. He didn't feel like rehashing the whole thing. The guy wasn't worth the hassle.

A few weeks later, Washington learned the troublemaker had been removed, transferred out of the house. It should have fallen to the officers of the firefighter's company to mete out that punishment, but none of them bothered with any disciplinary action. The transfer request came from Lieutenant Boldi, who quietly made some phone calls and put a firm word in a few ears. He never brought it up to Washington, and it wasn't something they had to discuss. Once, during one of their wandering chats, Boldi in his blunt way summed up the basic reality of Washington's everyday firehouse life.

"Paul, these guys ain't ever gonna like you. You're just too proud of being black," the lieutenant said. Washington laughed, recognizing his mother's attitude in the truth of Boldi's words. Around 1995, Boldi was promoted to captain. Not long after, he was diagnosed with cancer. The sickness ate his formerly hearty frame down to a husk but—as Washington learned during his hospital visits—didn't diminish his spirit. During one of their talks, Boldi surprised Washington with a gift.

"Here, I want you to have these," Boldi said, stretching out his hand. The young firefighter saw two slim pieces of silver lying in Boldi's palm—his lieutenant's bars. Boldi knew that Washington had taken the lieutenant's exam and his promotion was imminent. The inheritance was an old fire department tradition, one set of bars handed down from an officer to another as a special token. Washington was touched and proud that Boldi wanted to share it with him. When he made lieutenant, Boldi's bars were the ones pinned to his collar to designate his new rank. His former boss lived just long enough to see it.

In Washington's experience, there were very few white men like Boldi in the fire department, or elsewhere. But he never had a problem looking young black recruits in the eye and promising that if they took the job, they'd never regret it. Some of them were bound to have some bad luck and get stuck in a firehouse with a less-than-stellar company. But the Vulcans would be there to help them find a way out. "You won't ever have to worry about going through this stuff alone," Washington would say, and it was 100 percent the truth. The organization had been forged out of the virulent racism of the Jim Crow era, when the few blacks who were brave enough to try out for the job endured terrible treatment. Wesley Williams founded the Vulcans with the hope that no other black firefighter would ever feel as isolated and vulnerable in a firehouse as he did his first few years.

CHAPTER 5

THE SLOW BURN

Little Italy
January 1919

DAINTY QUEEN ANNE LEAFWORK AND ORNATE CARVINGS ADORNED THE pretty limestone and ruddy brick exterior of Engine 55. The graceful arch over the vivid red door was topped by an elegant curlicue of black wrought iron, a shapely branch sprigged with young shoots. The decorative outer flourishes were a sharp contrast to the spartan sight that greeted Wesley Williams inside his new firehouse. Light streamed from the two round front windows across a concrete floor to illuminate a wide, square spare room. One of its rough walls was covered with racks holding rolled-up hoses. Another was crossed by a neat line of knee-length black jackets, each with a helmet hanging above it. Parked in the middle of the space was a hulking fire engine. A few benches were pushed off to one side, and a sleek metal pole bolted to the floor ran up through a hole in the ceiling and disappeared from Williams's sight. In one corner, tucked close to the kitchen, he spied a black piano, obviously secondhand but polished until it glowed in the bright light. It was 8 a.m. on January 10, 1919, and fireman Wesley Williams was reporting for duty.

The men who'd been in the act of stacking their clothes on the shelves beneath the jackets turned in the doorway as Williams entered. Others were lounging on the benches, swapping stories. The room grew quiet. As the clock chimed the hour, an older man emerged from the staircase and strode to the middle of the room.

"Roll call," he barked, and the men broke their statue-like poses.

"Clifford, M'Bride, Radigan, Chacon, Daley, Hopkins, O'Toole, Shields, Tussi, Carlin," the man snapped out. The firefighters jumped to attention in two military lines in the middle of the room. Williams counted nearly 20 of them. Dropping his bag, he joined the nearest line. The man, obviously an officer, stopped in front of him.

"Williams," the officer ground out.

"Present," Williams responded.

"Fall out," said the man, who Williams surmised was the fire-house captain. The officer marched out of the room.

The men relaxed their stiff shoulders and a few wandered back to the benches to sit down. But still, nobody spoke. Williams set his duffle down by one of the empty pegs on the wall just as the captain reappeared. He gripped in his hand a bag not unlike the satchel Williams carried.

"Well, men," the captain said, into the expectant silence. "I wish you the best of luck." And with that, he walked across the floor and out the front door. Williams was the only person in the room who didn't know that the captain was gone for good. The day Engine 55 learned it was going to have to swallow the stigma of working with a black man, the captain put in for a transfer—along with every single firefighter in the company. An order came back swift and stern from FDNY headquarters: the Negro stays, and so does everyone else. Knowing that if they let any of the firefight-ers switch assignments they'd never be able to keep a full roster, the FDNY decided to declare a moratorium on transfers out of Engine 55 for one year. When the captain was told he would not be allowed to transfer, he put in for retirement instead. He made no bones about the fact that he'd rather end his career than try to fight fires alongside a black man. He complained bitterly to his higher-ups that he was getting a bum deal. Williams should be sta-tioned up in Harlem, the captain insisted. But FDNY brass didn't think it was a good idea to have Williams in a black neighborhood, where he might end up having his friends come around. That left

Williams stuck in Little Italy in a now captainless firehouse, alongside two lieutenants, three steamer engineers and 15 firemen—none of whom wanted him there.

One of those men, apparently a lieutenant, shoved himself off the wall he was leaning on.

"Show probationary firefighter Williams where things are and give him a bed," the officer said to the firefighter nearest him. "Everyone else, you know your assignments. Get busy."

Williams took out the thick, long black jacket he was told to buy and hung it on the wall. Then he started arranging the rest of his clothes on the shelves underneath, like some of the other men had been doing when he came in.

"Say, can you play the piano?" asked the firefighter who'd been told to show him the ropes. "Do you sing and dance too?"

Williams lifted his head. An Irishman who answered to the name O'Toole during roll call regarded him balefully. But the others appeared to be at least curious about him. Some, no doubt anticipating an entertaining way to spend the long evenings when no fire calls came, looked at him hopefully.

"No, I can't sing, can't play the piano. I don't dance either," Williams answered in his easygoing way, and saw disappointment cross a few faces.

"But you all sing and dance and make music," the firefighter protested.

"Nope, not all of us. I don't, for one," Williams replied. That was the last thing anybody said to him.

Despite the earlier orders from the lieutenant, nobody showed Williams where he should sleep. He explored the upstairs quarters on his own, after the entire crew spent the morning cleaning and scrubbing and then retreated into the kitchen for a shared communal meal. Williams didn't venture in to join them. He had already gotten the message that proximity to the white firefighters' food was a bad idea. He'd stepped into the kitchen midmorning to get a drink of water and when he set his cup down, one of the firefighters came in behind him and without a word swept it into the trash can. During lunch, he went upstairs and took his first look at his new sleeping arrangement—one large dormitory room full of military-style beds. The men sent the lieutenant to tell him he wasn't welcome there.

"Listen here, Williams," the officer said. "We'll make a deal with you. We'll start talking to you and let you eat with us on one condition. You take your bunk, you carry it downstairs and you sleep in the basement."

Williams briefly considered the offer. The idea of being segregated to the basement held absolutely no appeal.

"I don't think so," Williams replied. "I'm not sleeping in the basement. I'm a firefighter in this company now, and I'm sleeping up here."

He wound up getting assigned the bed in the least comfortable spot in the entire dorm, right next to the creaky bathroom door and positioned in such a way that the latrine light glared upon it. It certainly didn't give Williams the feeling that he'd be getting a good night's rest.

He expected his first days to be challenging and they were. The silent treatment continued, but the crew wasn't as openly antagonistic as he'd feared. Nobody had tried to hit him yet. But the seething antipathy coming from several of the men wasn't something to be ignored, especially since everybody else in the company seemed likely to develop a sudden case of blindness or deafness should things turn really ugly. It didn't really matter to him if anyone in Engine 55 spoke to him or not. None of the men struck him as worth getting to know anyway. They continued the ridiculous ritual of breaking any dishes or cutlery that he touched, or just pushing whatever items he used into the garbage. Whenever he entered a room, they all stood and walked out. They'd decided to do their best to force him out, and that was fine by him. He'd already made a few discoveries on his own that made life inside the firehouse infinitely more palatable. The best part of Engine 55 for Williams was its deserted, wide-open roof. He found the small staircase above the third floor during one of his early solo explorations of the quaint firehouse. He stepped outside and took a deep breath of the biting January air, relieved to have a few moments far away from the crew downstairs. The shouts and yells from packed Broome Street called him to the parapet edge, and he peered over the side to get a view of the corners crowded with fast-talking immigrants. He didn't know downtown as well as he knew Harlem and the Bronx, and a sense of excitement flowed into him as he watched the people hurrying on their day-to-day business. The street traffic was enticing as it hummed along, full of young school kids running home; Italian and Jewish housewives on errands, dressed in modest but spotless clothes; men of all ages and backgrounds either selling something or standing on street corners looking for work. Most of the buildings around him were taller than pocket-sized Engine 55. Clotheslines were strung outside of back windows, a fluttering backdrop to the cramped tenement walk-ups. A cart loaded with fresh fruits and vegetables rumbled along the street, and Williams had felt a growl in his stomach when he saw it. He went back downstairs and ran to the first floor. The rest of the crew was still eating lunch, but he opened the door to the street and stepped outside. He only had to wait a few minutes before another street vendor came along. Williams waved him over to the firehouse and, by dint of gesturing and pointing, got some vegetables he could eat.

Even with the frigid cold, Williams spent plenty of time in his airy retreat. The roof held a large, circular structure shaped like a grain silo. It was the hose tower, where the crews hung their 50-foot water lines to dry. Williams turned the small vertical space into his own private weight lifting and workout area. It also became a haven for his books. He spent hours tucked inside, reading and studying how-to manuals on firefighting. When he emerged, he would pump out some jumping jacks and toe touches. Then he was ready to return to the tension on the main floor.

As his first week passed and he settled into his role as house pariah, Williams was grateful he'd gotten the ten days of training at the probationary academy, because nobody showed him anything. The all-white crew of Engine 55 treated him like a melanoma that had to be excised. Williams was acknowledged at the daily roll calls and assigned a large number of household chores. It was the usual subservient role for a probationary firefighter, except the men in Engine 55 went out of their way to make his list of unpleasant tasks utterly onerous. But to Williams's surprise, as much as he was hated inside the firehouse, he was embraced outside its doors. The largely Italian community surrounding Engine 55 had their own history of culture clashes with the Irish. The firehouse, as always, was one of the focal points of the community. Very little went on inside that the Italians outside didn't hear about, one way or another. Williams went out into the street as often as he could. Usually it was in search of food, because he decided it was too risky to eat anything that came out of the communal kitchen. Not that he could if he wanted to—the firefighters refused to let him contribute to the pool of money they used to buy the food they cooked and prepared themselves in the kitchen. But even if he'd been invited to participate in the family-style meals, he would have declined. He was sure that, given a chance, one of the firefighters would slip him something to make him sick—or, even worse, hide something truly vile in his food and let him eat it, none the wiser. It would be a good joke that they would all laugh at later, and soon the story would spread through the entire fire department that the crew at Engine 55 had gotten that black man, and gotten him good.

Williams came to rely on the agile street boys. They were always eager to run and buy him lunch or dinner in exchange for a few coins. After a couple of days they learned to wait for him at certain times, craning their heads to get a look at the heavy-framed fire truck parked inside. Sometimes, when he was assigned to polish it and the weather wasn't too cold, Williams would roll it halfway out the front door. The machine was a magnet, attracting every unemployed neighborhood man and curious boy. He liked to talk to the people as he worked and ask questions about the ever-changing enclave. And many of the Italians who hung around Engine 55 had a few of their own kind in the fire department: Antonio Pepe, for one, was in Williams's very own firehouse. They usually knew more about the state of race relations inside Engine 55 than Williams himself.

"You know, word is they're going to try and burn you up," one of his errand boys told him one day, as Williams came out to send him off for food.

"That so?" Williams replied, fishing in his rough work pants for the coins he kept there. "Whaddya hear?"

"I just heard that, they're looking to burn you up. My daddy heard it himself from someone who works in the company, they said, 'We're going to burn this nigger up.'"

"They said you're gonna go out in the first big fire they get, 'cause you can't take the smoke 'cause your nostrils are too wide," the boy added.

Williams stared at the urchin thoughtfully, and dropped an extra coin in the sticky palm cupped before him. "Here you go, kid," he said. "You don't worry about me. I can handle myself."

Even though Williams wasn't getting any real hands-on instruction on how to work in a fire, he was getting a crash course in how to survive in the actual firehouse. When the company ran drills he watched carefully, mimicking the other firefighters. No one talked to him or offered tips, but a few, especially if O'Toole wasn't around, would make their movements slow and deliberate so he could follow them better. Williams saw O'Toole was best avoided. A former cop, he got a thrill talking about all the niggers he beat up whenever Williams happened to be within earshot.

The company went out on a few small calls. Located as it was close to the garment district—a section known as Hell's Hundred Acres—the firehouse got its share of action. But so far nothing truly raging had come in. Yet even those minor runs caused the acting officer of the house serious agita. Engine 55 had a potentially humiliating problem—one that was even bigger than having a black man in its ranks. This problem threatened no end of embarrassment if it ever got out, and it would bring down the wrath of fire department headquarters too. Nobody in Engine 55 had any finesse with the hulking metal apparatus that was their fire engine. The fire department was in the process of phasing out its horse-drawn fire rigs—in fact, they all should have been gone by 1917. But, as the frustrated chief in charge of the training would admit to himself in private, the firemen, never ones to embrace a new way of doing things, showed a maddening obtuseness with the newfangled machines. The FDNY was several years behind in replacing horses, and even further behind in training the willfully Luddite firemen how to drive. It didn't help that the fire trucks were clumsy and slow to respond. Steering was a challenge, and making a quick stop almost impossible. The men identified to take over as drivers were those who had a background as dock workers or trolley car operators. They lurched and burped through the streets, trying to get comfortable with the unwieldy clutches and bucking engines. In densely crowded Little Italy, driving Engine 55's truck was a nightmare. Running children, loose dogs and cackling chickens abounded, and they were just as likely to dart into the street as stay on the sidewalk. Taking the fire truck out of Engine 55 was a nerve-racking experience, but the real fear came when it was time to return. That meant somebody had to drive the fitful machine in reverse, easing it backward, carefully, through the single-door archway of Engine 55 at a slight angle so it would slide between the two walls with just inches to spare.

Not long after Williams got on the job, the humiliating situation that Engine 55's lieutenant desperately hoped to avoid arrived. The men went out on a run, and upon their return the perspiring driver behind the wheel couldn't find the right angle to fit the fat machine back in the firehouse. A snickering crowd of voluble Italians amassed on the street around them.

"I'll do it," Williams volunteered, as the lieutenant stared in exasperation at the capricious machine.

"Yeah, let Williams do it," another firefighter said, overhearing the offer, and soon the rest of the company was adding its approval.

"Let him try, Lieutenant, if he wants to," smirked one of the crew.

"All right, Williams, get up there," the officer told him.

As the grateful driver climbed down, Williams hopped confidently into the seat. None of the other firefighters knew he had driven a post office mail truck for six months. He'd also had ample time to study the fire truck and its clutches and pedals during his regular washings, when he rolled it part way out of the firehouse and then pushed it back in. He knew exactly what angle to take to make the machine slide home. He revved the engine over the clapping and shouts from the Italian mob around them. Williams smiled to himself. Damned if he wasn't going to take a chance to rub this in the rest of the firefighters' faces, he thought. Signaling with his hands to clear the street in front of him, Williams pulled the machine forward, nose pointing so that it looked like it would go right into the big brick tenement across the street. After taking a last look over his shoulder to make sure nobody stood behind him, he swiftly and surely backed the fire truck through the narrow doors of Engine 55. Cutting off the engine, he jumped down and walked back outside, where the locals cheered and laughed, immensely tickled by the display. The lieutenant motioned him over.

"You can drive," he said, and Williams nodded. "Fine. That's your assignment. From now on, when that truck goes out, you're driving it."

"Yes, sir," Williams replied. The position of driver was a highly visible and prestigious one. He knew it was going to infuriate the rest of the crew, and likely make the festering animosity finally explode. He couldn't wait.

Williams's first six months on the job were punctuated by infrequent visits home, when he'd have to shake every hand on the block and reassure his wife and his worried parents that things were going well. His appointment to chauffeur was still eating at his colleagues in Engine 55, and in fact incensed firefighters throughout the department. When he'd first driven the rig to a second-alarm fire on Canal Street, the FDNY Assistant Chief of Department Patrick "Paddy" Walsh had thrown up his hands in disgust.

"Of all the men in the fire department, he's got to pick that man to drive the apparatus," Walsh snarled to his personal driver. Walsh, who went on to become fire commissioner in 1941, never dreamed his chauffeur, Augustine O'Connor, would one day work alongside Williams and relate the anecdote to him. At the time, Williams was still an outcast in the firehouse and within the department. Nobody figured he'd make it that long. He was not to be addressed or spoken to, except in the case of a direct order; and he was more convinced than ever that keeping his food separate from the others was the safe thing to do. He'd ventured a few times into the communal kitchen where firefighters sat for long hours on cold winter nights talking endlessly about the job, politics and women. But his entrances caused such painfully abrupt silences that he stopped doing it.

He'd learned a few other valuable lessons too, like never to leave his equipment hanging in the communal lockers. After he was appointed driver, the first time an alarm bell rang in the house, he jumped up and sprinted to his gear. He grabbed his black jacket and tried to shrug it on while climbing behind the wheel, only to end up in a tangle of fabric. Someone had taken a razor and carefully sliced his jacket to ribbons and hung it back on the peg so he would grab it without knowing. Other times he'd race to find his gear during an alarm and discover it tossed in a heap at the foot of the basement stairs. He couldn't leave his helmet out either, because in the chaotic rush it often got kicked out of sight—sometimes even under one of the rig's wheels, to be crushed to pieces. Slimy chicken entrails got dumped inside his boots. Complaining was useless, Williams knew, so he kept his mouth shut even as he started securing all his gear in a locked box. It was the only way to avoid having to pay out of his own pocket to replace what got destroyed. He didn't complain when the firefighters, who still wouldn't speak to him but had no problem speaking of him, made racist remarks within his hearing. He didn't even complain when most of the firefighters took to using the firehouse spittoons as their own private urinals. He was pretty sure they were led by firefighter O'Toole. They all knew the probie had to clean every inch of Engine 55, and that included the toilets, the bathroom floor and sink, and the many spittoons put out for those who chewed tobacco. The noxious stench of urine mixed with the charred stench of smoky saliva was enough to turn Williams's stomach. But he scrubbed uncomplainingly, even knowing the spittoons would be filled up with piss and spit again the next day.

He hadn't forgotten the warning from the Italians who had hooks in his firehouse that some of the men were looking to "burn him up." So far, they hadn't gotten a chance. But they worked in a busy industrial area, close to the Triangle Shirtwaist Factory that went up in flames in 1911, killing 23 men and 123 women, some as young as 14. A big blaze was inevitable. It finally came, a terrible fire down near the Bowery. Something combustible caused a massive explosion inside a tenement, and Williams's engine company roared up, among the first to arrive. Grabbing a hose line from the fire engine, Engine 55's men prepared to attack: they were ordered into the cellar. Williams was shoved to the front and handed the nozzle.

"Get in there and show us what you can do," one of the men yelled at him. The rest of the crew lined up tight behind him, body to body, as they braced for the rushing power of pressurized water. The men had only fire helmets, rubber boots, gloves and their long thick rubber coats as protection. There were no air masks, no fire-proof bunker gear and no radios or emergency buttons to push for help. The crew advanced down the dark steps into the cellar, choking in the smoke and glowing flames that licked the walls and ceiling. A gas meter had exploded, and as Williams led the crew into the room, spraying water everywhere, another gas ball erupted.

The young probie couldn't see or hear anything beyond the screaming pitch of the backdraft that rolled over his head, a furious twister of black smoke and writhing red tendrils. He instinctively dropped to his knees. When he slowly straightened into a half crouch, he struggled to keep hold of the wild hose that threatened to knock him down again. Looking behind him, he realized he was alone. Engine 55 had pulled out. They'd left him behind.

A flight above, the men of Engine 55 spilled out onto the street. Whether they deliberately chose to abandon Williams or he simply lacked the experience to know when to run, they broke a cardinal firefighting rule. A battalion chief strode over, addressing the lieutenant who, as an officer, should have been the first in the cellar and the last to leave.

"Are all your men accounted for?" Chief Ben Parker asked sharply.

"No. Williams is down there," answered the lieutenant.

It was a fortunate break for all of them that Williams, still down in the basement, was putting a final spray on the last burning embers. Had he died, it's unlikely that even the Tammany clannishness would have convinced the fire department to look the other way, or that their own firefighting brothers would have excused them. It was a grievous dereliction of duty—and a betrayal of the deeply held bond of brotherhood—to abandon a fellow Bravest, even a black one. Thankfully, the great ball of fire that roared over Williams's head depleted itself along with the rest of the flammable gas. Aided by judicious hits from his nozzle, Williams had succeeded in containing and extinguishing what remained of the flames. He climbed wearily back up the stairs, sweaty and smoke-stained.

"So, men, you were gonna burn him up," Battalion Chief Parker said to the disgraced crew as Williams's sooty figure emerged. "Looks like he burned you up instead."

By rights, Williams's bravery should have earned him a break back in the firehouse. Instead, the hazing intensified. But others in the fire department were impressed by his staying power, and word started to circle that maybe the new black recruit would be all right. Back at the firehouse, the haters in Engine 55 decided to up the ante.

A heavy, long-handled wrench somehow slipped from someone's hand just as Williams was sliding down the shiny metal pole from the second floor to the main room below. The tool crashed on his head as his feet touched the ground, striking a direct blow to his forehead, right above his eye. His blood splattered across the firehouse floor. Williams staggered to stay on his feet, clapping a hand over the gushing cut. A warm crimson flow trickled over his eyelashes and through his fingers.

"Who did that? Who threw that?" he demanded furiously. The firefighters, rushing to get on the truck, ignored him.

Another time, as Williams enjoyed his airy perch atop the firehouse roof, one of the firefighters stumbled out to join him. He was a taciturn, hulking fellow, the one Williams privately called the big Bohemian, because of his German heritage and massive bulk. The man didn't speak, just stepped close to where Williams stood. Watching him carefully, Williams understood this wasn't to be a friendly visit. When the man sprang at him, Williams was ready. He grabbed the larger man in a viselike headlock.

"You better not try it," Williams said, squeezing the man's windpipe until he gasped and wheezed. "Now you listen to me. You tell all your buddies downstairs to never approach me on the roof again, here or at any fire. Any of you think you're going to throw me off a roof you better know this: I'll take every man around me over too. At least one of you will go down with me."

That was the last visit Williams ever got. And at fires, his colleagues gave him wide berth. Most of them likely would have been content to just leave him be, Williams thought. But there was a core clique in Engine 55 that was determined to break him—and nobody else in the house would buck them. It was time to address the ringleaders, Williams realized. In the age-old firehouse tradition, that meant only one thing: a bare-knuckle fistfight.

Long before the days of human resource offices and departments of personnel, fire department problems were solved by brawling, preferably in the firehouse basement. It was an all-male world, and one with a liberal policy on alcohol consumption. Fistfights were not uncommon, and they were generally treated like family affairs. The fire officers looked the other way, the firefighters took bets on who would win, and the two combatants—who might be sworn mortal enemies at the moment but would drop their ill feelings in a heartbeat if an alarm bell rang—would go to the basement and square off. The rest of the crew waited upstairs to learn the outcome. The winner was always the first to come up. The loser stayed down below to wash the blood off his face and the floor.

It was time to show the bigots in his firehouse exactly what they were up against, Williams decided. They'd tried to freeze him out, hound him out, smoke him out and throw him out—well, now they could try to beat him out. He knew an opportunity to get angry over something would present itself soon, and he was right.

It came during a routine inspection of the fire engine. The finicky machine, unhappy with the winter cold, let out a cough and then refused to turn over when Williams pressed the starter switch. One of his tormentors wandered over to watch him.

The fireman muttered something behind him, and Williams caught the words "kinky hair."

"What was that?" Williams said, swinging around.

"I said, 'Use some kinky hair on that and it would turn,'" the man answered, for the first time addressing Williams directly. Williams set down the rag he had in his hand and leaned back against the machine, hooking one ankle across the other.

"You want to go down in the cellar with me?" he said, staring into the fireman's bright, watchful eyes.

"Yeah, I'll go down with you," came the reply. The fireman smiled at the others who, sensing a fight, started to gather. "Let's go."

The two men walked over to the small door that led to the dank cellar below Engine 55 and disappeared. The others headed to the kitchen to keep an eye on the small opening. But they didn't even have time to make coffee. A few minutes later, footsteps bounced up the basement stairs and the door swung open. Williams stepped out and took in the air of stupefied shock spreading across the room. He had not a mark on him, save for the halfway healed cut above his brow. His shirt, which he'd taken off downstairs before the fight, was carefully tucked in and as wrinkle-free as ever. He didn't look like he'd done much more than take a short walk in the park. Smiling at them, Williams returned to his task of checking the fire truck. The white firefighter was downstairs where Williams had left him, struggling to get up off the floor to wash his face.

Williams wasn't naive enough to think this was the end of the firehouse hazing. Once the crew recovered, someone else would come around to make sure this fight hadn't been a fluke. But the fireman he'd bested wouldn't be able to tell them much in the way

Wesley Williams scored a perfect 100 on the FDNY physical exam in 1919. Photo credit: Charles Williams, Family Collection, Schomburg Center.

of useful information to better prepare against him. Williams had made sure of that. He had two secret weapons in his favor, and he meant to use them to his advantage for as long as necessary. The first was simple: nobody in the house realized he was a natural lefty. He wrote and did most things with his right hand—thanks to his grammar school teacher—but he had a southpaw's mean hook. It came out of nowhere and could knock a man flat. The firefighters also didn't know that for months before he entered the fire department, some old-school black prizefighters had given him boxing lessons.

Sam Langford, an all-time great boxer known as the Boston Bonecrusher—the only fighter world heavyweight champion Jack Dempsey said he ever feared—and sturdy Joe Jeanette, the most terrifying inside boxer of his day, were familiar figures at the colored Y. They approached Williams one day in the locker room after he finished his daily laps. News of his appointment had just started making the rounds in black newspapers, and congratulations were flowing in. He looked up in awe at the legendary prizefighters when they approached.

"Boy, you're going down to work with the Irish. You're going to need to know how to fight," Langford told him bluntly. "You're going to get lessons from us."

The men had taught him well, and they'd done him a big favor. They'd taken his natural strength and speed and added a layer of devastating power and skill. Williams was sure he could go toe-to-toe with just about anybody and win, which was a good thing since it was now clear he was going to have to spend a lot of time fighting more than fires. And if he had to whup every man in the company—or even the fire department—to get them to understand that he was not quitting, he would.

CHAPTER 6

GET OUT OF THE KITCHEN

New York City
1920s

AS TOXIC AND MALIGNANT AS NEW YORK CITY FIREFIGHTERS' REACTIONS were to Wesley Williams, they were not out of step with the larger racial realities of 1920s America. Some black firefighters had slowly infiltrated fire departments in many major northeastern cities but in very small numbers. Chicago created all-black firehouses in 1872 with Engine Co. 21. Its official paid professional status came a year after black firefighters fought valiantly alongside whites in the Great Chicago Fire of 1871. Chicago's black firefighters invented the sliding pole that allowed a quick drop to the main floor from sleeping quarters above, although most credit Boston with creating it.[1] In Los Angeles, two firehouses in an emerging minority neighborhood were staffed with Mexican and black firefighters, over the protest of white smoke eaters. Cambridge, Massachusetts, led the nation in appointing the first black fire chief, Patrick H. Raymond, on January 5, 1871. The son of an escaped Virginia slave, Raymond worked as a journalist before becoming a fire chief. When Cambridge was absorbed by Boston's fire department, blacks were quickly isolated and in many cases, well into the 1970s, knocked out of the running for jobs despite what was supposed to be a fair-minded civil service system. Around 1912, black inventor Garrett Morgan devised an air mask for firefighters, a forerunner of the high-tech systems in use today. But just like in the FDNY, the all-white fire departments weren't ready to eat, sleep and work around the clock with black men. The U.S. military hadn't even broken that racial barrier yet, and wouldn't until after World War II. America was still many pitched battles away from willingly sharing public space among races—let alone welcoming a black man into the ranks of their neighborhood heroes.

In New York City, it wasn't just ignorance that stood in the way of progress—politics did too. Tammany Hall still ruled much of the city and in fact was firmly in control of the FDNY. The civil service system embraced by Teddy Roosevelt was intact, and had actually grown larger and more efficient. But that didn't mean there weren't ways around it. One such tool was known as the one-in-three rule. The bosses at city agencies succeeded in getting a measure passed that allowed them to choose only one out of every three candidates on a hiring list, if they were so inclined. In practical terms, that meant fire department bosses could cherry-pick which names they wanted—and those passed over got no reason for their exclusion. They did not even have to be notified of it. Ostensibly, the rule was to help department heads have more control over which officers got appointed to the very highest positions. But the rule applied to rank and file too. It was also possible, in civil service's early days, for creative grading and other string pulling, predicated mainly on the "who you know" theory of advancement. Calls between family friends could be made, favors were granted. It was a pattern that would stay with the fire department for the next 100 years. It was also a pattern that Wesley Williams was able to exploit, thanks to his father's powerful connections, and he did so many times throughout his career.

When Williams took the fire department test in 1918, firefighters had to produce a character letter. His father, James, contacted Roosevelt, the granddaddy of civil service. Roosevelt, at that point in waning health but still politically active, had written hundreds of such letters in his career: odes to the moral qualities of fine young men who, through merit-based examinations, were getting a fair shot in life. The old Rough Rider was more than willing to pen one for Williams. But even armed with a character reference from a former U.S. president, Williams almost didn't get on the job. He was wait-listed for about a year despite his impressive scores on both the physical and written exams. The rest of the men who took the test with him were hired. Ironically, Williams's breakthrough rested upon the benevolence of Tammany Hall and his father's connections. The now gray-haired Red Cap reached back to his youth and contacted his old boss, flower shop owner Charles Thorley. Thorley, over the course of 20 years, had become a major political player inside Tammany, mainly through his heavy fund-raising and generous donations. Thorley had always championed progressive causes, and so when James Williams asked for a little help getting his boy a leg up, Thorley responded. He let it be known to Tammany leaders that his annual $50,000 gift might disappear if the son of a dear old friend was passed over for selection. The Tammany order went down to the FDNY: pick the Negro from the list. Privately, the Tammany machine didn't give him much chance of flourishing in the firehouse, but they made it clear he was to get his shot. The man who took Tammany's order was the agency's chief of department, John Kenlon.

Kenlon, born in 1861 in County Louth, Ireland, left his mule, his plow and his not-so-fertile fields behind to try life on the high seas when he was 13 years old. He sailed into New York and landed in the FDNY in 1887. By 1911, he was the chief of department, the highest-ranking uniformed position within the agency. Kenlon couldn't protect Williams in the firehouse, but he emphasized to other top brass that Williams had friends in high places. When the FDNY finally did appoint a new captain to Engine 55 to replace the one who abruptly retired, the officer went to Kenlon to get his orders.

"What am I to do with the black man?" asked the new captain, John J. Brennan.

"He stays," Kenlon said bluntly. "Those are the orders, but I am sending you there because I want you to handle the affair in the right manner."

Kenlon had chosen wisely in Brennan, a man who respected effort and work above all else. As Brennan got to know Williams, it no longer mattered that he was there under Tammany's directive. Brennan came to respect the young smoke eater's spirit and determination. One day, as Williams performed his usual task of polishing the firehouse rig, the captain of Engine 27 drove up. It was Thomas O'Toole, the brother of fireman John O'Toole, the main instigator of trouble for Williams. Addressing Captain Brennan, who stood outside, Thomas O'Toole gestured at Williams.

"What are you doing with this nigger? If he worked for me, he'd be gone by now. I'd keep him going night and day and he'd quit in three weeks," Captain O'Toole said. "He would never have a chance to stop."

Brennan just shook his head. "He'd do everything you tell him. You'd never make him quit," Brennan said. With Brennan's arrival, the worst of the firehouse hazing stopped. But by and large, the men still refused to speak to Williams. He'd taken a few more of them down into the basement too, until they'd gotten tired of being smacked around. Williams showed his white firefighting brothers no mercy, drilling them with punches until they dropped to the floor. Soon, nobody challenged him anymore. They still didn't socialize with him, but that didn't bother him. He spent most of his free time on the roof in his hose tower space, working out or reading. He was a student of history, philosophy and also the fire sciences. He was determined to take and pass the civil service exam for officer when he was eligible in 1924.

"You'll be a boss over white men when black crows turn white," jeered one of the men, when the Engine 55 crew spotted him reading a training manual. Williams just shut his book and went upstairs. He'd gotten used to being laughed at, but mostly he was just ignored. The Fire Department persisted in overlooking him even when he logged a spectacular rescue—which he'd done several times by then. The first one came after a few months on the job, and it made a big splash, in the black newspapers at least. His officers, however, were unmoved. Williams had been walking in Harlem with his dad when shouts of "Fire!" broke out near 187th Street and St. Nicholas Avenue. Even though he was off-duty, Williams ran over. Hook & Ladder 40 had already responded and the men were raising an aerial ladder up to five screaming children trapped on an upper floor. Williams darted up a scaling ladder and was nearly at its top when the oldest boy, a white teenager named William Thompson, hurled himself from the window, aiming for the aerial ladder nearby. He made a clean jump, but couldn't hold on. As his sisters and brothers screeched in horror, the teen's grip slipped. Just as he started to plummet, Williams made a superhuman save, plucking the falling youth from midair as he launched himself from one ladder to the next. Clinging to the boy with one hand and the aerial ladder with the other, he got his legs wrapped around the rungs, and succeeded in hoisting his passenger over his shoulder for a safe descent. When Thompson was on the ground, Williams went back up the ladders to help firefighters bring the other four children to safety.

Later, he asked the officer in charge if he might get written up for a commendation. "Nah, that was just regular duty. Nothing special in that," the officer replied. It was an answer Williams would hear several times over the next few years.

He was getting recognition for one thing though—his boxing. He continued to train with Joe Jeanette and Sam Langford at the colored Y on 135th Street in Harlem. He also got additional instruction from "Panama" Al Brown, a devastatingly fast lightweight who'd moved to New York City from the Caribbean. Captain Brennan told the chiefs at FDNY headquarters about Williams's annihilating skills, and that got him an invitation to enter the city's Municipal Athletic Association's boxing tournament on behalf of the department. Given his proficiency, Williams decided he should fight in the heavyweight division, even though he was a trim 180 pounds. He took the championship two years in a row, to the delight of the FDNY brass and the disgust of some of his Engine 55 brothers.

In between boxing bouts and fire calls, Williams joined his newfound Italian friends in a little black market business. Prohibition was in full swing, which meant the illegal liquor trade was booming and New York City was lousy with illicit speakeasies. Many of the Italians around the firehouse dabbled in the lucrative underground market for booze. Williams soon realized he could score a little cash off it too. At first the Italians were interested in him because of his uptown connections in Harlem, where the nightlife was going full bore. But once they realized he also had a link to Grand Central Terminal, his popularity really soared. The train hub got cars coming in from all across America, including Canada. The bulk of the travel was done on Pullman railways, which were staffed by black porters. The trains took the black porters all over the country, making them a perfect network to pick up moonshine, corn liquor and green river whiskey and bring it back to the city. The Italians hooked Williams up with a truck and a driver, and when a haul came in he'd head off to Penn Station or Grand Central Terminal to load up the hooch. The contraband wound up in Harlem's many backroom social clubs, netting Williams $300 to $400 a pop.

It also won him increased protection and affection from the Italians around Engine 55, which was a good thing to have in the violent 1920s. The Italians sometimes sent him messages warning him to keep away from certain stores or restaurants at specific times, or when to stay inside the firehouse because something violent was going down on the street. Decades after the repeal of Prohibition, when Williams was safely retired, he would tell the story of two FDNY officers who took a long-planned vacation to Italy with their wives. One night, they ate at a restaurant owned by an Italian immigrant who had moved to New York and then returned home. Hearing that he had New Yorkers in his eatery, the owner stepped out to chat, and upon learning they were firefighters, he clapped his hands in excitement.

"You must know Wesley Williams!" the man cried, beside himself with joy when both men nodded their heads.

"But you know he was the biggest bootlegger in Little Italy," the man exclaimed. "He is a great friend of mine!"

As much as the older Williams laughed, later in life, about his days on the wrong side of the law, his bootlegging sideline was a significant risk for him as a young firefighter. There were any number of people who would have loved to turn him in and blot out his career in a dark cloud of disgrace.

Williams counted his blessings that his family connections meant many eyes were upon him. It afforded him a small measure of protection—a luxury the black firefighter who came before him, John H. Woodson, never had. Woodson had been all alone, stationed in the hinterlands of Brooklyn and Queens. After Williams got on the job, he made it his mission to track Woodson down, and the two met up in Grand Central Terminal to swap stories and talk. It was then that Williams learned he was technically the third black firefighter in the FDNY—and actually the sixth if you included civilian jobs. Like the rest of the world, Williams had always seen the FDNY as Irish, with a decent smattering of British, Germans, Italians, Eastern Europeans and even some Jews. That was true, and in

Wesley Williams with some members of his all-white crew at Engine 55 at 363 Broome Street in Little Italy, New York, circa 1920s. Photo Credit: Charles Williams, Family Collection, Schomburg Center.

Manhattan, no other black man had entered the hallowed FDNY before him. But in Brooklyn, he learned, it was a different story.

Before it was annexed into New York City in 1898, Brooklyn— a key stop on the Underground Railroad—had built up a small black political patronage mill. Through the Republican Party, a few black leaders had been able to dole out some decent-paying laborer jobs. Charles Anderson, a key black official in the Republican Party, claimed to have gotten blacks 697 positions in 1913, mostly with the Postal Service.[2] Blacks weren't a significant presence in the FDNY, but between 1898 and 1913 there was a black inspector of combustibles, a clerk and an oil inspector.[3] The earliest-known paid black man hired at the rank of firefighter was William Nicholson, a former cement tester from Virginia. He was appointed by a high-ranking chief in 1898, just before Brooklyn merged with New York City. He lived with his wife and two young children at 260

Myrtle Avenue and was assigned to Engine Co. 6, on High Street. His salary was $800 a year.[4]

Nicholson never once put water on a flame, or got to work as a firefighter. Rank-and-file opposition was so stiff, he was greeted by a new department order on the first day he showed up at Engine Co. 6 to work: "When William H. Nicholson reports for duty, send him to Headquarters. He is detailed to the Veterinary Department in Manhattan."[5]

Nicholson spent his career shoveling manure and feeding horses after being warehoused in the vet's unit. By the time the 1910 census rolled around, he had moved his expanding family to Fort Greene Place in Brooklyn. On the census records, Nicholson's job as "fireman" stands out. He was the only black male in his immediate area working for the city, but probably few people in his neighborhood knew it, since Nicholson wasn't allowed to fight fires. The only exception came every year on July 4, when the department insisted all able-bodied firefighters suit up in preparation for 24 hours of firecrackers and other explosive celebrations. On that day, Nicholson was allowed to appear in public as a firefighter. Nicholson left the FDNY in 1912 as quietly as he entered it, when he was just shy of 13 years of service. The reasons aren't clear—some records say the 41-year-old suffered a career-ending injury from a swift horse kick in the knee. Other reports indicate he had heart disease. In either case, the only newspaper that noted his departure was the *Chicago Defender,* which revealed he was retiring on a pension of $700 a year—a hefty sum. Records also indicate that after he passed away, his widow got a firefighter's pension.

Likewise, the appointment of John H. Woodson is somewhat shrouded in mystery. Woodson, also from Virginia, worked in Brooklyn's Postal Service in the early 1900s. In 1914, when Woodson joined the FDNY, the city was in the grip of a three-party race for mayor—and Tammany Hall was starting to grapple with Roosevelt's Republican Party for the black vote.[6] Brooklyn blacks had long been loyal to Republicans, but Tammany Hall leaders were making overtures—heralding the big switch that would come in the 1920s, when black voters started to turn out for Democrats in large numbers. Woodson's appointment might have been part of a deal brokered by a black Republican leader, who abruptly switched his allegiances and began to campaign for the Democratic candidate for mayor. Woodson's appointment to the FDNY has been seen as a reward to George Wibecan. A longtime postal worker and Brooklyn's most powerful black leader, Wibecan didn't shy away from using his clout to get blacks jobs.[7] As part of the agreement to get a black man into the FDNY, Wibecan and Woodson agreed not to publicize his new appointment for fear of upsetting white voters.[8]

Somehow the news trickled out though, for in the October 24, 1914, edition of *The Gazette,* an African American newspaper in Cleveland, Ohio, this item appeared: "The first Afro-American to become a member of the New York City Fire Department was appointed by Commissioner Adamson recently. He is John Woodson and he has been assigned to duty with Truck 106, at 124 Greenpoint Ave, Brooklyn. He was third on the civil service list and successfully passed through the school of instruction."[9]

Woodson appears to have fared well in his firehouse, known officially as Hook & Ladder 106. An article three years later in *The Bee,* a black newspaper in Washington, D.C., lauds him for a tremendous rescue that almost killed him. The newspaper interviewed FDNY Fire Commissioner Robert Adamson for the article, who recalled how Woodson came to join the 5,200 all-white Bravest.[10]

In 1914, Adamson said, he'd been talking over the latest recruits with Chief Kenlon and recalled the "whimsical" look on the officer's face when he pointed out that there was a "Negro on the list."

"You know what that would have meant in the old days," Kenlon commented.

"If the Negro ever got on the eligible list there was always the department surgeon or surgeons who could be relied upon to find him too flatfooted, or would prove him unfit," the commissioner replied.

"Well, what will you do about it, Commissioner?" Kenlon asked. The two went on to discuss Woodson's various merits. Kenlon described him as a "regular Jack Johnson" physically, a reference to the first African American world heavyweight boxing champion, a man from Texas who held the title from 1908 to 1915. But Woodson's civil service score was not extraordinarily high, Kenlon noted.

Adamson, after careful thought, replied to Kenlon that "if Woodson met all the requirements, I would make him a fireman regardless of the fact that he was a Negro."

Nearly three years later, with Woodson getting one of the FDNY's highest awards for his amazing save of a shrieking mother and her baby trapped in a blazing building, the fire commissioner was impressed with his own perspicacity.

"It seems to me that this [rescue is] a good answer to those who might question the wisdom of my appointing a Negro," Adamson recounted for *The Bee*.

When the newspaper's reporter stopped by Hook & Ladder 106 to interview Woodson, the young firefighter gave him some carefully calibrated words.

"I have been on the force 3 years nearly and never asked a man for his friendship or association. I made up my mind that I wouldn't thrust myself on anybody. If they don't like my skin, alright," Woodson was quoted as saying. "But they have treated me square. I come and go like the rest of the firemen here. I see now that I am in the department what a tremendous undertaking it was for a man of my color to get in. I don't think it could be done under another commissioner."

Not long after his quote appeared in print, Woodson was transferred to Engine Co. 5 in Manhattan. He stayed only four months. Then he was moved to Queens. He was transferred several times over his career and no reason was given for any of them except one: in 1934 he was charged with insubordination. The accusation came from a lieutenant, and Woodson was dragged into a departmental hearing. What happened behind those closed doors is unknown, but in the end Woodson was cleared of all charges. The lieutenant, however, was found to have committed an act that brought "discredit to the uniform of the department."[11]

Woodson's struggles were well-known to Williams—and to Williams's Red Cap dad as well. All three had a shared ambition to get more blacks in the Fire Department. But first they had to ensure Williams's illegal extracurricular activities didn't interfere with his career. The striving young smoke eater had already put himself in line for a promotion—something that would have gone up in flames if department chiefs caught him importing moonshine through a network of black railway porters. Protestations from nearly every corner of the fire department started rolling in the minute it got out that Williams was serious about taking the next promotional exam. For three years, Williams took private civil service classes at a school known as Delahanty's on 15th Street and Fourth Avenue. Started by an old Irishman, it claimed to prepare students for the rigorous civil service examinations. It also encouraged cop and firefighter applicants to run through simulated physical tests in its gym.

Williams sat for the lieutenant's exam in 1924, the first year he was eligible for it after joining the force. He didn't have any seniority points—given to men who had been longer on the job—to carry with him into the exam. Nor did he have any points for award-winning rescues. But he wasn't worried about failing the test or not scoring well. What he did fear was that racism in the ranks would force Tammany leaders to pass him over for promotion, using the one-in-three rule. As soon as he took the exam and saw his list number, Williams took a preemptive strike against the forces he knew were consolidating against him.

"The Civil Service List for Fire Lieutenant has just been promulgated; and my name is on this list, also in such a position that it will be reached long before said list expires. That is why I am writing you," Williams said in a letter dated August 8, 1925, to the editors of the *New York Age,* one of the nation's most influential black papers.[12] The one-page, single-spaced, typed letter ran down the highlights of Williams's career—his 1919 appointment, his numerous impressive rescues, his boxing titles—before getting to the heart of the matter.

"List for the promotion to Fire Lieutenant was established Wed. August 5, 1925. The examination was held Sept. 11 and 12 of 1924. There were 3,010 men who competed—1,220 failed, 920 withdrew. I was 189th on the list with a final percentage of 89.12. A difference in one point would mean a difference of about 100 names in the standing on the list. The list is good for about four years, during which time they use 275 to 300 men on it . . . I am in the money," Williams wrote.

"Now, will they promote me when my turn arrives? I believe in preparedness, so I am notifying the Negro Press now as I expect a fight about it later on. Although they will not reach my name for a year to 18 months, don't you think I am right in getting prepared now?"

Williams's wariness was well-founded. But as it turned out, the opposition came not from within the FDNY, but from another quarter. His list number came up in 1927, just as he predicted it would. The FDNY knew that blocking his appointment outright would result in great pushback from black leaders at a time when Tammany was wooing their voters. But department heads couldn't ignore the outraged reactions from within its rank and file. White firefighters were incensed at the idea they'd have to answer to a black officer. So the department proposed a simpler solution. They'd make Williams a lieutenant in Harlem. James Woodson, the other black firefighter still on the job, would be transferred to Williams's firehouse. So would the two other blacks who'd recently gotten into the FDNY: Arnold Joel and Edward Bantry. They were both in Engine Co. 17 at 91 Ludlow Street on the Lower East Side. Some more blacks could be hired and funneled up to Harlem. That way, Williams could be an officer in an all-black firehouse, and no white man would be subordinate to him. It was the perfect solution, except Williams wasn't having it.

"I have had to take orders from a white man, and now the white men will have to learn to take orders from a black man," he'd said, when approached by the FDNY.

That put the FDNY bosses in a real pickle. Williams had some influential hooks in Tammany, and there were progressive forces inside the political club that had a vested interest in his success. In the end, relying on some of the less forward-thinking elements within Tammany, the powers-that-be went over the local party bosses' heads. Democratic governor Al Smith, a Tammany man and a longtime friend of Williams's father, was vying to become the party's presidential nominee in 1928. Smith, a champion of progressive reform, was already facing anti-Catholic opposition in the South. Word started to filter down the Tammany structure that Smith didn't need the added baggage of having allowed a black firefighter with less than ten years on the job a promotion over well-deserving whites.

While it was highly unlikely that the fate of one black man in the FDNY would sway the outcome of a presidential election, some in Tammany were willing to play that political card. Pressure was applied to new Fire Commissioner John J. Dorman from all sides. But they hadn't counted on the wide-ranging connections of Grand Central's chief Red Cap, James Williams. Recognizing the political chess game lining up against his son, Williams decided to knock

Tammany off the board completely. The FDNY had appealed to its higher power in the governor's office, now he would appeal to his. On September 9, 1927, from his Grand Central Terminal office, he dashed off a quick note to his dear friend, the Catholic archbishop of New York, Cardinal Patrick Hayes.

"Your Eminence:—my son Wesley Williams, a member of the New York Fire Department, is shortly to be appointed to a Lieutenancy and as he especially desires to continue his labors at his present location (Engine Co. 55,–363 Broome St.) may I take the liberty of appealing to you to intercede with Commissioner Dorman on his behalf so that he continues there. A word from your Eminence would be the determining say so," the elder Williams wrote.[13] He signed his letter "respectfully and gratefully, your humble servant." Once again, the FDNY found itself outfoxed by the wily old Red Cap.

On September 21, 1927, Wesley Williams became the first black man to ever hold the office of lieutenant in the FDNY. He was kept at his old firehouse, Engine 55 in Little Italy, despite fervent and angry protests from the men. The FDNY abandoned its immediate plan to segregate blacks in Harlem. And as an added bonus to Williams, his longtime firehouse nemesis, John O'Toole, walked off the job when he heard the news. It was a fireable offense to go absent without leave, but O'Toole couldn't stomach the alternative. Two days later, thanks to some backroom intervention from his well-connected family, O'Toole was quietly reassigned to a marine unit. He wasn't punished for going AWOL, but he never returned to Engine 55.

"Good riddance," Williams said when he heard. O'Toole's hatred for him had been a festering cancer that sickened the whole firehouse. Things still weren't going to be easy in Engine 55, but they likely wouldn't be as bad, Williams thought. Now it was time to concentrate on his next goal: to get more blacks in the fire department. Only then would the provincial firehouse culture truly change.

CHAPTER 7

THE CAN MAN

New York City
Fall 1998

PAUL WASHINGTON WALKED INTO THE LOUD CLATTER OF A LOCAL DINER IN Brooklyn to find Michael Marshall waiting for him at a table by the window. He was glad that Marshall got there early; Washington was headed back into the firehouse to start a 24-hour shift, and he had something important to discuss with his fellow Vulcan.

Things had been good for the young lieutenant over the past decade, and headed into the final few months of 1998, he was on the brink of some life-altering changes. He'd begun dating a beautiful young Brooklynite named Tabitha. He had his eye on a three-story brownstone on a shady, tree-lined street in Bed-Stuy. The idea was to fill it with kids and family. He was on the list to make captain too. His personal life was right on track, but in terms of the goals and expectations he and Marshall set for themselves and their organization to bring in more blacks, the 1990s had been pretty brutal.

"How you been, man?" Marshall asked, as Washington slid into the empty booth bench across from him. They hadn't seen each other in a few weeks. Washington had taken off on a solo trip on his motorbike. He spent some time at Virginia Beach by himself, just thinking. He went to Florida, too, to visit two retired Vulcans who'd done their time back in the 1960s and '70s. Vincent

Julius and Jim Lee had been in the thick of the Vulcans' decision in 1972 to file a civil rights discrimination lawsuit against the city and FDNY. Washington wanted to talk to them about their choices, and what—if anything—they would do differently today. He listened carefully, and he thought a lot, and he made some decisions. It was time to tell Marshall about them.

"Good, I'm good. The trip was great," Washington said. "Got some things to talk to you about."

"I'm listening," Marshall replied, leaning his elbow on the table and taking a sip of his tea. He waited patiently while Washington ordered his usual sandwich.

"I'm going to run for president," Washington said, once the waitress disappeared. "I want the Vulcans to push harder on getting blacks on the job. The way we're doing it isn't making enough of a difference. We're getting maybe 20, 30 guys on every four years. It's just never gonna add up to any real kind of change. For every few we get on, some others retire."

Marshall nodded.

"I made a plan while I was down in Virginia. It's a three-part plan on how we can bring more pressure on the department to hire more blacks," Washington said. "The first part is media. We need to do more press and speak out more. We gotta stand up more on our issues. Then we need to get some political support, you know, tap into the City Council and community leaders and get them to start talking to the fire department for us. Something really grass-roots," he said, pulling out the notes made in his Virginia Beach hotel room while staring across his balcony at the white-capped waves outside.

"And the third?" Marshall said, putting down his cup. Washington leaned forward a little bit. He already knew what Marshall's response would be when he heard number three.

"The third is a lawsuit. We have to bring a lawsuit," Washington said.

"Haven't I been saying that all along?" Marshall chuckled. Then he made the offer—a touch reluctantly—that Washington had hoped for.

"Okay, if you're going to run for president, I'll stand with you," Marshall said. "Count me in for vice president."

Both men knew their decision was going to be controversial—and could potentially cause backlash for their organization. The Vulcan Society remained steadfast in its determination to bring in more blacks, but not everyone agreed on how to achieve that goal. Washington had been on the executive board since 1990 and he'd learned that among such a relatively small group of firefighters, there could be great diversity of thought in how to accomplish things. It didn't bode for an easy presidency—especially since he was determined to shake up the status quo.

He and Marshall and other Vulcans poured tremendous energy and resources into the black recruits who took firefighter exam 0084, administered in 1992. Washington found a YWCA they could rent in downtown Brooklyn and—over the misgivings of the super—Marshall put his carpenter skills to use, pounding nails into floors and walls. With the help of Washington's cousin Gary, they constructed a lifelike facsimile of the physical test given by the FDNY. It was rudimentary, but it got the job done. It took Marshall and Gary two hours to put it up every Tuesday night for the training classes, and 15 Vulcans came in to help students run through it. One of the obstacles required candidates to crawl on their hands and knees, wearing a blackout mask and an air tank, through a wooden tunnel that snaked across the floor. Another section taught candidates how to best use a sledgehammer. It wasn't an exact replica of the FDNY test, but it gave everyone a good sense of what awaited them. The kids who showed up had already taken the FDNY's written exam, and the Vulcans had tutored some of them for that too. Washington personally called all the high-scoring candidates to make sure they stayed on track. The hopeful candidates would ply the Vulcans with questions about their chances. For the old hands, it was an easy equation: anyone with a written score below a 95 was in doubt, and anyone below 90 was a longshot. The city set its passing grade at 70, but that was just a formality. Thousands passed the test with much higher scores and never got called. But the Vulcans encouraged everyone. Life was always a crapshoot, even with civil service exams. Many candidates, thousands actually, got washed out between the test and probie school by the lengthy background checks. The attrition rate was so high that FDNY investigators called in 1,000 candidates at a time, figuring roughly 300 would make it through. There was always an outside chance that the FDNY might reach someone with a score in the mid-80s on the hiring list—although it was pretty unlikely.

There were plenty of bright, standout guys training with the Vulcans in 1992, but everyone had especially high hopes for Keith and Kevin Maynard. Identical twin sons of an FDNY captain, the Maynard men scored exceptionally well on the written exam. Kevin, the older of the two, got a 97. His brother got a 98. Their father encouraged and helped them both through the process. A Vietnam vet who joined the FDNY after serving overseas, their dad never sugarcoated life inside the firehouse. He warned his sons that they'd have to keep to themselves sometimes, and be prepared to speak up in self-defense other times. He told them about his first day as a lieutenant, when he showed up at his new assignment in the Bronx. The FDNY sent him to one of its rowdiest, most rebellious crews and told him to prove how good an officer he was by taming them. When he arrived at the door and rang for entry, nobody would come down to let him in. Whether they deliberately locked him out or just glanced through the window and—assuming the black man there was a neighborhood scruff—decided not to open the door was unclear. He had to walk to a pay phone and call FDNY headquarters to get them to order someone to unlock the door. He told his twin boys it would be challenging and at times daunting, but rewarding in ways they could never imagine. A Vulcan himself, he kept tabs on how many of the training tutorials they attended in preparation for the test.

In 1992, the city had 8,682 firefighters. Three hundred thirty-five were black, around 3.87 percent. Forty thousand people applied to take that year's firefighter exam. Following the usual pattern, white men made up 73 percent, roughly 30,000 of the applicants. Blacks were 8.4 percent, with 3,395 applicants. Latinos had slightly more, 9.3 percent, or 3,736 applicants. A decent number of women also applied: 1,260. It was a good start—but the Vulcans knew there would be a significant drop-off by the time test day actually came, especially among candidates of color. Too many just never showed up for the exam. This year was no different. Despite all the outreach and follow-up the Vulcans did, only 1,995 of the nearly 3,500 blacks they'd registered for the test actually showed up and took it. The same high attrition rate plagued Latinos and women, whose actual test takers dropped to 2,613 and 675 respectively. White men showed only a slight drop off. That still made them more than 75 percent of the total test takers.[1]

Kevin and Keith Maynard, who both got perfect 100s on the grueling physical, were about to find out what a difference a point could make on the highly competitive FDNY civil service exam. Keith, with his 98, was called to join. Kevin, who got a 97, was not. Within that one point were thousands of other applicants. Some might have scored lower than Kevin Maynard on the written test, but gotten extra points for military service that put them ahead. Others might have gotten his exact same score—which happened frequently on the cookie-cutter exams. The FDNY broke scoring ties by listing applicants according to the numerical value of their Social Security numbers. A random mathematical sequence might have dashed Kevin Maynard's dreams of an FDNY career. Whatever the reason was, it wasn't explained to him. His brother was selected and put into a training class in 1999.

The whole family, a tight-knit group from Montserrat, got up early on Keith's first day of probie school to see him off from the kitchen. Kevin Maynard sat at the table watching his mother make sandwiches for his brother's lunch, while his dad paced the floor, eager to see his youngest off to the academy. Kevin Maynard never heard from the FDNY again after his initial score came back. Nobody had the answer for why his list number didn't come up. The FDNY may simply have stopped hiring before they reached it. Kevin's bad luck was reflected in the overall results for blacks in FDNY hiring in the 1990s: out of the 31,000 people who took exam 0084, only 2,692 got a firefighting job. Out of the 1,995 blacks who actually took the FDNY exam, only 53 became firefighters—less than 2 percent.[2]

Even with the disappointment over Kevin Maynard and the bleak showing in general, the Vulcans made sure to congratulate the black candidates who did squeak through. Among the new recruits were John Coombs, then just a fast-talking, no-nonsense rookie not long out of college, and Regina Wilson, one of a few black women firefighters in the FDNY's history. There were other things to be cautiously optimistic about as well. In 1994 the city began to put its own type of pressure on Fire Commissioner Howard Safir, an appointee of new mayor Rudy Giuliani. The Republican mayor took over the city from outgoing Democrat David Dinkins, and immediately got to work on his campaign pledge to crack down on crime and improve the quality of life for New Yorkers. With Police Commissioner Bill Bratton at the helm of the NYPD, the Giuliani administration implemented the "broken windows" theory of crime fighting. It was the first of several steps down a road that would eventually erase the derelict, gritty, graffiti-covered city of the 1980s, but not without creating some hostility and rage among heavily policed minority communities.

Mayor Giuliani had bigger concerns to tackle than the lack of diversity in the FDNY, which in any case was not cause for complaint within the fire department itself. The city's Equal Employment Practices Commission, however, was concerned. In 1988, under Mayor Ed Koch, the city conducted a study on the under-representation of certain ethnic and gender groups in its workforce. To nobody's surprise, the FDNY was the biggest offender: 94 percent white, in a city that was only 50 percent white. That was enough to send the EEPC—charged with keeping New York compliant with civil and human rights laws—poking around on its own.

In August 1994 the EEPC wrote to Commissioner Safir to alert him to the serious deficiencies of the FDNY's minority recruiting effort. The recruiting division had only been in existence since 1988, cobbled together in the wake of Koch's diversity study. The FDNY sent a few members to recruit minorities ahead of the 1992 exam—with abysmally low results. But that didn't stop the FDNY from telling the EEPC that its recruitment effort was successful.[3] The EEPC found it decidedly not so.

"It is the unanimous position of this Commission that the FDNY must develop and implement a more effective recruitment program to attract women and minorities," the EEPC scolded Safir.[4] The FDNY skimped on recruiters, signing up only four firefighters. It allotted only two vehicles and "both were in poor condition." It did the bare minimum on flyers and banners, which did little to attract attention at job fairs, while the Metropolitan Transportation Authority and NYPD came with flashing lights and elaborate displays. The budget for the entire recruitment program was $450,000, of which $300,000 went to a consultant to design the brochures. Most disturbingly, FDNY senior staff admitted to the deficiencies in interviews with EEPC, but then refused to follow up when asked to improve the program. The EEPC deemed the whole effort "grossly inadequate."[5] The end result was that minority participation in 1992 actually dropped from the test given four years earlier—down to 5,597 from the 7,788 minorities who took the firefighter exam in 1988.[6] Given that, the EEPC wrote, it had appointed its own advisory committee and would be sending recommendations to Safir on how the next recruitment drive should be run. The EEPC followed up in October 1994 with another letter to Safir, informing him the advisory committee was ready with a list of recommendations.

Safir had already decided to add a residency credit to the next firefighting exam. It was designed to give a boost to any city resident applying for a city job. The Vulcans hoped it would help improve diversity too. But its guidelines were lax and enforcement of it loose. Moreover, the five bonus points for residency didn't get applied until the very end of the process, when the FDNY was ready to start hiring. That didn't make it very much help to the city kids competing to be among the top 5,000 scorers.

The Vulcans contributed to the EEPC's list of recommendations along with several other FDNY fraternal groups—which included not only the United Women Firefighters Association, but also Polish, Norwegian, German, Irish, Catholic, Hispanic and Italian groups, plus the firefighters' unions and a few other associations. With so many voices in the mix, the Vulcans soon grew unhappy with the glacial pace of Safir's changes.

In April 1995, Vulcan president Delbert Coward, a battalion chief in Queens, wrote to the EEPC and advocated for continued hiring from the list established in 1992. If the FDNY hired one more class off that list, another woman and three more black men would be among those eligible for the job, Coward said. "We do not agree with the Fire Commissioner's notion that the candidates at the top of the list are inherently better quality than those now being reached on the current list. We must all remember: the entrance exam only allows you to TRAIN as a firefighter. It is not a guarantee that you will ever be a firefighter. And, your position on the entrance list is not a gauge of how good or bad a firefighter you will be," Coward wrote.[7] In those few lines, he neatly summarized the heart of the Vulcans' main argument: the civil service exam used to whittle down tens of thousands of applicants to the few thousand needed every few years was an incomplete indicator of a person's job-related skills. It was a snapshot of how well someone performed on that test, on that day, not an accurate measure of firefighting aptitude. It was not a popular perspective inside FDNY headquarters, or inside the roughly 200 firehouses of the Bravest. The civil service system had been the litmus test for city hiring for nearly 100 years; nobody in the FDNY saw a reason to change it.

Commissioner Safir didn't stay in the FDNY long enough to worry about the EEPC's sudden and determined interest in his department's diversity problem. In 1996, he was already moving on—but just a short distance, to the NYPD. The departure of Howard Safir was one of the worst-kept secrets in the FDNY; it was common knowledge he was taking Police Commissioner Bill Bratton's job. The real gossip centered on his replacement: tongues wagged in speculation about which chief or deputy commissioner Giuliani would pick. Little did the rumormongers know the choice had already been made—and it was the last person anybody expected.

The day Safir's NYPD move was to go public, Tommy Von Essen jumped to answer his phone at 6:30 a.m. before it woke his sleeping wife. A former firefighter who'd worked as the "can man," the smoke eater assigned to haul a bulky, heavy fire extinguisher into every blaze, he'd risen up the ranks to become president of the Uniformed Firefighters Association that represented the city's 9,000 Bravest. He and Safir sat across the table from each other on union and management business for the past two years. When he recognized the voice of the fire commissioner, he groaned into the phone.

"You're leaving, aren't you?" Von Essen accused. He'd heard the rumors. He was sorry to see Safir go. Traditionally, union heads and management were sworn enemies, but he and Safir got along. He started to offer congratulations, but Safir cut him short.

"Yes, I'm leaving, but there's a second part to this. How would you feel about being fire commissioner?" Von Essen heard him say. The labor leader immediately shushed him.

"You're crazy. You shouldn't do that. I have an election coming up. Don't put my name out there, that'll be a problem," the union head said.

"No, no, no, there's nobody else. The mayor's going to call you in half an hour and ask if you want the job. I just wanted to know if you are interested first," Safir responded.

Von Essen croaked out an affirmative and ended the call. Just as Safir said, Mayor Giuliani called him about half an hour later.

"Come to City Hall this morning," the mayor said in his peremptory way, after the usual pleasantries were dispensed with. Von Essen was vetted that same day by Giuliani's team in the city hall basement. Later he found out that some tried to nix him, despite Safir's recommendation.

"The best guy over there is the union guy," Safir had said, when asked by the mayor who he would pick. Some key Giuliani aides immediately said no.

"We can't do a union guy," they protested.

"Great, let's do the union guy," Giuliani responded.

Von Essen inherited a department rife with problems, not the least of which was shoddy equipment, antiquated technology and—over time—a corrosive resentment of his appointment among high-ranking chiefs. Von Essen, formerly known as "Tommy the can man from the South Bronx," had cut his teeth at Ladder 42 during the War Years. He was stationed in La Casa del Elefante, named for the five or six burly firefighters there who were so large they dwarfed his six-foot, heavyset frame. Von Essen proved himself a deft and dependable firefighter many times over, but after 20 years on the job, that's all he was: a firefighter. He considered it the only title worth having. But the fact that a lowly smoke eater vaulted to the head of the department as fire commissioner rankled the FDNY's top brass to no end. Among the firehouse troops, who'd gotten used to Von Essen as their union leader, his switch to management was cause for sad celebration. They didn't like to see him go, but everyone got a kick out of having a labor leader take over as commissioner. At last, a fox in the henhouse, his union buddies crowed. But when he started butting heads with old friends, his defection turned into a deep wound. Tommy the can man, who'd battled his way out of countless blazes in the South Bronx, soon found himself in a real hot spot.

Amid all the tension around him, the last thing Von Essen needed was more emphasis on the nearly all-white makeup of the FDNY. It was a divisive issue no matter who raised it. In Von Essen's Bronx company, there'd been a few black firefighters, including a beloved lieutenant who died just before he arrived. But he'd be a liar if he tried to pretend the racial prejudices and animosity found in the world at large didn't also exist inside the brotherhood. He'd heard it and experienced it himself. Firehouse talk often fell outside the boundaries of the politically correct, and he was okay with what he called the "grab-ass" pranks that firefighters loved to play on each other. But he had a real problem with the officers in the firehouses who turned their backs and pretended not to hear racist slurs. These were the same officers, he found, that feigned ignorance about the 20-ounce plastic tumblers that held beer and not water at the dinner table and claimed not to know when someone put in for medical leave on a phony injury. Every battalion had a few of what firefighters called hairbags—those who were looking to game the system in some way. The real cheats usually got weeded out, but the ingrained firehouse culture of taking care of one's own left plenty of wiggle room for mischief and, in some cases, even malfeasance.

Von Essen stepped into the FDNY at a time of great upheaval—and he only had a few short years before the city started gearing up for its next firefighter exam, number 7029, to be administered in 1999. The normal timing of FDNY hiring got bogged down when a group of suburban candidates from Long Island and Westchester, Putnam, Rockland and Orange counties threatened to sue over the five-point residency credit applied to exam 0084. Some 17,000 applicants applied for the credit, claiming they were or would be city residents by the time they were hired. But a group calling themselves Committee for Fairness for FDNY Test 0084 went to court to try and halt the program, claiming it put them at a disadvantage. At the same time, angry firefighter candidates from the earlier exam, number 7022, were furious the city wasn't continuing to hire from their list. A group known as #7022 Eligibles Association began agitating to keep their list open. They peppered City Council members and the press with outraged letters, all in an effort to influence the new commissioner.[8]

Even as Von Essen grappled with a surfeit of problems, he was quick to make some fairly significant overhauls to the FDNY. Some were good and some were bad, depending on who you asked. Among them was a 30-college-credit requirement for all new firefighter hires. Von Essen hoped bringing in recruits with better education and exposure to different ideas would help break up the narrow, cliquish mentality that dominated most firehouses. Plus, the NYPD now required 60 college credits, and Von Essen was not about to let the FDNY fall behind the cops in any way. His only concession to the EEPC, which feared the college credits would be another deterrent to minorities, was to cap it at 30.

Mayor Giuliani had also annexed the city's beleaguered 911 Emergency Medical Services corps and folded its operations into the FDNY in 1996. With that move, Von Essen was handed a workforce that was far more diverse than the fire department. The EMS rank and file was heavily populated with blacks, Latinos and women, and what the FDNY needed was a way to siphon off some of those numbers. Von Essen created a special promotional civil service exam just for EMS members that put them on a fast-track for firefighter positions. When hiring time came around, the candidates on the EMS promotional list would be called first. The promotional exam was meant to be a benefit to minority applicants—but it didn't work out quite as intended.

Von Essen also came up with a supplemental plan to bring in more minorities—a Fire Cadet program to get young kids in school interested in joining EMS. The idea was to train minorities so they were ready to join EMS after completing school—and from there, hopefully, they'd eventually follow the promotional path into the FDNY. Both the fire unions—the UFA that Von Essen once led and the officers association—hated the idea. Von Essen ignored them. He brought in Sheldon Wright, a Vulcan, to coordinate. The black lieutenant had earned his firefighting bona fides holding his own in Brooklyn's busy Ladder 111 before an injury took him out of active-duty rotation. As a general rule, Von Essen didn't care much for the Vulcan Society. To him, the black firefighters seemed determined to bring another lawsuit, no matter what the FDNY did to appease them. But Von Essen trusted and respected Wright.

Wright had his own views on what the FDNY needed to do in terms of diversity recruitment, and it wasn't always the same opinion espoused by the rest of the Vulcans. He'd been a young father of twins in the late 1970s, taking part-time college classes and working two jobs to earn $13,000—barely enough to keep his family together—when he'd been approached by a black firefighter on his Queens College campus. The firefighter had bent his ear for nearly half an hour about joining the FDNY, and in the end Wright agreed to file an application just to get him to stop talking. Wright was $5 short on the application fee, so the Vulcan offered to put up the money if Wright gave him his word he'd follow through. The young man reluctantly agreed, and when the time came he took the FDNY civil service test. Obligation completed, he moved on with his life. The FDNY packets that came to his grandmother's house in Queens were dumped in the trash. Before long, he'd moved to a new Brooklyn apartment and the FDNY mail ceased. His firefighting career might never have gotten started if two years later, a black captain named Fred Fowler hadn't shown up at his grandmother's house one Sunday morning during a torrential rainstorm. The Vulcans had gotten a list from the FDNY of blacks on the 1977 test and were systematically tracking down all those who fell by the wayside. By the time Captain Fowler got hold of Wright, the young father was working the midnight shift in the psychiatric emergency room at Queens Hospital and weekends at a different guard job—and still unable to do much for his growing family. The firefighting career he'd thrown away now sounded like a pretty good deal. By 1982, Wright was riding the back of an engine and hanging tough through his inaugural year of firehouse hazing. He made $32,000 in his first 12 months, thanks to generous overtime.

Wright understood better than most the challenges facing young inner-city kids, who were the bulk of the Latinos and blacks the FDNY was targeting. The hiring cycle of the FDNY took forever; four years often passed before recruits were called, sometimes longer. Too many kids couldn't wait around without a job. They needed something that would pay them immediately. And they barely knew anything about the benefits and joys of joining the FDNY—hardly any of them knew a firefighter or had one in their family. It was a real disadvantage, compared to the kids who grew up seeing dads and uncles with time to coach Little League, hold down a second job, and serve the public. Those kids had a real fire in the belly to join the FDNY. Wright's aim was to invoke the same fervor in the minds of inner-city kids, in part by introducing them to the unique culture of the FDNY—a huge, dysfunctional family, to be sure, but one that always took care of its own. In a firehouse, crews shared the highs and the lows of life. If somebody's father died, the company showed up at the funeral in their crisp dark blues. If someone got married or a child had a first communion or a bar mitzvah, everyone celebrated. Wright grasped just how much it could help the inner-city kids he knew to feel that they belonged to something larger than themselves and had a place in the world. After some trial and error, he devised a cadet program that gave members about $10 an hour and got them trained and prepped to take the state's Emergency Medical Technician (EMT) exam. If the kids didn't know how to drive—a requirement for the FDNY—Wright got them out to Fort Totten in Queens, where he set up a driving course. He targeted kids in two-year associate degree programs and community colleges, and memorized the 200-plus names of all his cadets. To get them in shape for the physical test, Von Essen's new deputy commissioner, Lynn Tierney, requisitioned a training facility on Randall's Island. It was modeled after the course used by the fire department in the actual physical exam. An ex-firefighter and football coach named Pudgy Walsh ran a similar course out on Long Island. Many fire-fighters paid to get their kids into his classes. His course would have been perfect, but it was too far away for Tierney and Wright to use. Tierney's training facility had the funding it needed and the fire commissioner's support—now the fire department's unionized carpenters just had to get the thing up. The carpenters—probably taking their cues from the fire unions—did everything they could to stall, including questioning why it had to be built at all. The bellyaching dragged on until Tierney despaired of ever making progress.

Frustrated, she put in a call for help. Tierney had been around the fire department long enough to understand what was going on. She needed support from someone whose reputation in the field would transcend the union bickering and racial resentment. Among firefighters, grit on the job trumped just about everything.

"Lee, would you lend your reputation to this?" Tierney asked. She'd called Lee Ielpi, a highly decorated firefighter who'd worked

out of Rescue 2, one of the most respected and sought-after units in
the department. He'd amassed so many credentials and honors over
the years that if he pinned them all on his jacket he'd be wearing
close to ten pounds of metal. Ielpi knew right away what Tierney
needed.

"No problem. I'll be there," he said. Ielpi showed up the next
day, bringing Marty McTigue with him. If it was possible, McTigue
was even more well-known throughout the department than Ielpi.
A captain out of Rescue 4 in Woodside, Queens, the father of four
nearly died in 1992 while responding to a Con Edison explosion
on Manhattan's East Side. A pipe burst inside the plant, releasing
a massive gush of deadly, 500-degree steam. A Con Ed worker was
instantly killed. McTigue, searching through the plant for survi-
vors, got his air straps tangled in a stairwell. While four other firefighters fought to free him, the steam enveloped him, melting skin
off bone and—as he inhaled—burning him internally. His survival
was miraculous, and his rehabilitation long and painful. When he
was as healed as he could be, McTigue went around to individual
firehouses and told his story. It was a firehouse tradition to share
knowledge, especially about mistakes made in the field. It might
prevent the same thing from happening to someone else. When Ielpi
showed up at Tierney's barebones training course with McTigue at
his side, ready to build, the union resistance evaporated.

Just as the city was prepping for the 1999 exam, and Washington and Marshall were busy building a foundation for their Vulcan
campaign, the city erupted in racial angst again, as it had regularly
in the latter half of Giuliani's second term. An annual Labor Day
parade in Broad Channel, Queens—a sequestered, mostly white
waterfront community with a heavy concentration of city employees—caused a horrified sensation. A cop and two firefighters decked
out in blackface were videotaped tossing watermelon slices to the
crowd and bouncing basketballs on a parody float titled "Black
to the Future." At one point one of them pretended to be dragged
along behind it—a grotesque satire of the death of a black Texas
man, James Byrd, who was killed just that way a year before.

Giuliani, branding the float a "disgusting display of racism,"
immediately called for the cop and firefighters to be fired.[9] The initial fallout was worse for the NYPD. The Broad Channel incident

came just a year after a vicious attack on Abner Louima, a Haitian immigrant beaten by four officers and sodomized by one of them with a plunger's wooden handle. The Broad Channel float added to the rancorous feelings.

But the FDNY didn't escape censure either. Inside the department reactions were mixed. The float itself was widely panned as repugnant. But Giuliani's call for summary dismissals raised hackles. The float was meant as a parody, after all, and the same men won first prize with similar floats in the past that mocked other minorities, including ones called "Gooks of Hazzard," "Hasidic Park" and "Happy Gays." Nobody had objected to those.

Von Essen once again found himself caught in the awkward overlap between his past and present. He deplored the stupidity and bigotry the men displayed in creating the float. Yet he'd met with both firefighters and their union lawyers, and he could tell they were good guys. It was the sort of stupid firehouse prank that sometimes went wrong, and they deserved to be punished. But was it a career-ending mistake? After meeting with them, Von Essen was inclined to say no. Giuliani was far less forgiving.

"Tommy, you have to fire these guys," the mayor told him, when he called Von Essen to discuss the incident.

"Why? They're just dopes," Von Essen replied.

"Yeah, but it's not about them being dopes. It's about the image of the fire department, the image of the city of New York. We don't condone that kind of behavior. We have to take strong action against it," Giuliani responded. Von Essen stepped back to consider the mayor's words. He'd been viewing the men's actions through the firehouse prism, but as he reflected on it he realized he had to act as the fire commissioner. Giuliani was right. The city couldn't keep employees who made it look like the FDNY didn't care about minorities. The men were fired, and the union howled. The men filed a First Amendment lawsuit to get their jobs back.

The discord and fury continued into the New Year and cast a pall over the city's last-ditch efforts to increase minority turnout for exam 7029, which was scheduled for February 1999. But it galvanized the Vulcans, which Washington and Marshall took control of that January in uncontested elections. Washington was ready to set a new tone inside the organization and push its views on the city at large. He knew that David Floyd, president of the Vulcan Society for part of the 1980s, had used the press to heighten the group's profile. Floyd had also been president of the International Association of Black Professional Firefighters, and from them Washington learned about other black struggles around the country. He gained a new appreciation through the IABPFF for the support of a strong union. The Vulcans and the UFA were hardly bosom buddies, but New York City firefighters had a lot more freedom of expression because of their vocal union. Washington met other blacks through the IABPFF who were putting far more on the line when they spoke out.

He also modeled himself after an emergent NYC grassroots group, 100 Blacks in Law Enforcement Who Care, led by Eric Adams, Marquez Claxton and Noel Leader. The NYPD officers managed to operate as community activists while being cops—and were clever about getting the media to carry their message. As he prepared for the day he would give his own press conferences for the Vulcans, Washington studied what the cops wore, the locations they chose, even how they ordered the speakers. Realizing it would help to have a signature touch, something to help people recognize him, he decided to let his Afro grow. He liked that it would be distinctive and add a flare of 1960s and '70s militancy. Plus, it was a nice way to pay tribute to Jimi Hendrix. Washington was a fan.

A few weeks before the city gave firefighter exam 7029 to 17,151 applicants, a young African immigrant named Amadou Diallo was killed by four elite NYPD cops who were roving a broken-down section of the Bronx looking for an alleged rapist. Diallo, 23, from Guinea, was gunned down in a blaze of 41 bullets. The cops spotted the young man in front of his building around 12:40 a.m. and, identifying themselves as NYPD, yelled at him to stay there. Instead, a bewildered and frightened Diallo ran up the stoop, where he turned to face the cops and pulled out his wallet. Amid the darkness, the confusion and the adrenalin, the cops made a terrible mistake. "Gun," one of them shouted, as the lead officer advancing on Diallo tripped and fell. Assuming he'd been hit by Diallo, the officers behind him opened fire, shooting wildly. Diallo was struck by 19 bullets out of the 41 shots fired before the cops finally stopped.

For two weeks after Diallo's death, huge crowds of protestors appeared daily at 1 Police Plaza, usually led by the then plump and pugnacious Reverend Al Sharpton, the civil rights activist and leader of the National Action Network. Diallo was a detonator that set off years of pent-up fury and frustration among minority communities, who claimed the Giuliani administration's tough-on-crime regime made targets out of young black and Latino men. Inside Vulcan Hall in Brooklyn, Washington and Marshall watched the daily news coverage with amazement. Tens of thousands of New Yorkers of all races were turning out daily, and it wasn't just community leaders and committed activists speaking out. It almost seemed like the whole city was up in arms, one way or another. Diallo's death had stirred up huge controversy about lack of diversity in the NYPD. As the Vulcans joined the various protests, they couldn't help but wonder what the public would do if it realized the fire department was far more racially unbalanced than that of its brothers in blue.

CHAPTER 8

BLOWBACK

New York City
1999–2001

THE HORROR OF AMADOU DIALLO'S DEATH GRIPPED THE CITY FOR MONTHS, and with so much going on, only the Vulcans noticed when the results of firefighter exam 7029 came back. They were extremely depressing. The exam attracted 17,151 test takers overall and 75 percent of them were white. Even though the FDNY claimed to have spoken with 8,000 minority candidates during its recruitment phase, only 1,700 blacks sat for the exam, roughly 10 percent. Hispanics came in at 12 percent with just over 2,000. Women, as always, lagged the farthest behind. Ninety-seven percent of test takers were male; only 473 women took the exam.[1] Just like the prior firefighter test, 7029 was a bust, at least as far as the Vulcans were concerned.

For reasons that were never explained to the Vulcans, the Department of Citywide Administrative Services—the new name for the old Department of Personnel that handled civil service exams—decided to alter the passing grade for the 1999 firefighter test. Instead of setting it at 70, which was the usual cutoff mark, city exam experts in DCAS, as the agency was known, pushed it up to 84.75. Any score below that was considered a failing grade. The change was made even after DCAS was warned by one of its own analysts that the higher benchmark would hit minority candidates the hardest. The largest clumping of blacks typically fell in the mid-80s, the analyst said. The response from DCAS was a collective shrug; the passing grade was 84.75.

As a result of that decision, the pass rate for whites on exam 7029 was 89.9 percent, while the pass rate for blacks was 60.3 percent. Blacks who did score above the cutoff mark were still ranked on average 630 places lower than white candidates on the eligibility hiring list. Of the 3,027 firefighters ultimately hired by the FDNY off list 7029, only 99—3.1 percent—were black. Hispanics got 269 hires, 8.4 percent.[2]

Among those who didn't make it were Rohan Holt, a 25-year-old from Queens, and Jose Ortiz, a 26-year-old Bronx resident who dreamed of joining the FDNY or NYPD like many of his friends and family. Holt earned an 88, well above the cutoff mark. But when he checked in with the FDNY a few months later, he was told his grade was so low he likely would never get called. He finally took a job with the Metropolitan Transportation Authority as a bus driver. Ortiz, who eventually moved out of state, was never contacted after he took the test. He never learned his score.

Determined to use the weak numbers to create more traction through the press, Paul Washington tracked down a newspaper reporter at the NY Daily News and fed him the figures. Black candidates were being knocked out of contention for a great job because of a written exam that did nothing to measure how good a firefighter they'd be, Washington argued. It was like the Yankees giving an SAT test to pick who would play shortstop. The story appeared May 2, 1999, a two-page spread that caused a big splash. Washington considered it his preliminary shot across the city's bow. The reporter, David Saltonstall, did his due diligence and included quotes from Tommy Von Essen and his deputy commissioner, Lynn Tierney. Saltonstall noted their determined outreach to minorities through the cadet program and recruitment events at community centers and black churches, plus a $250,000 ad campaign. It was a miniscule figure compared to the NYPD's $9 million ad budget, but then again the police department was four times larger than the FDNY. The NYPD had also taken a far more progressive and aggressive approach to diversity under former commissioner Ben Ward, appointed in 1984 and the first black to lead the police department. The FDNY had already broken that barrier—appointing its first black commissioner, Robert Lowery, in 1966, and then a second, Augustus Beekman, in 1978. Lowery, the first black fire commissioner in any major U.S. city, served seven years. Beekman followed from 1978 to 1980. Both their appointments were a tremendous boost symbolically and emotionally for the black firefighters. Among the white majority, some embraced Lowery and Beekman, some tolerated their appointments, and a few grumbled that the FDNY was kowtowing to black groups. For all their good intentions—especially Lowery—neither man achieved the same impact as Ben Ward in the NYPD. He hired a special team to tackle the department's lack of diversity and studied other agencies like the Department of Corrections, which had a heavily minority membership. Things still weren't perfect in the NYPD either, as Diallo's death showed. But Ward's determined inroads in the 1980s made a big difference. Between 1986 and 1996, the number of Latino cops in the NYPD grew by 74.5 percent, Asians grew by 127.5 percent, women by 62.5 percent and blacks by 18 percent. The number of white cops decreased by 13.4 percent.[3]

Saltonstall also included Von Essen's deep-seated opposition to any talk of a hiring quota—even though two court-ordered quotas briefly improved the number of blacks, Hispanics and women when they were applied to the FDNY some 25 years earlier. For the Vulcans, it was a familiar story: the FDNY applauded itself for its minimal efforts to improve minority turnout, but flat-out refused to consider any change to the traditional way of hiring. From what the Vulcans could see, updating the written civil service exam was the biggest remedy that could bring more blacks on the job.

"I can't think of a worse solution . . . than to impose a quota," Von Essen said to Saltonstall. "We have a very dangerous job, and to not reach out to find the very best in every population would be a serious mistake."

Washington wasn't surprised by the commissioner's quote. Like every fire commissioner before him, Von Essen clung to the popular firehouse myth that the standardized tests ranked merit. In reality, the test did a decent job of weeding out the functionally illiterate; what its ranked results truly revealed about the skills of each candidate was anybody's guess. Not even the city's own test experts knew. The exam questions and testing methodologies evolved, piecemeal, from the days of Tammany Hall, when fire-fighters themselves composed exams. The development process for each test became slightly more sophisticated over time, especially after the first legal challenges in the 1970s. But the city never hired an outside expert to find out how effective the make-or-break exam was in filtering candidates so the best came out on top. Once DCAS took control of the exams, the contents were fiercely guarded to avoid allegations of cheating. But the basic format was well known: about 100 questions, heavily weighted toward cognitive ability and reading comprehension. Sample questions were readily available.

"Firefighters are at the scene of an uncontrolled fireplace fire. They have followed proper procedure and have just found that the fire has extended into the wall. The next thing the firefighters should do is: A. Tear open the wall with axes. B. Put out the fire in the fireplace. C. Put out the fire in the wall. D. Make sure the necessary equipment is ready for use. (The correct answer is D)," said one.[4]

"While inspecting an automobile repair garage, Firefighter Morales observed the following conditions: A. A mechanic is re-pairing a hole in a half-filled gas tank while smoking a cigarette. B. A heater is being used to heat the garage. C. A mechanic is chang-ing the tire on a van while smoking a pipe. D. There is no fire extin-guishing equipment in the garage. Of the four conditions observed by Firefighter Morales, which is the most dangerous fire hazard? (The correct answer is A)," said another.

Candidates had about two hours to finish, and many questions focused on memorization. Applicants were shown a drawing of a fire scene and allowed to study it for five minutes. Then they had to turn the page—no looking back—and answer a series of questions about what they had observed, such as how many victims were in-volved, where the fire hydrants were located and whether it was an apartment fire or a commercial fire. Another segment showed them a grid of city streets, with arrows indicating which routes were one-way traffic only. Candidates were asked to show how they would travel from the firehouse to an emergency a few blocks away, and to pick which types of tools they would use for different types of firefighting tasks. Was a hammer or a Halligan tool better to make a hole in the wall? The test wasn't particularly challenging—nor was it particularly good at discerning who had the best temperament for firefighting.

Washington's first round of media success soon led to another. In July 1999, the *New York Times* ran an article about three black FDNY lieutenants who filed a civil discrimination lawsuit after they were denied transfer requests to desirable posts. All three were Vulcans. One of them, Edward Alston, a 37-year veteran, said a white man with less seniority got his requested transfer. The FDNY admitted that the transfer Alston wanted was given to a more junior man—but it was because he had experience on a naval patrol boat in Vietnam. Lieutenant Rod Lewis was a veteran firefighter with tons of seniority, and his requests were turned down three times in favor of white men with fewer years on the job. Lieutenant Michael Cuttino had similar complaints. The allegations were under investigation, said the fire department, which made a point of criticizing the black lieutenants for wasting taxpayer money. That frugal attitude didn't last long. In the decade to come, the city and FDNY would throw away millions fighting the Vulcans' discrimination lawsuit.

Washington was pleased. The media attention flushed out some helpful politicians, and by September 1999, Von Essen was summoned to a City Council hearing to testify about FDNY recruitment. Washington's right-hand man, Sheldon Wright, was at his side. Wright wasn't completely convinced a lawsuit would get the Vulcans where they wanted to be. It was expensive and time-consuming, and the last suit the Vulcans pushed forward had only resulted in minimal gains—while creating a tidal wave of resentment. Its effects hadn't lasted long either: the federal judge only imposed the hiring quota for four years. Blacks jumped to 6 percent of the FDNY because of it, but now that number had drifted down to less than 3 percent. It was far more effective, in Wright's mind, to keep the specter of a lawsuit hovering over the FDNY. He was happy flexing the power of the threat.

"Trust me, you do not want a solution to this problem to be imposed on you," Wright was fond of reminding FDNY and city officials when the topic of diversity came up at interdepartmental meetings. He knew nothing scared them more that the Q-word— a quota. He also freely shared his opinion that the written exam should be thrown out entirely. He found its whole creation and application absurd.

"We've got the college credit requirement now, and if anything we should require more. If someone can get themselves through college with at least a C average, why do you need this exam to tell you that they're worth hiring?" Wright argued. Plus, whoever heard of setting the passing grade based on how many hires a department needed to make?

"It's just a bad test," he'd say. Von Essen didn't view the test as all that awful, but in his opinion if it was a bad test, at least it was bad for everyone. But he did dig around in his budget to produce enough money for Wright to buy new recruitment vehicles.

Washington and Michael Marshall agreed with Wright that the test was generally useless, but without a lawsuit they didn't think it would ever disappear. They weren't getting anywhere with finding a lawyer, however, and it was starting to cause some concern. Then Washington got a good tip. Kevin James, the president of the FDNY's Islamic group, suggested he call a lawyer at the Center for Constitutional Rights (CCR). Washington and Marshall weren't aware of the firm, or its origins in the Civil Rights Movement. William Kunstler, the radical lawyer who became one of the most venerated and hated legal figures of his time for his defense of groups like the Black Panther Party, Attica prisoners and the Weather Underground, was among its founders.

Marshall and Washington were unaware of CCR's illustrious—or infamous—roots. But they were happy to find a law firm willing to listen. The search for a gung-ho legal team was harder than either man expected. Not only were they getting turned down by just about everybody, they discovered a clump of naysayers within the Vulcans who disliked anything their outspoken new president said. The far more serious deterrent, however, was financing, because the Vulcans had very little. In their first few months in office, Washington and Marshall conducted business in a freezing cold hall, with members shivering inside their tightly wrapped jackets, gloves and hats. The old, three-story brownstone in Crown Heights along Eastern Parkway in Brooklyn was like a sieve, letting what little heat there was seep through porous windows and creaky door frames. The Vulcans bought the single-family home in the 1960s, moving their headquarters from Harlem. By the late

1980s the ramshackle building was badly in need of renovations. Washington gutted it and made a top-to-bottom overhaul his first priority when he took over in 1999. But landing a law firm was a close second.

The CCR lawyer who called them in was Stanford-educated Barbara Olshansky. She was slender and intense, with a riot of dark curls sitting on her head, and she cursed more than any firefighter Washington or Marshall had ever met. She dropped f-bombs with a ferocity that made them laugh, and they liked her immensely. Olshansky hacked through the Vulcans' dense legal tangle in just a few quick meetings. They could build a strong legal argument that minorities were disproportionately hurt by the civil service exam just on the hiring results alone, she said. But there was an intriguing glimmer of an even larger claim lurking in the FDNY stats, Olshansky realized. It was hard to believe an agency had remained 94 percent white for nearly 150 years in a place as diverse as New York City purely by accident. But the Vulcans had a lot further to go if they wanted to prove the FDNY's exclusion of blacks was intentional.

"I need evidence. Bring me evidence, examples of ways blacks are getting weeded out beyond the initial exam," she told Washington and Marshall. Olshansksy had no doubt she could bring a discrimination lawsuit against the city using Title VII of the 1964 Civil Rights Act. She only needed to figure out the best approach.

Marshall had evidence—reams of it. For many years, he'd been the self-appointed advocate for black candidates who got turned away by the FDNY during the background investigation phase. Marshall didn't have the same direct ability to steer candidates through the system that Henry Blake did in the 1980s, but he could and did go to FDNY headquarters to follow up on guys who were dropped from the list. The Vulcans had long suspected that more minorities got rejected for minor blips in their personal histories than whites, and Marshall amassed all the information he could.

The Vulcans had suspicions about other parts of the hiring system as well. The five-point residency program was an ongoing point of contention. The extra credit was designed to go to applicants who grew up in the city. But the way the regulation was written, a candidate only had to show they'd been a resident for one day to get the five points. Then there was the promotional

Emergency Medical Services exam created by Von Essen that fast-tracked EMTs and paramedics into the firefighting ranks. The Vulcans noted that plenty of young white EMS workers used that route too—and a lot of them had the same last names as high-ranking FDNY officers. The Vulcans never expected the fire department to limit residency points or the EMS promotional exam to blacks and Hispanics only, but it galled Washington to watch both programs push even more white firefighters into the firehouses. He didn't like the cheating but couldn't blame the kids alone. He understood as well as anybody that fierce drive to follow a family tradition. But he did fault the FDNY brass who knew what was happening and still refused to cut off the pipeline.

He and Marshall pulled together a list of about six black applicants fighting with the FDNY over their background investigations and brought it to Olshansky. One of them, Damon Alston, took the firefighter exam in 1992 and was just on the brink of being permanently ejected from the hiring list. At 31 years old, he was running out of time in other ways too. Alston was embroiled in a lengthy back-and-forth with the white female investigator, and he couldn't get a handle on what was holding up his appointment. Finally, he went to FDNY headquarters to speak to her in person, and she let him know what the problem was: he had a sealed arrest in his past, she said.

"You're kidding, right?" and incredulous Alston said. His lone arrest was for jumping the turnstile once as a teen. The only other blotch on his record was a summons given to him a few years later by a cop who spotted him dumping some traffic tickets out his car window.

The investigator told him the two incidents were "cause for concern." Alston left the meeting dispirited. He'd known it was a difficult process going in, and at that point he had no reason to think he was being held to a standard that was any different for anybody else. He shrugged his shoulders and prepared to move on, but decided to let the Vulcans know it was over for him. He'd kept in close contact with the group since first taking their tutorials for the test, and periodically showed up at Vulcan Hall to help out with events. He reached out to Michael Marshall, who quickly set him straight.

"No, that is not normal, and those two things should have no relevancy to you now," was Marshall's firm response. "Let me make a few calls."

Two days later, Alston was summoned back to fire department headquarters. The FDNY had just sworn in its latest class of probies and he'd missed the cutoff. But Alston hoped his investigator was going to say he could join the next class in six months. To his shock, he was ushered up to the eighth floor and into the office of Fire Commissioner Von Essen, who was waiting to swear him in. The private ceremony was over in minutes, and a businesslike Von Essen politely showed him the door. Alston's background investigation was never brought up again. He was hustled into the probationary class that had just started, and he dedicated himself to being an eager and grateful student. But as he got to know some of the other probies, almost all of them white, he heard some disturbing information. Quite a few of the other new hires also had stains on their records—and most for things much worse than Alston's turnstile jump. There were drunk-driving arrests, collars for bar fights, even some domestic violence assaults. Those who'd gotten through had signed a "stip," something he knew nothing about.

"You sign it if there's something in your background that makes the investigator think twice about hiring you. It says you can be hired on the stipulation you maintain a clean record and agree to random drug tests for a while," one guy explained to him as they sat in the locker room after a workout. Alston was stunned. The word *stipulation* never came out of his investigator's mouth. The revelation soured him slightly. When the Vulcans called to ask him to meet with their new lawyer and share his story, he said yes. The other blacks had experiences that were remarkably similar to his, including one who'd scored a 98.25 out of 100 on the test and wound up ranked in the sixtieth hiring spot. He was held back because of an eight-year-old infraction on his military record. He'd been charged for insulting an officer in the navy, but was later cleared of the insubordination accusation. Yet that incident was cited by the FDNY as an issue in his delayed hiring when he went down to ask what was taking so long.

Olshansky was stunned to learn the FDNY didn't need to provide applicants with a written letter explaining the reason for their rejection. Thanks to the one-in-three rule instituted a century ago by Tammany Hall, the FDNY was free to choose one candidate out of every three if it wanted to. Those not picked got bumped to the next spot on the hiring list. If they were passed over two more times, they fell off the list for good. All the FDNY had to do was issue a letter saying they'd been "considered but not selected." The evidence was compelling enough to give the Vulcans another avenue for a discrimination lawsuit, but if they chose that path the half-dozen candidates they'd brought to Olshansky would never get on the FDNY. By the time litigation got done, it would likely be too late for them.

"We can't take that chance," Washington said to Marshall, who agreed. Besides being unfair to the waiting men, it was counterintuitive for the Vulcans to do something that would keep eligible blacks from joining the FDNY. Instead, they worked out a system with Olshansky. She agreed to write letters to fire department officials on behalf of all those still sidelined. At the same time, the Vulcans requested sit-downs with FDNY chiefs to go over each applicant's history. It didn't take long for the FDNY to start moving its creaky bureaucracy; one by one, the men previously on the verge of getting tossed out were able to move forward.

"You know, if we hadn't gotten all these guys this help, we'd have a better chance at our lawsuit. We just undermined one of our own claims," Marshall joked to Washington. "We're too good for our own good."

Even with the success of specific cases brought to Olshansky, Washington wasn't ready to let the FDNY off the hook. He and Marshall decided early on to take a good-cop/bad-cop approach with the department. Washington had no difficulty playing the hardball role, or saying the abrasive truths in meetings and to the press that annoyed Mayor Rudy Giuliani and the fire department leadership. He'd learned that getting the FDNY to agree with the Vulcans' points didn't mean anything would actually change. In his view, the only way to achieve his goals was through a forceful media campaign and pressure from friendly politicians. Marshall had the role of the affable, reasonable Vulcan, the one who could be counted on to respond in a way FDNY officials found rational. Few people realized that underneath his easy grin and cheery moustache, Marshall's militancy matched his partner's. As Von Essen's

The dynamic duo at work. Lieutenant Michael Marshall on a rare detail to Captain Paul Washington's Brooklyn firehouse, Engine 234. Photo credit: Vulcan Society.

day to testify to the City Council approached, Washington played his role to the hilt, unloading a fresh fusillade of criticism at the FDNY, again through the *NY Daily News*.

"Bravest Hard on Minorities; More Candidates Rejected On Character, Health Issues," trumpeted a September 26, 1999, headline. Washington fed the reporter some of the backstories of black applicants he and Olshansky were helping. The FDNY had also handed over what scant data it had on its background screening process—and the numbers weren't good. Since 1995, the city greenlighted 2,501 white firefighters—but 8 percent were ultimately weeded out by problems with their background checks. In the same time frame, the city had deemed 212 minority firefighters eligible, but 11 percent were eliminated through background checks. The same pattern held true for medical disqualifications: 4 percent of whites were washed out compared to 7 percent of minorities.[5] Washington knew that if the FDNY had released numbers just for blacks—instead of clumping minorities together—the disparity would have been even more glaring. The article succeed in turning up the heat on Von Essen during his City Council hearing two days later, although he didn't deviate much from his planned testimony.

"Before we begin I would like to state that as it is, hiring at the New York City Fire Department is a fair and competitive process," Von Essen began. "The way to get a job in the Fire Department is to score high on the written test and to score at the top of the physical test. . . . Also understand that before you start comparing this job to other civil service positions in the city, this universe is very different. Traditionally, we fill only about 500 positions a year. Not thousands. Over the life of a list that can be 6–7 years, we may hire only 3,000 people."[6]

Von Essen also added that they'd tightened up the criteria for the five residency points amid allegations of widespread abuse. "Applicants must prove residency for a period of at least one year . . . we believe it's a much more stringent requirement that will be harder for the applicant to prove but easier for the Department to verify," he said.

He went on to detail his team's efforts to increase diversity through the Fire Cadet program, noting that its participants were city residents attending a city college, and they had to have at least 30 college credits, and were recruited over a ten-month period. The first class in 1996 was 70 percent minority, and the second class nearly the same—probably about 60 minority kids in total. It put them in an ideal spot to join EMS after graduation, and from there springboard off the EMS promotional exam into the FDNY, he said.

"We firmly believe that making these positions eligible for promotion will help us to attract qualified candidates into the ranks of firefighter," Von Essen said.

The Vulcans were pleased with the more restrictive five-point program, until they read the fine print. The city mandated that an applicant had to be a resident for a year. But a kid from Long Island could apply for the test, and as long as he said he'd lived somewhere in the five boroughs during the period required by DCAS, he could get the extra credit. There were plenty of ways to cheat too. Some candidates got together and rented a cheap place in the city, so they could show they got their mail delivered to an NYC zip code. Others relied on a city-living aunt or uncle who would let them put a utility bill in their name, another way to prove residency. The FDNY investigators were supposed to thoroughly go over each claim, but it was common knowledge that many applicants found a way around it—and nobody was all that worried about catching the violators.

The Vulcans' concerns were waved away. But another embarrassment for the FDNY was coming. Two months after Von Essen's testimony, a red-faced city had to defend itself after a *NY Daily News* exposé detailed dozens of relatives of white firefighters who'd taken the streamlined route through the Fire Cadet program to get into the FDNY—including the sons of four high-ranking fire officials. Even the son of a Uniformed Firefighters Association official—the union that had fought so hard to block Tierney's training course at Randall's Island—was found in the Cadet Corps ranks. The promotional pathway meant for minorities had become a backdoor route for the well-connected few.

"The reality is that [the relatives] got into the program on the same basis as everyone else," a defensive Giuliani told the press. "[They] had to be accepted because otherwise you would have a very serious reverse-discrimination case if you didn't accept them."[7]

Not long after the city gave exam 7029 in 1999, the Equal Employment Practices Commission that had audited and found fault with FDNY recruitment under Commissioner Howard Safir in 1994 began another audit of FDNY recruitment practices. It took a look at exam 7029 and how it was constructed. By the next year, the EEPC was hectoring Von Essen for a meeting to discuss its audit results, which were not good. From the written correspondence that followed, the meeting did not go well. The fire commissioner and EEPC spent most of the year sniping at each other in memos. On July 14, Von Essen wrote to point out several "factual inaccuracies" and differing interpretations of data that needed to be cleared up.[8] The EEPC responded a month later, criticizing Von Essen for giving half-answers to questions about FDNY recruiting and skipping others entirely. The committee also accused him of reneging on promises he'd made to the EEPC earlier to implement certain diversity recruitment steps.

"Given these facts, this Commission has determined that your response letter is inadequate and therefore unacceptable," the EEPC said. The fire department's recruitment for exam 7029 "will have minimal impact on diversity" within the FDNY, the agency said.[9] By the fall Von Essen adopted a much more conciliatory and cooperative tone. He provided a detailed description of the FDNY's actions and responses to the EEPC's recommendations. But he still resisted two key suggestions: he refused to hire experts to study the FDNY's written exam and its college credit requirement to judge if they unfairly hurt minorities' hiring chances.

"The Fire Department should conduct an adverse impact study based on the results of the written examination. If the department's study reveals that the test disproportionately screens out minority or female candidates, FDNY should conduct a validation study in accordance with the federal government's [procedures]," the EEPC wrote.[10]

Adverse impact was by then a well-established part of employment law, having grown out of a 1970s discrimination case brought by a North Carolina laborer named Willie Griggs and 12 other blacks who worked in a hydroelectric plant. Blacks at Duke Power Plant were limited to menial labor in one department until the Civil Rights Act of 1964 opened new pathways. Duke came up with two hiring and transfer prerequisites: a high school diploma or a high score on a general intelligence test given by the company. The new criteria meant no blacks could transfer into higher-paying positions. Griggs filed a discrimination lawsuit that went all the way to the Supreme Court, and won. The Supreme Court found that the intelligence tests and diploma requirement had been implemented to limit minority hiring, and had nothing to do with actual job performance. *Griggs v. Duke Power* made it illegal for a company to impose arbitrary criteria, unless it could be proven that the standards were job-related—a process called validation. Von Essen was not about to tie up precious FDNY resources in one of those studies—especially when it was clear results wouldn't be good.

"Not applicable," Von Essen answered. He pointed the EEPC to DCAS. That was the agency responsible for designing and administering the civil service test, he said.[11]

The back-and-forth culminated in a meeting just before Christmas in 2000 between EEPC officials and Von Essen. Amid the wide-ranging discussion, which touched upon the five-point residency credits, mentoring and other recruitment efforts, a new fact emerged: the civil service exam administered in 1999 was based on the same material used in the prior exam from 1992. This same material was also going to be used as the template for the next scheduled exam going forward, sometime in the early to mid-2000s. Yet at no time had the city hired outside experts to assess how well the test was designed.

The testing material as it existed actually only measured nine cognitive abilities deemed important to being a firefighter—even though there were nine others considered equally important. DCAS had gotten its information from several Bravest, who gave them feedback on the qualities they deemed most relevant to the job. The firefighters said that oral comprehension and oral communication were the two most important qualities of all—and they were completely left off the DCAS test. The other seven important qualities were also left off, because it was not within DCAS's standard operating procedure to test for them. It seemed the only thing the city learned from the Vulcans' 1970s discrimination lawsuit was that it didn't like court-imposed hiring quotas. It certainly hadn't figured out yet that the way it made up the FDNY civil service tests was fatally flawed.

Although the exchanges between the FDNY and the EEPC occurred largely outside of the public eye, Washington and Marshall couldn't have been happier with how things were shaping up. They continued to work closely with Olshansky and another bright young lawyer she'd brought in, Shayana Kadidal, from Yale. Moreover, the city's political landscape was taking on some interesting dimensions. A longshot billionaire candidate, Michael Bloomberg, appeared on the scene. He was a Democrat in Republican's clothing, having switched parties to stand out in the crowd. Few pundits gave him much of a shot. The real race was in the tense, divisive Democratic primary that pitted public advocate Mark Green against Bronx Borough President Fernando Ferrer. Two other candidates were also in the field, Council Speaker Peter Vallone and City Comptroller Alan Hevesi.

In the middle of the city's run-up to the 2001 primary, the Vulcans got wind of a new FDNY hire. One of the four Street Crime cops who had shot Amadou Diallo was joining the Bravest. Edward McMellon had taken the firefighter exam before the fateful night he and three colleagues shot and killed the African immigrant—and the FDNY had reached his list number. An upstate jury had acquitted McMellon and the three other cops of second-degree murder and other charges, but the NYPD was still working on its own internal investigation. The fire department's review board cleared McMellon for hire anyway. It was time for the Vulcans' first major news conference, Washington decided.

On April 14, 2001, Washington stood outside Vulcan Hall with Diallo's father, Saikou Diallo. They were backed by Michael Marshall and a dozen other black firefighters, including Keith Maynard, whom Washington was grooming as a future Vulcan leader. Washington had a short press release, typed out for him by his new wife, Tabitha. He'd been nervous thinking about his first real foray in front of the press as the Vulcans' leader—and half afraid no reporters would show up. When he saw all the cameras and notebooks, the nerves disappeared.

"If a black man had ever murdered somebody and went to trial for murder, no matter what the circumstances, that man would not be allowed to be a firefighter," Washington said to reporters. "Officer McMellon has easily shown that he has poor judgment. This is not the type of man we want to put in life-and-death situations," he said, noting that McMellon pulled the trigger for 16 of the 41 shots fired at Diallo.[12]

As the press conference hit the evening news and made headlines the next day, mutterings of what many saw as the Vulcans' hypocrisy flew around the department. If a black man was put on trial for murder but cleared of all charges, the Vulcans would have been first in line to demand the FDNY hire him, whispered more than one high-ranking official. The FDNY chiefs weren't the only ones paying attention to the press coverage. Public advocate and mayoral candidate Mark Green added his voice to the Vulcans', telling the *New York Post* that it was "wrong . . . to transfer one of the officers to the Fire Department so that the [Police] Department's investigation of him may never be completed."[13] Green later asked the Vulcans for their endorsement. They didn't grant it, but they did pass along the latest figures on FDNY diversity.

Headed into a difficult primary against Fernando Ferrer, who had large support in Hispanic communities, Green was more than willing to get on the Vulcans' bandwagon. He took their information and ran with it, crafting a letter of concern to Von Essen. It spelled out all the stats that Von Essen already knew by heart: white men make up 93 percent of the FDNY, while minorities rank significantly lower. Green added a new twist by including a graphic of minority representation in other uniformed city agencies: the numbers for Latinos, blacks and women were in the double digits for the NYPD and the Sanitation and Correction Departments, Green noted—and in some cases were more than 50 percent. In the FDNY, no single minority group cracked 5 percent. He also factored in black and Latino representation in fire departments around the country, noting that the FDNY was woefully out of step with other major cities. Los Angeles, Houston, Philadelphia, San Antonio—much smaller departments overall—had at least four times the diversity of the FDNY, and in some cases much more. Even Chicago, which for decades had a deliberate policy of discrimination, had jumped from 5 percent to 29 percent following an aggressive affirmative action program.

Calling on the FDNY to end "this long and unacceptable history of de facto and formal segregation of one of the city's largest and most vital uniformed services," Green proposed creating two new fire science high schools dedicated to feeding students into the Cadet Corps, then EMS and then the FDNY.[14]

These were all good things as far as Washington and Marshall were concerned. In just a few short years, they'd moved their agenda ahead significantly. They'd put the FDNY on notice of the seriousness of their intentions and found a dedicated, gutsy lawyer to handle what they anticipated would be a major civil rights discrimination case. They had only high hopes for the future, and Washington was already pulling together the different pieces for his next round of attack. And then, on September 11, 2001, two commercial airplanes plowed into the Twin Towers and changed the city and the FDNY forever.

CHAPTER 9

AMID THE EMBERS

9/11

IN THE DARK AND TERRIBLE DAYS AFTER 9/11, THE CITY AND THE WORLD cried like never before for the New York City fire department. Nearly 3,000 innocents were killed when terrorist-hijacked planes crashed into the World Trade Center and the Pentagon in Washington, D.C., and into a field outside of Shanksville, Pennsylvania. Among the dead were 343 members of the FDNY, who perished amid the rubble of the collapsing Twin Towers.

Grief was a numbing pall that shut down almost everything related to fire department business save for two things: responding to the immediate needs of the city, and retrieving the remains of the fallen 343, all those who died trying to save others, and the bodies of the victims themselves. The city's Equal Employment Practices Commission (EEPC) shelved its questions about FDNY diversity and recruitment. The Vulcans set everything they were doing to one side. Among the lost Bravest were 12 of their members—including Keith Maynard, the Vulcan whose brother missed getting into the FDNY by one point. His twin Kevin Maynard, working at Continental Airlines in Houston, Texas, spent frantic hours looking for news of his younger sibling. He wept into the phone when he finally got through to his twin's firehouse, Engine 33, around 1 a.m. on September 12. Keith Maynard was missing and presumed dead, along with several other members of his company.

In Brooklyn, Paul Washington steeled himself to pick up the phone and call Ruth Powell, whose son Shawn Powell ran into the towers with Engine 207 and never returned. Washington had helped him get on the job. Ruth Powell recognized his name right away when he called.

"You recruited my son," she said to Washington. To his relief, it was just a gentle statement of fact, not an accusation. Losing someone he'd brought in to be a firefighter had always been one of his worst fears. He talked to the grieving mother for a few minutes, and hung up with a promise to visit. There really was nothing anyone could say to any of the 9/11 families to alleviate the despair.

Amid the raw anguish, Fire Commissioner Tommy Von Essen found himself fighting to keep the fire department functioning. In one day, the FDNY saw its troops seriously depleted and a significant number of its senior men—beloved and seasoned leaders—wiped out. Those who survived labored at Ground Zero, and dedicated every other spare minute to the families of their fallen brothers. Von Essen and the department were running on fumes. In the chaos, Von Essen stopped for one second to do a favor for a friend. Ten days after the attacks, he wrote a memo to the FDNY's Department of Personnel: "As per Commissioner Von Essen please appoint this candidate in the next class. List No. 933. Name: Loscuito, Anthony S." Loscuito was the son of Von Essen's driver, who'd asked for help getting his son into the FDNY. As he had with black firefighter Damon Alston, Von Essen used his clout to move the connected candidate ahead—but the differences ended there. Loscuito, who was rushed into the October 2001 class, had serious drug charges in his past. He was arrested in 1998 and pleaded guilty to charges of possessing meth and marijuana. He should have at least been subjected to heavier scrutiny from the FDNY investigators. But armed with Von Essen's waiver, he waltzed through unchallenged.

At any other time, the Vulcans would have seized upon that detail, if the information had gotten back to them—as it probably would have in the gossip-driven FDNY. But like all the fraternal organizations and the department at large, they were overwhelmed. The heavy loss Washington felt over the death of Maynard, a close friend, as well as all the others who died on 9/11, didn't ease. Three months before the tragedy, he and Tabitha welcomed their first child, a boy named Julius. When he cradled his young son, brushing his face against the newborn's downy skin, Washington seriously questioned whether he would want his children to be firefighters. It no longer seemed worth the risk. His firehouse tasks became mundane and meaningless. The bleak feelings only began to lighten incrementally a few weeks after 9/11, when he responded to a fire in the second-story apartment of a Queens building on Jamaica Avenue. Washington pounded up the stairs and through the black smoke with two other firefighters, his inside team. Dropping to their knees, the trio crawled through the apartment, feeling their way into the rear bedroom as they went. Washington tried to peer through the new thermal imaging camera the FDNY just started issuing Ladder company officers. But he was unfamiliar with the heat-seeking technology, and he impatiently cast it aside. He resumed the old-fashioned method of searching with an outstretched hand. As he neared a window, he heard a frightened cough. Stretching further, he felt the soft contour of a body. Tiny hands came out of nowhere and grabbed his neck. He got to his feet, hoisting the slight weight of a small child. The terrified boy wrapped himself around Washington and clung hard, burying his face in the firefighter's scratchy black coat. When Washington felt the boy's small arms twine around his neck and the skinny legs squeeze his waist, a glimmer of his former joy in the job came back. It felt so right to make a rescue. He carried the boy down the stairs while the other firefighter followed with the child's mother. Washington held tight to that small flicker of passion over the heartbreaking months of almost endless memorial services and funerals. In the firehouses, the atmosphere remained highly charged. The littlest thing could set off a gush of emotion, as the Vulcans discovered when they sent out flyers for their annual memorial service. It was a smaller version of the fire department's own ritual of commemorating its dead with a private, secular ceremony every October.

"What about the white guys????" someone scrawled across one of the leaflets which bore the names of the 12 black Bravest who died on 9/11. The defaced flyer was posted on a wall in a Brooklyn firehouse, where a Vulcan firefighter saw it.

"Lick me," said another scribble, and "Please, no white guys."

Underneath the name of the guest of honor—former mayor David Dinkins—other names were inserted. The Jackson Five,

FDNY Captain Paul Washington, from Engine 234 in Brooklyn, former Vulcan Society president, September 2014. Photo credit: Mariela Lombard.

Gary Coleman, Buckwheat and Al Sharpton were a few. As soon as he heard about it, Washington went down to the firehouse with Ronnie Greene, a Vulcan and retired firefighter, and spoke to the officer in charge, a battalion chief. The chief investigated and discovered who did at least part of the defacing. The person was punished and Washington saw no need to make his complaint official. The FDNY was still in mourning; the Vulcans let the matter drop.

The FDNY didn't even begin to emerge from its shell-shocked state until the New Year, and by then a new mayor was in charge: billionaire businessman Michael Bloomberg. His improbable run—so unlikely just months ago—got a huge boost from the endorsement of Republican mayor Rudy Giuliani. The tough-on-crime mayor's many leadership excesses while in office were shoved aside in the days after 9/11, and he emerged as a major national figure. It also didn't hurt that Bloomberg bankrolled his own $74 million campaign, and that the last-minute voter-turnout push from Democratic candidate Mark Green got scuttled by nasty infighting with former rival Fernando Ferrer.

Von Essen, undone by the toll of 9/11, communicated to Bloomberg that he wasn't looking to stay in his job. The FDNY was in tatters emotionally, devastated physically and drained of resources, yet he felt no qualms about stepping down. There would be any number of people eager to fill a post that now carried immense, worldwide prestige. But Von Essen was as surprised as anyone by Bloomberg's pick: Nicholas Scoppetta, a 70-year-old lawyer whose government career dated back to Mayor John Lindsay in the 1950s. He was undeniably experienced in many things, but Scoppetta had never fought a fire in his life.

Avuncular and soft-spoken, Scoppetta overcame a poverty-stricken childhood that included nearly a decade in foster care, after his Italian immigrant parents had to give him and his two brothers up. His personal experience made him a natural fit when Mayor Giuliani needed a reformer to take over the city's Administration for Children's Services. ACS was a perpetually struggling agency, charged with the difficult task of monitoring child safety in the gargantuan city. Although Scoppetta was a fixture in city government off and on for many years and was a high-profile member of Giuliani's staff, he never crossed paths with Bloomberg. After the billionaire announced his mayoral ambitions, Scoppetta was surprised by a phone call from a former Giuliani staffer who'd taken a well-paid gig on Bloomberg's long-shot campaign.

"Mike Bloomberg would like to talk to you about something," the staffer said.

"Oh?" Scoppetta replied. He searched his brain but couldn't recall a single meeting with the billionaire.

"He wants to talk to you about putting together a fusion ticket. You could run for city comptroller. Would you like to run for comptroller?" the staffer said, almost coaxingly. "He can't give you the money, but he could raise the money and help you raise money so you wouldn't have to worry about funding it," the staffer added.

Scoppetta had never entertained any aspiration to be the city comptroller, but he couldn't help being curious about the offer. The plan was to forge a fusion ticket between Bloomberg, himself as comptroller, and a third well-known official who would round out the ballot by running with them as public advocate.

The phone calls continued for over a week, and Scoppetta's interest grew. But his wife, Susan, was already telling him, "Don't you dare." Plus, he had lined up some teaching work at Fordham University. He was planning to give classes at both its law school and social work school, two topics that were close to his heart. Scoppetta had zero belief that Bloomberg's fusion ticket would win. But he'd never run for elected office and he thought it might be fun, especially if he didn't have to do much fund-raising. It certainly would heighten his profile as his tenure with the Giuliani administration wound down. On the other hand, it might not heighten his profile in the ways that he wanted if he became known as the guy who ran on Bloomberg's failed platform. Scoppetta decided there was only one way to make up his mind, and that was to meet the man himself. He put in a request for a sit-down with the staffer who'd been his only point of contact with Bloomberg so far. A few days later, on a sunny, early summer Saturday afternoon, Scoppetta was happily engrossed in his favorite hobby, gardening outside his Long Island home, when Susan urged him inside. He had a phone call.

"This is Mike Bloomberg. I understand you want to get together?"

"Well, don't you think we should?" Scoppetta replied.

"I agree. How about dinner tonight?" Bloomberg offered. Scoppetta looked down at his grass-stained knees and the fine layer of dirt that stuck to his grubby hands and forearms.

"I'm out in Amagansett. I have to get cleaned up and drive into the city, so it's going to take me a few hours," he said.

"No, no. Stay where you are," Bloomberg instructed. "We'll come to you. We'll be out in 45 minutes or so. Give me a restaurant I can't possibly miss."

By the time Scoppetta and his wife made themselves presentable and pulled up to the Palm restaurant in East Hampton, Bloomberg had arrived in his private helicopter. He was seated at a table and flanked by a bevy of advisers that included political heavyweight consultants David Garth and Bill Cunningham. It was still early and the airy restaurant was empty, but the group was tucked into a discreet table cornered far away from the windows. The men made no concession to the beachy Hamptons atmosphere; all of them wore dark-colored suits. When everyone was seated, Bloomberg jumped right to the point.

"What's the hesitation? We'll raise the money and all," he said to Scoppetta. "I promise you that every single piece of campaign literature I put out will have your name on it. If you're interested in running for office, this is as comfortable an offer as you could possibly get," Bloomberg added, as the discussions went round and round.

"What do you think?" he finally said to Susan, who had been silently taking it all in as the meal progressed.

"Truth?" she said. Bloomberg nodded.

"Not much," she said, matching his bluntness perfectly.

"Well then," Bloomberg said, a small smile on his face, "how would you like to take a trip around the world until primary day?"

The joke lightened the mood at the table and the talks ended with laughter. A week later, Scoppetta called and declined the offer, but wished Bloomberg the best of luck.

When Bloomberg emerged in the weeks after 9/11 as the winning candidate, Scoppetta turned to his wife. "How do you like that? And I said no," he laughed.

"Yes, but you would have had to be comptroller for four years," Susan shrugged.

Scoppetta soon learned that Bloomberg was not done with him yet. The mayor-elect was moving decisively to pick his new staff, and he wanted Scoppetta's experience somewhere on his roster. Not long after his election, political insider Nat Leventhal, who'd been around since the Ed Koch days and was handling Bloomberg's transition, started calling Scoppetta with offers. He sounded out Scoppetta's interest in heading a number of city agencies. The fire department was not among them.

Scoppetta, for his part, had his eye on a position that seemed a perfect fit for his love of gardening: head of the Parks Department. Leventhal signaled that his chances were good. But late in the game, another idea came to Bloomberg. On the Friday before his January 1, 2002, inauguration, the mayor-elect called Scoppetta at his ACS office.

"Can you come up to campaign headquarters? I want to talk to you about another job," the almost-mayor told him.

When Scoppetta arrived, the two sat down inside a quiet office for a conversation. Bloomberg remembered that Scoppetta planned to go into teaching when he left public service, and he used that to frame his offer. "I need you to help me out here," said Bloomberg. "Come run the fire department, and after a year, if you don't like it or I don't like you, you can go teach."

"You know I have a lot of experience in law enforcement with police and prosecution, but nothing in the fire department," Scoppetta said.

"I don't consider that a handicap," came the reply. Bloomberg gave him the weekend to decide, and Scoppetta went home. The next morning Scoppetta had breakfast with Von Essen, who encouraged him to take the spot. Scoppetta needed little urging. As soon as Bloomberg made the offer, he felt a tug of response. Firefighters always joked that theirs was the last noble profession, and in the months after 9/11, their love and dedication to each other was there for the world to share. Scoppetta saw honor and privilege in the chance to lead the department out of its decimated state. He decided that he couldn't say no.

He was sworn in as fire commissioner on Tuesday, the same day Bloomberg was inaugurated as mayor. After the short, businesslike ceremony, he and Susan went to a nearby firehouse. Battalion Chief Joseph Pfeifer, whose firefighter brother Lieutenant Kevin Pfeifer had worked and died with Keith Maynard in Engine 33, lent them his tiny office to change out of their formal clothes. Then they were taken on a tour of Ground Zero that included a stop at the famous 10 House, home to Engine 10 and Ladder 10. It miraculously survived the destruction even though it stood right in the shadow of the Twin Towers. It was being used as a pit stop for crews still searching for firefighter remains. Scoppetta exchanged words with some fathers, a few of them retired smoke eaters, who came daily to look for their missing sons. It was a slow and sorrowful beginning to what would be a tumultuous eight years in office.

Racial politics came roaring back to the FDNY two weeks after Scoppetta's swearing in, and the flashpoint was an iconic 9/11 photo of three white firefighters raising an American flag. Taken by photojournalist Thomas Franklin, it caught dust-covered Dan McWilliams, George Johnson and Billy Eisengrein in a poignant and patriotic moment against the somber backdrop of twisted metal. When it appeared in the *Record,* a Bergen, New Jersey, newspaper on September 12, it flashed around the world and gained instant international acclaim. Not long after, a wealthy New York developer who wanted to create a 9/11 memorial statue decided to use the all-American image as a template. Bruce Ratner, who owned the buildings in downtown Brooklyn that housed the FDNY's administrative center, commissioned the artwork with the idea of placing it right at the entrance of 9 MetroTech. It would be a daily visual paean to the lost Bravest, right in the fire department's nerve center. Ratner's vision called for a 19-foot-tall bronze statue of three men raising the American flag. Unlike the original image, which captured three white firefighters, the trio in Ratner's statue would be black, white and Hispanic. It was meant to be an homage to the varied backgrounds of all the Bravest who made the ultimate sacrifice. But as word trickled out about Ratner's plan, it was met with widespread disdain inside city firehouses. Firefighters accused the developer of sacrificing historical accuracy on the altar of political correctness. The ruckus reached the ears of outgoing Mayor Giuliani and his replacement Bloomberg, but neither made a move to dissuade the developer.

In early January, not long after Scoppetta's swearing in, a feisty firefighter named Steve Cassidy from Engine 236 in Brooklyn showed up at a union meeting called to discuss the statue. The slow-acting Uniformed Firefighters Association wasn't doing enough to derail the project in the eyes of the unhappy membership. Cassidy, as the UFA's Brooklyn delegate, was part of the leadership team. But even he had to shake his head in disgust at the union's limp response. Its members were passionately opposed to altering the photo in any way, yet even in the face of their emotional pleas, the UFA leaders just grumbled that nothing could be done. When the meeting ended and the men from Engine 236 assembled again back at the firehouse, Cassidy spoke up.

"If we could get a reporter to write up this story, that we're gonna do something about this statue . . ." he mused.

"What are you gonna do, Steve?" asked one of the other men hopefully.

"How about we start an online petition?" said Cassidy. "Let's call up a reporter and say that we're going to start a firehouse petition against the statue."

Within days, Cassidy and a tech-savvy firefighter hooked up an online form that could be downloaded, filled out and faxed back to either Engine 236 or to FDNY headquarters. Cassidy made a quick phone call to reporter Michelle McPhee, who covered cops and firefighters for the *NY Daily News*. The next day, January 15, McPhee wrote about the firefighters' effort to sink the statue.

"We have no problem with our African-American and Latino brothers being represented, just not with that image," Captain Kevin McCabe of Engine 236 said in the article. "That image is sentimental, and to change it is to tamper with a part of the Fire Department's history."[1]

The online petition also had an open letter to Mayor Bloomberg, written by Cassidy. It included his suggestion that a larger memorial be built that included firefighters of all races and genders toiling at Ground Zero. Within a few days, more than a million signatures had been collected, with participants from all around the country. Completed petitions were coming in with such speed that Cassidy feared Engine 236's antiquated fax machine would catch fire. Soon the *Today* show called and asked him to appear on a live debate with Elinor Tatum, publisher and editor of the *New York Amsterdam News*, the city's oldest black newspaper. The two faced off, with Cassidy invoking the spirit of the famous marine picture of the battle of Iwo Jima as an example of historical accuracy, while Tatum argued in favor of creating a more inclusive public memorial.

By January 17, a second article appeared in the *NY Daily News,* and to Cassidy, it signaled the FDNY's surrender. Developer Ratner was quoted as saying he'd follow the fire department's wishes, and—contrary to its stance of just a few days ago—what the FDNY now wanted was for all discussion about this statue to just quietly fade away. Plans were scrapped, the idea was dropped and nobody within the FDNY ever mentioned it again. Cassidy, a torrent of twitchy energy packed into a wiry, five-foot-ten frame, filed the experience away. It was a valuable lesson on the power of the media, something he didn't think the current union leadership tried to exploit enough for its members. He was already mulling over a run for the UFA presidency, and the statue experience sealed it for him. He'd spent the last few months watching firefighters toil in the grim sludge of Ground Zero, some already taxed by a nasty, spewing cough. He was convinced that before long firefighters were going to need someone at the union helm who wasn't afraid to speak up for them, no matter how controversial the topic.

Nicholas Scoppetta, sitting in his new office on the eighth floor at 9 MetroTech, spent the last few days feeling slightly at sea. He was two weeks into his first term as fire commissioner, and the volcanic media scrum and the intensity of the blowback seemed to him all out of proportion for what was a well-meaning and thoughtful proposal for a memorial statue. Moreover, he was reluctant to abandon the idea just because some firefighters were grandstanding in the press. But if he dug in his heels the fight would continue, and the last thing he wanted was to spend his first month trading grenades with the UFA, especially on a topic as dicey as departmental diversity. As it was, Scoppetta winced every time someone repeated that the FDNY was just 3 percent black—a factoid the Vulcans emphasized at every opportunity and that the press corps seemed to regurgitate in an endless loop. When in doubt, like most lawyers, Scoppetta fell back on expert counsel, in part because he believed in the value of gathering different opinions. Through a staffer named Liz Squires, Scoppetta hit on the perfect person: Maya Lin. If anyone could offer insights on navigating the rocky emotional landscape of post-9/11 New York, it was the sculptor whose Vietnam Veterans Memorial had been dubbed the "Black Gash of Shame" and the "Degrading Ditch" by detractors when it went up in the 1980s.

The artist agreed to meet Scoppetta at a popular spot in the West Village, a cozy, romantic French boîte called Provence. The fire commissioner enjoyed it so much he later set up a lunch meeting there with Bloomberg's new police commissioner, Ray Kelly. When Kelly's wife found out, she couldn't resist teasing her ex-marine husband about joining the fire commissioner in the dimly lit, atmospheric restaurant. "You met Scoppetta at Provence? How about one of these days you take me to Provence?" she said to him, looking at his afternoon schedule. Scoppetta laughed heartily when the police commissioner shared the joke with him. Soon after, the two moved their meetings to the manlier and more private Harvard Club.

When Scoppetta sat down with Lin and Squires inside the hushed, flower-filled restaurant, they engaged in a deep discussion that left him with profound misgivings about the statue.

"Don't do it," the artist warned him. The controversy would never really go away, and instead of creating a public memorial to honor the brave 343 who made the ultimate sacrifice, he'd build a permanent reminder of the very dispute he was trying to bury.

Scoppetta knew enough to realize that the firefighters' opposition wasn't something to take lightly—he could easily imagine them lining up to picket the statue's unveiling, its dedication ceremony and so on. And then there was the Vulcan Society to consider, as well as the Hispanic Society. The Hispanic Society was keeping clear so far, but Washington went on both CNN and NY1 to argue in favor of including black and brown faces. And at a later panel discussion, he expressed his frank opinion that if the Semitic figure of Jesus could be remade into a blond man with blue eyes, it couldn't be that historically inaccurate to include a representation of the firefighters of color who died on 9/11. Scoppetta didn't need the controversy to get any louder—and it would if those groups really dug in. It wasn't worth the potential embarrassment and pain. The new administration had much bigger things to worry about.

One of those things was replenishing its diminishing ranks. The FDNY was facing an exodus of historic proportion, and the root cause was money. Many firefighters saw their six-figure salaries—and by extension their retirement pensions—boosted to dizzying heights by the round-the-clock overtime right after 9/11. For those eligible to retire, now was the time, because they'd never match those earnings again. Within the span of a year, several hundred Bravest of all ranks, each with at least 20 years' experience and wisdom, were going to be checking out. In their place, the FDNY was going to have to hire fresh young firefighters, many of whom applied in a swell of patriotic fever. If 9/11 ripped the guts from the fire department, the mass exits that followed were an institutional lobotomy.

The hiring process started in February 2002, when the FDNY's assistant commissioner for human resources, Sherry Ann Kavaler, wrote to the Department of Citywide Administrative Services to request that it post a notice for an upcoming firefighter exam, likely in late September or early October. The FDNY had already set up a recruitment drive, with the theme "Heroes Wanted." There was only one potential fly in the ointment: the loaded question of how well DCAS had vetted its entrance exam—if it had at all. The FDNY, legally prohibited from getting involved in any process of the exam creation and rollout, did the best it could to find out.

"Who will determine the validity of the written exam? We understand some questions have been raised about its fairness/bias," Kavaler asked in her memo.[2]

The same concern was also raised by the Vulcan Society, which was quietly angling for a sit-down with Scoppetta and Bloomberg. The rapid rate of FDNY hiring was cause for alarm. They wanted a meeting, and fast. They caught a break through Charles Billups of the Grand Council of Guardians, who had a tight relationship with the new mayor. Billups, a black man whose group had many black members, was a strong believer in the Vulcans' cause. His organization, an umbrella group that encompassed several large law enforcement unions in the city and state, had been one of the earliest uniformed agencies to endorse Bloomberg. Billups had paved the way for him at black churches and with black community leaders ahead of the general election. Bloomberg remained grateful for Billups's early support, and when the Guardians' president called City Hall to speak to the mayor, he got put straight through. Billups raised the issue of fire department diversity to Bloomberg not long after his first month in office, and the mayor was eager to learn more. "I'd love to have a meeting with the Vulcans," he told Billups. "Let's set one up."

In the month that passed before the new mayor and the Vulcans found time to meet, the FDNY had to absorb a few more broadsides from the city's EEPC. Even accounting for 9/11-related delays, the agency was fed up with the fire department's indifferent attitude. The department continued to ignore several key EEPC recommendations on ways to improve its diversity. As far as the FDNY was concerned, all test questions needed to be directed to DCAS, including validation issues. The EEPC, in a sharp memo, tartly reminded the FDNY that it was responsible for its own compliance, regardless of which agency designed its tests. The back-and-forth between the FDNY and DCAS had the EEPC feeling slightly crazed.

"The Department should conduct an adverse impact study to determine if the new educational requirement disproportionally screens out members of historically under-represented groups. If the study reveals such disparate impact, the Department should conduct a validation study," the EEPC wrote to FDNY Deputy Commissioner Doug White in a stern memo on March 14. "The

Department should retain a consultant to develop the tutorial for the next written firefighter's examination."[3]

The FDNY had also fallen behind on its monthly reports on diversity recruitment compliance—even after it was given two months' grace because of 9/11. The FDNY under Von Essen had also promised in meetings to undertake the adverse impact studies, and yet as far as the EEPC could see, nothing had been done.

"No such reports were submitted," the EEPC said accusingly to White.

As the debate raged on, Washington and Michael Marshall, unaware of the bureaucratic backlog, walked up the steps of city hall on April 29, 2002, for a 3 p.m. meeting with Mayor Bloomberg. They were accompanied by two other Vulcans, Fred Taylor and Larry Brown. The mayor's infamous bull-pen arrangement—the circle of desks where his eager young staff beetled away—was not quite fully formed yet. The Vulcans were escorted past the beehive of cubicles until they reached a large round table in a corner of the busy room. Bloomberg and Ed Skyler, one of the mayor's most trusted aides, greeted them genially.

"Can I get you some coffee, tea? Would you like something to eat? We have some chips here," Bloomberg offered, standing and gesturing to a sideboard as if he meant to serve his guests himself. Fire Commissioner Nick Scoppetta, who arrived 15 minutes earlier to brief the mayor on the FDNY's history with the Vulcan Society, shook their hands. Washington had come in with an agenda of things he hoped to get the mayor to commit to, but it soon became clear there would be no negotiating.

"We'd really like to change the written test to a pass/fail score and put more emphasis on the physical exam instead," Washington said.

"I'm not sure that can be worked out with DCAS," Bloomberg said mildly.

"It would also help if you would beef up recruitment," Washington said. The mayor nodded in a noncommittal response. Whatever his thoughts were on the topic of diversity, he was keeping them to himself.

The four Vulcan men were silent as they walked out of City Hall into the bright summer sunshine 40 minutes later.

"Well, we got absolutely nothing out of that meeting," Fred Taylor said, when they reached the bottom of the wide marble steps. Washington had to nod in agreement. He wasn't optimistic in general about the state of race relations in the FDNY, or in the larger world, for that matter, but talking to Bloomberg brought his usual pessimism to a new low. In his experience and from what he knew of history, even the smallest change took a lot of fighting, and what he and the Vulcans wanted was no small thing. It was going to take more than a polite conference room chat to convince a new mayor to attack the root of the FDNY's diversity problem—especially since the department was now practically enshrined in the eyes of the public.

Over the next few months, Bloomberg settled into office, and the city and the FDNY pressed ahead with exam 2043 over the EEPC's objections. For the Vulcans, the meeting with Bloomberg accomplished one thing: Scoppetta approached Washington and asked him to head the FDNY's recruitment program. It was an offer Washington found hard to refuse. He would have loved to take things over and do it all his way. He also got a friendly call from prominent black businessman Earl Graves, advising him to take it. But he didn't trust the FDNY's motives, and he was leery of stepping into an underfunded program that was already halfway completed. What the FDNY defined as a success to him was laughable.

The more he saw of the effort, the more he was convinced the FDNY wanted to set him up for failure and muzzle him at the same time. Once he took the job, it would effectively stifle his ability to criticize the department. He called Scoppetta and declined, news the fire commissioner received with a tinge of resentment. Scoppetta felt the department was making every good faith effort to get along. Washington's rejection stung.

Not long after, the Vulcans got word that Steve Cassidy, the fast-talking firefighter from Engine 236, was the newly crowned president of the UFA. The Brooklyn-born son of a firefighter, Cassidy had first worked on Wall Street before deciding to follow in his dad's footsteps in 1988. His decisive pushback on the 9/11 memorial statue gave him something of a profile, and he rode it to the presidency. It was fairly unprecedented for a borough delegate to make the leap to union leader. Cassidy had done it against three other candidates, although it took a runoff election. The day after his victory was announced, Cassidy called Washington to request a private sit-down.

"Yeah, let's do that," Washington said. He had a couple of things he was eager to say to the new union head. The meeting happened in Vulcan Hall a few days later, and the two men sized each other up over the large table in the old building's first floor. Washington got right to the point he wanted to make.

"You know you used race to get attention in your election, whether you believed what you said about historical accuracy or not," he said bluntly. The union leader wasn't fazed by his direct approach.

"I did what I thought was right," Cassidy responded.

"If you don't help us do this," Washington said of the Vulcans' diversity effort, "we're going to one day wind up in front of a judge and then the union and the fire department are going to regret it."

The short meeting broke up with an invitation to Cassidy to return to Brooklyn for a Vulcan Society meeting. Washington thought it would be good to clear the air with the black firefighters, since rank-and-file Vulcans were part of the UFA too.

The night Cassidy appeared, he strode to the front of the room and gave a short speech on what he thought were the department's biggest challenges, including diversity. For him, the issue was pretty straightforward: between the two tests, he thought the physical exam was far more vital in picking the best people for the job. So if the Vulcans wanted change in the name of diversity, let it be on the written exam. In the back of the room, firefighter Regina Wilson, one of just a few black women—or women, period—on the job in 2001, listened intently. She and John Coombs had been in the same 1999 probie class at Randall's Island, although not in the same rotation. While Coombs's group was doing physical training, Wilson's was in the classroom. At midday, the groups switched. The two met often after the end of classes to compare notes, and neither was surprised when it emerged that some instructors were going extra hard on Wilson. Exercises that Coombs and his all-male class would only have to do for a few minutes—like going into the smoky, claustrophobic simulator that mimicked a real fire—she would have to do for much longer. He urged her to file a protest, but she didn't want to complain. They often passed each other during the day, as one group jogged off the training field and the other came on. Coombs would raise a fist to his chin, a silent salute of encouragement. She'd send the same signal back. Wilson, like all the women, knew not to look for much institutional support, and that included keeping a wary distance from the firefighters' union. None of them had forgotten the terrifying incident that befell Ella McNair, one of the first black female firefighters hired in the 1980s. McNair only had a few years on the job in 1986 when she entered her firehouse, Engine 207 at Tillary and Gold Streets in Brooklyn, on June 7 and found a derogatory article about women firefighters pinned to the wall. Annoyed, she reached up to pull it off—and discovered it was glued in place. McNair marched into the kitchen for a knife, then returned to the clipping and started scraping it down. A male colleague, who was drunk at the time, tried to stop her. He grabbed the knife to yank it away and sliced her fingers. McNair filed charges against him, and a city judge found firefighter Greg McFarland guilty of harassing her. The judge recommended his immediate dismissal, both for the assault and for being intoxicated while on duty—but the FDNY instead fined him $15,000 and suspended him without pay for six months. But McFarland didn't suffer. The union, which rallied behind him to fight what most saw as an unduly harsh punishment, took up a collection on his behalf. In no time, the UFA gathered more than enough to cover his $15,000 fine. McNair, however, was left mostly on her own. Her experience still resonated with Wilson. Given the UFA's questionable history on gender equality, she had a keen interest in what Cassidy had to say.

"The most important thing is a competitive physical exam," the new labor leader declared. "My view is that there's going to be change sometime, so which test do you want to compromise on? I believe you couldn't compromise on the physical component, so I maintain that if you score well on a high pass/fail on the written, that's good enough. I want athletes that are smart. I don't want mediocre athletes that are really, really smart," Cassidy said.

As welcome as his position on the written test was to Washington and Marshall, it put them in an awkward spot with Wilson and other women firefighters. The women on average scored really well on the written exam. Any proposals that downplayed its importance while stressing a tougher physical wouldn't make them happy.

Washington spoke up.

"What about the sisters?" he asked Cassidy.

"What about them?" Cassidy responded. "If the department can recruit and target women from the right places, go to the athletic directors of high schools and colleges, go to the gyms and look for female athletes, they'll find women who can do it. But make no mistake about it, just handing out applications to the average woman walking down the street is not going to generate a high success rate of finding ones who can do this job. It's just not gonna happen."

The meeting wrapped up not long after. Washington and Marshall had no expectation that the UFA was going to get in the Vulcans' corner, but they were happy to have at least established some common ground on the written test. Their tentative accord, however, was viewed with deep suspicion by the women firefighters.

With a month to go before the end of the summer, Washington got a call from the Center for Constitutional Rights. The Vulcans' federal discrimination claim against the FDNY was ready, his lawyer said. One humid day in August, he presented himself at CCR's offices near SoHo. He flipped through the eight-page affidavit that would go to the federal Equal Employment Opportunity Commission, the first step of many in pursuing a possible civil rights claim. The complaint was nothing more than a legal, cut-and-dried summary of everything he and the Vulcans had been saying for decades, but he still had to take a minute when he reached the last page. Staring at the small space reserved for his signature, Washington felt a squeeze of loneliness. The enormity of his next step tightened his chest. It was no minor matter to file a civil rights charge against the FDNY. His mind flashed to his father, who had passed away in the summer of 1999. Cornelius Washington never talked much about what being a Bravest meant to him, but he'd worn his firefighter's uniform with distinction and pride.

"The best type of job you could do is a job where you help people," he'd said once to his youngest son, and it had stuck in Washington's head. His father's voice echoed in him again—along with the defiant reverberations of his spirited mother. He gripped the pen and, in his spiky handwriting, spelled out his name.

CHAPTER 10

FIGHTING THE FIRE WITHIN

New York City
1928–1944

THE FIRE BROKE OUT, AS MOST OF THEM DO, IN THE DARKEST, COLDEST
hours between midnight and dawn. It was April 27, 1928, and less
than a half-mile from Lieutenant Wesley Williams's cozy firehouse,
a nasty restaurant blaze was cooking under the tiles of the dining room. Inside the small space between the basement ceiling and
the first floor above, the hidden flames fed greedily, fanning out
sideways.

Four blocks away, Williams and his firemen slumbered bliss-
fully. Only the on-duty house watchman, maintaining his solitary
vigil of the hushed streets, was aware of the world. The fire-box
alarm was a violent intrusion that jerked the sleeping men upright.

The firefighters leaped into the practiced disorder that had
them outside, rubber coats flying, helmets clapped to their heads,
in less than two minutes. The blare of the fire truck sounded extra
loud in the light air of the frosty spring night.

"Let's get moving," Williams said. The rig rounded the corner
of Broome Street in a matter of seconds. It slid to a halt in front of
472 Broadway, which appeared dark and deserted. With the night's
patrons long since gone home and the kitchen staff dispersed, the
smoldering flames might have gone undetected for hours, save for

the sensitive nose of a passerby who sniffed the pungent char. In Hell's Hundred Acres, fire was a familiar smell.

Williams and his men plunged into the basement to start the exhausting task of pulling down the ceiling. It was grueling, sweaty work amid the choking fumes, which billowed out of the cracks in the red-hot beams and plaster overhead. Again and again the men drove their long, hooked pikes upward, then tugged sharply down. Each yank yielded a cascade of grimy material and more vented smoke, but no fire. The crackling flames danced away.

"All out, men, all out!" shouted Williams. He counted his crew as they passed by, then followed them up the stairs. Outside, the overheated firemen pulled off their helmets and tried to clear their lungs in the acrid air as they leaned against their fire apparatus. Williams conferred with another officer who'd arrived on the scene. His men were trying to find the fire from above. They were gingerly breaking holes in the dining room floor, mindful that it could give way at any moment.

"All right, Engine 55, on your feet. We're going back in," Williams said, and his weary crew hoisted their pikes again. They knew they'd be back and forth between the basement and the street as many times as it took for the fire to be extinguished. That was firefighting, and they loved it.

Williams was in love too, with many things. He'd been a lieutenant for about six months, and he reveled in his authority at Engine 55, where time had mellowed some of the more resentful firefighters. Those who couldn't reconcile themselves to working with him were mostly gone. He loved his children, of course, and now had a little girl as well as his two boys. His wife, Peggy, remained a dear companion, although their relationship was not what it had been. The spirited 16-year-old girl he'd married had grown into a fretful, anxious woman who suffered from an unspecified nervous condition. The marriage endured. Their romantic affection for each other did not. Along the way, a beautiful, dark-haired Italian woman named Frances captured the fireman's heart. He met her through his Italian connections in the neighborhood, and from his first glance, he was hopelessly attracted to her. But Williams was not the type of man to abandon his family. Peggy needed his care and support. He maintained the facade of the marriage and returned to the Bronx to be with his kids every chance he got. But when he was in Little Italy, he belonged to the woman he called Fran. Theirs would become a lifelong love affair known to intimate family and close friends. In 1928, their relationship was just blossoming, at the same time the handsome young lieutenant was finally getting a chance to let his talent shine in the FDNY.

The black press celebrated his recent promotion with story after story, and even the *New York Times* wrote about the first Negro officer in the FDNY. The supporters Williams had in the fire department were happy to champion him, although at times the praise was lukewarm at best.

"Williams is a regular fellow, able and efficient. He is one of the best amateur wrestlers in the city and sometime ago he won the boxing championship of the Fire Department," Lieutenant Walter Kavanaugh told the *Chicago Defender*.[1] It fell to the paper to note that Williams, also an amateur scholar, had stocked his hose tower study room with works by Nietzsche, Schopenhauer and other philosophers.

A year after he made lieutenant, Williams also marked his tenth anniversary in the FDNY, all of them spent at Engine 55. Few if any men worked that long in Hell's Hundred Acres. Most were rotated out of the busy division after two years. Fire Commissioner John J. Dorman made sure to commemorate the moment to the black press. "Williams is a fine man, comes of a fine family, and is an excellent officer. His men like him and he stands well at Headquarters. He is in line for another promotion," Dorman told the *New York Amsterdam News*.[2] It was a rosy picture that the FDNY painted, but not an accurate one. Williams had support from some of the very top officers, but most in the upper ranks were boiling. Williams was surprised when, after getting promoted, he got an invitation in the mail from the Lieutenants' Association. The prestigious group—the first of several fraternal groups that were separated according to rank—only sent invitations to those lieutenants with the best social and political connections. Nobody could ask to join the Lieutenants' Association. They had to wait to be invited. Williams filled out the enclosed application and sent it back in with his membership money. The group's goal became clear when they returned the payment to him, with a note that his application was spurned. Only white men were welcome in the Lieutenants' Association, the rejection letter said.

"They wanted so badly to hurt me," Williams said of the incident. And it did hurt. He didn't forgive them that petty slight.

The officers didn't stop there. They transferred a screwup firefighter to Engine 55, a well-known troublemaker named Frank Abbott, and told Williams to deal with him. Abbott had been shuttled in and out of 30 different fire companies. His father was a captain in the fire department and a leader in the Greenwich Village district run by Charles Culkin, a top Tammany Hall man. That meant Abbott was protected, as protected as Williams himself. Abbott was also an alcoholic, a hard-core one. Williams knew a complication when he saw it, and he went down to Commissioner Dorman.

"You're sending him to me? I got enough problems as a black man. I'm in a unique situation, as an officer of these white firefighters. Why does he have to become my problem?" Williams asked.

"We want him with you because if he can't make it with you he can't make it with anybody," was Dorman's short answer. In all likelihood, the FDNY bigwigs probably figured Williams was the only officer in the whole fire department that wouldn't feel Tammany's wrath if he brought Abbott up on charges.

Williams returned to his firehouse and grabbed hold of Abbott. He brought the unsteady man to an out-of-sight spot to tell him how things were going to go. Abbott had a long history among his other firehouses of getting so sodding drunk that he couldn't climb on the rig when the alarm bells sounded. Williams wanted him to know straight off that wouldn't be tolerated under his command. "Look, fireman Abbott, I want you to make the apparatus. I know you're a drinker and you can drink all you want. There are some men in the department who drink and do better work than they would if they were sober," Williams said. "But don't miss the apparatus. Obey orders and do what you are supposed to do. You must not drink so much that you are unable to respond," he warned.

Abbott took Williams's warning to heart. The lieutenant often found the firefighter stretched out on the concrete firehouse floor in subzero temperatures, clutching his bottle. Abbott reasoned if he passed out for the night in front of the truck, decked out in boots and his rubber coat, the firemen would choose to wake him up rather than run him over if a call came in. That way he was assured that he would never miss an alarm. Of course, the plan had some flaws, like the nights Abbott passed out before he got his boots on. Several times Williams found him clinging to the fire truck as it raced to a blaze, high as a Georgia pine and wearing his rubber coat and helmet, totally barefoot because he forgot his boots.

As long as Abbott got on the firehouse rig, Williams left him alone. Until the day came when he ordered Abbott to wash the outside of the upper firehouse windows and the man said no. It turned out that Abbott was deathly afraid of heights, but he refused to explain himself to Williams. The lieutenant had never brought charges against any fireman, letting it be known that he preferred to solve problems in-house. But he couldn't ignore a fireman who bucked his authority. He brought an insubordination charge against Abbott, even though the firefighter was considered untouchable within the department. FDNY brass hit Abbott with the highest fine known in the department at that time: two weeks' docked pay.

The official department order went out the next day, and to make sure everyone got the point, it was also published in the *New York Times*. In private, to his friends and family, Williams admitted his deep relief. The FDNY had made it clear that when Williams gave an order, it was to be followed.

"I would have had to put my hat on and walk out of the fire department if no action had been taken," Williams said decades later. "No white man would have paid any attention to my orders."

Within four years, by August 1933, Williams was a captain. That put him in charge of the entire firehouse. He'd taken the civil service test and scored well. And this time he didn't have to turn to his father's connections for help. His appointment went through without any outward opposition. But resentment toward him lingered amid the general resistance to Negro firefighters. There were still only four black men on the job, including Williams, out of 6,717 Bravest. Between 1928 and January 1937, not a single black firefighter was hired.[3] In Depression-era New York City, where one-sixth of the population was on the dole, that fact stood out— so much so that the *New York Amsterdam News* launched its own probe of the FDNY in 1934. The paper wondered how, in the age of civil service tests, "no one has yet come forward with a plausible explanation as to why Negroes have shunned this branch of city service."[4] The paper noted that there "must have been 50 applicants for places on the Police Force as against every candidate for the Fire Department," and the same held true for the Sanitation Department. The answer might be found in the experience of a young, college-educated black man who told the *New York Amsterdam News* what happened to him when he went down to FDNY headquarters to ask about applying. The man in charge of examination registration told him his chances weren't good.

"Well, you probably know the answer as well as I do, pal . . . I'm not trying to discourage you. But I'm just telling you confidentially that they will do everything to flunk you in the examinations. And if they can't do that, they'll make your life miserable on the force, send you to a station a heck of a distance away from your home, and you catch the devil from every superior officer. They would have to put you in a station full of white men because we have no Negro station," the FDNY official said, according to the young man. The black applicant went ahead with the exam anyway, and got a failing grade. Whether he was deliberately flunked or just did poorly on the test, the result was no surprise to New York's legions of unemployed immigrants and blacks. The so-called merit system used by the city to hand out jobs tilted inexorably toward those who backed Tammany Hall, and while there were some poor blacks, Italians and others in the mix, it was still mostly Irish Catholics.

The virtual blackout on Negro hires ended on December 14, 1937, with the appointment of probationary firefighter Walter Thomas, who was assigned to Ladder 41 in West Harlem. Thomas, who took college classes at night and later pursued an advanced degree, was a literary smoke eater. He wrote down the experiences of black firefighters as they gradually infiltrated the FDNY over the next ten years. The surge came after Tammany Hall mayor Jimmy Walker—done in by his Tweed-esque corruption—was ousted and fusion ticket reform candidate Fiorello LaGuardia swept into office. Short and stocky, with an impressively large head, LaGuardia was a fierce lover of firefighting, and often jumped in his car and raced to fire scenes to watch the action firsthand. He belonged to a breed known as fire buffs, men who loved everything related to the job—except actually doing it.

LaGuardia knew that Tammany loyalists were nested throughout the entire civil service workforce, and to control the city he had to be in control of its employees.[5] He tore apart the existing civil service department that was rife with Tammany rot and created a new civil service commission. In theory and to some degree in practice, it was a more impartial and equitable way to distribute jobs. It mandated the public announcement of upcoming exams, created tougher regulations on testing and grading procedures, and changed hiring so it was based on quantitative scores, reducing the influence of an applicant's political connections.[6] LaGuardia's reshaping of the civil service system might have done more for blacks had it not come in the depth of the Depression. In those harsh days of intense need every job, no matter how piddling, was a good job. As news of the mayor's reforms spread, applications flew in from all over the city, even from well-educated people who wouldn't have considered civil service jobs in other times.[7] In 1932, the last year Jimmy Walker was mayor, only 6,327 New Yorkers applied for civil service jobs. By the end of the decade, under LaGuardia, that number surged to 250,000.[8]

In 1937, the year Thomas was hired for $3,000 a year, LaGuardia got rid of the FDNY's two-platoon system that kept firefighters working nonstop for days at a time. Instead of having two crews of five or more men staffing a firehouse around the clock, LaGuardia decided to change to a three-platoon system. This meant more men available to work—and shorter hours for all of them. For the first time since 1865, firefighters had some semblance of a regular family life, instead of living in the firehouse with bi-monthly breaks to go home. The change created an instant need for more FDNY hires, and blacks benefited. After Thomas, another 50 or so got on the job, approximately .5 percent of the otherwise all-white department.[9] Those increases, though small, were enough to trigger a backlash. The creeping antagonism chronicled by Thomas started to solidify into department-wide practices. Segregation, the bastard creation of the Jim Crow south, reared its ugly head.

Black firefighters were often denied use of the firehouse table at meals, or told to eat at separate times. They weren't allowed to contribute to the commissary kitty or chip in for staples like sugar, salt and milk. It was an unwritten rule that the Negro firemen not be assigned to high-profile positions; no black man should be found at the fire-truck tiller steering the rig or operating its pump, or carrying certain tools. Blacks were assigned the meaningless grunt work, the onerous tasks firefighters were supposed to share.

"The most menial porter-type work was assigned to the Negro fireman . . . the toilet cleaning, furnace tending, ash removal or whatever work that was considered uninviting was surely to be assigned to the colored fireman," Thomas wrote. "With a great number of the officers spearheading the action or remaining neutral to it, there was no difficulty for many white firemen to add to this growing pattern of discrimination."[10]

Blacks detailed among different firehouses had to carry their own equipment back and forth. White firefighters wouldn't share or lend them any, although they commonly did it among themselves. Blacks got the silent treatment, and their salutes to officers were often ignored. White firefighters in line for promotion were permitted to act as officers on duty from time to time to get used to the skills. Black firemen were not, Thomas said. Such treatment went on "as much as the colored fireman would stand for," he noted.[11] The segregation wasn't just in the kitchen and the common room, but in the sleeping quarters too. As Jim Crow practices subtly took root, emboldened firehouses expanded the practice of black beds, where only the Negroes would sleep. White firefighters refused to use a bed after a black man, even though the linens were changed daily. In some firehouses with two blacks, the officers limited or changed the Negroes' working hours to keep them off night tour. That way there only needed to be one black bed to serve the firehouse. Generally, it was the bed closest to the toilet. In some firehouses, it was screened off, or moved to another room entirely.

Not every firehouse or officer tolerated the vicious Jim Crow behavior, however. Many firefighters had a "sense of justice and maturity [that] would not allow them to prejudge a man," Thomas wrote. He spoke of "great companies" that did everything they could to protect the blacks from the cruelty of the rest. "There were fair-minded individuals, many with brogues thick and intact from the counties of the old country, who would stand up and oppose the pattern. . . . These men . . . in instance after instance, gave the struggling Negro firemen inestimable encouragement and guidance," the young smoke eater wrote.[12]

White firefighters were drawing their battle lines, and the outcome was going to affect black smoke eaters for generations, Williams saw. It would also determine the shape and the spirit of the FDNY itself. Was the department to become a segregationist agency that opted to crowd its black firefighters into one or two small companies, or would it became a national leader in creating a fire department that had whites and blacks working together as equals? The fight was on, and Williams was determined to win.

In 1938, Williams was promoted to battalion chief. He'd climbed in rank three times since starting the job, but he was still the only "race" officer in the FDNY. His rank and seniority made him the unofficial ambassador for black firefighters, who came to him with complaints when they got stuck in a difficult house. The Chief, as he was known, would put in an appearance and try to reason with the officer in charge—often with limited success. By 1941, with approximately 80 colored men in the FDNY and his own job as battalion chief, Williams was having a hard time keeping up with the requests and demands. He called all the black firefighters to the Harlem Y. He'd been paying attention to the combined clout of the FDNY's fraternal associations, such as the Steuben Society, the Emerald Society and the Ner Tamid Society. The Jewish men of Ner Tamid worked together very effectively, Williams saw, to force the FDNY to accommodate their specific needs, like not working on the Sabbath.

"Men, let's form a society," Williams said to the black firefighters at the extraordinary gathering. He didn't make the suggestion lightly. He had his 20 years on the job and was virtually untouchable. He could retire the next day and walk away with his pension. The younger men had families to feed and bills to pay but no security at all. Organizing a fraternal society to combat firehouse racism was a considerable risk. They could face trumped-up charges or even more abusive treatment. The worst would be to get fired, because Williams knew that Depression-era jobs were difficult for anyone to get, but for a Negro they were just about impossible. He studied the problem from all angles before deciding to commit to forming a group. The black firemen had no political pull behind them, and that was their weak spot. To get it, they had to be organized.

Among the most fervid supporters for a black organization was an impassioned firefighter named James Strachan, who had been born in Harlem and raised in the Caribbean but returned to New York as a young man. He was almost court-martialed by the FDNY once for refusing to shine and carry his white captain's boots. Strachan spent hours in the library creating bylaws for the fledgling group, and, according to some, even came up with the name: the Vulcan Society, named after the Roman deity of fire. Will Chisolm, a black firefighter studying to become a lawyer, was named president. Williams vowed never to hold any position within the Vulcan Society; he was older than most of the black men and the day when he would be gone from the FDNY was not far off. He was determined to groom the next generation of black leaders to continue the fight.

To everyone's surprise, Fire Commissioner Patrick "Paddy" Walsh gave the Vulcan Society his eager approval. Walsh, who'd criticized Williams's appointment as driver of Engine 55 years ago, was known to comment, "I don't know why God made Colored people, but I guess he knew what he was doing."[13] The black men were shocked at his easy acceptance but also thrilled. It gave the Vulcan Society the same standing and access to FDNY headquarters that all the other fraternal groups had.

But not all black firefighters got behind the Vulcan Society. Brooklyn firefighter Willie Brent, known as Heavy Willie, and Edward Brantley, who was in line for lieutenant, both dissented. "We're only Jim Crowing ourselves with all this," Heavy Willie said to Williams.

"You don't have to worry, they'll Jim Crow you anyway," Williams retorted. He was perplexed by the black men among them who didn't see that they were being shoved to the bottom of the pecking order. "Are the Jewish men Jim Crowing themselves? Are the Irish men in the Emerald Society Jim Crowing themselves? They all have an organization and with an organization you can work your connections politically and socially. You can go ahead and do your job, but without an organization you're helpless. You are already Jim Crowed," Williams told Heavy Willie. The men declined to join anyway, but Williams wasn't bothered by it.

"Don't worry about those two," he told the rest of the Vulcans. "They'll be back."

While Williams was busy fighting on behalf of other blacks, his own struggles with the department continued. In the months before the Vulcan Society formed, he was embroiled in a dirty little war with Commissioner Walsh over his request to transfer to the Bronx. Williams was tired of the back and forth to Little Italy, a round trip of 44 miles. With the shortened platoon hours it was becoming too much. He also needed to be more available to Peggy, who wasn't faring well. His wish to be transferred to the Bronx, the first and only personnel request he ever made, was being blocked by Walsh.

It was time to use his father's Red Cap rolodex one more time. Williams appealed to the ex-governor, Alfred E. Smith, asking if he could take advantage of "your long years of friendship with my father" for an intervention with the fire department.

The letter started out sincerely enough, but Williams likely had to hold his nose as he wrote the last line: "Should you be kind enough to bring this to the attention of our very humane and just Commissioner Patrick Walsh, I am sure he will do it if it is possible."[14]

Not long after, Williams got the transfer he wanted, becoming a Bronx battalion chief. He took Fran with him and set them up in an apartment where she could enjoy the Italian enclave along Arthur Avenue and he could maintain contact with Peggy and his children. But as it turned out, Commissioner Walsh had more plans for Williams now that he was uptown. Walsh wanted to resurrect the idea of segregated firehouses. The department told Williams that since the Vulcan Society had been formed they realized that "you all prefer to be together."[15] The easiest way to achieve that was to put all the blacks into two Harlem firehouses and leave them there. It was also the perfect way to stifle black growth in the FDNY, because it immediately limited the number of black firefighters the department needed to hire. And it severely restricted the number of promotional opportunities, since two firehouses would only need a few officers. Blacks would be forced to compete for those slots against other blacks. No white man would lose a job because he was outscored on a test by a Negro. Williams was incandescent when he heard.

"Do you plan to put all the Germans in one company and all the Irish in one company and all the Italians in one company?" he said to FDNY Deputy Chief of Staff David Kidney. "No, you don't. The black men are just fine and they should be distributed all around. If you put too many in one company it's gonna cause that company to have a stigma, see?"

The FDNY did see, and that was exactly what some of them wanted. The Uniformed Firefighters Association created in 1917, got behind the idea. The union also decided to try and Jim Crow its new medical health plan for its members. Black firefighters would get a benefits card marked with a "C" for colored, so white doctors would know to refer them to a Negro physician.[16] Williams could barely contain his rage when he described life in the FDNY in a letter to a black firefighter buff named Al "Smokestack" Hardy.

"The colored men are assigned throughout the department just as are the Italians, Polish, French, German, Jewish, Greeks and Irish despite the fact that the latter feel that the Colored men shouldn't even be allowed in the department or else segregated like a lot of animals. We are human beings just as they are so why should they want to Jim Crow us? Talk about Hitler and the way he treats people, it could not be any worse than the way they treat we Colored Americans in this supposedly free and democratic country," Williams wrote.[17] He'd had enough of trying to appeal to the better natures of fire captains who allowed discrimination to flourish in the firehouse. It was time for the Vulcans to stop talking among themselves. They needed community and public pressure to help them fight back. Williams reached out to the National Association for the Advancement of Colored People.

The NAACP had a good relationship with Mayor LaGuardia, and so did an up-and-coming black politician from Harlem named Adam Clayton Powell Jr., who was just elected to the City Council. He was also a preacher at Abyssinian Baptist Church, one of Harlem's most powerful religious institutions. By dint of their combined pressure, the Vulcans forced the UFA to ultimately abandon its segregated medical plan. The idea of black firehouses also was grumblingly put aside. But the black beds remained.

The NAACP sent frequent reminders to Commissioner Walsh that under Section 222 of the FDNY's 1937 regulations, firefighters were strictly forbidden from doing anything that might incite "religious or racial hatred." And the FDNY's own officer guidelines stated that bed and shift assignments be rotated regularly and made impartially. The NAACP's nudging was ignored and the fire department—with more than 100 blacks in its ranks by 1944—continued to look the other way when Jim Crow disrupted a firehouse.[18]

On September 18, 1944, Williams called his Vulcan Society together. It was time for the men to decide just how much they wanted to fight. A few days earlier, in Engine 221, a white lieutenant named

Otto Claus ordered the company's two black beds removed from the main dormitory and placed right in front of the toilets.[19] The two black firefighters protested, with no luck, and then turned to Williams. The battalion chief took the complaint to Commissioner Walsh, who referred the incident to his deputy chief, a man named Petronelli. When Petronelli went to Engine 221, he only revved the racial hatred higher. It would be embarrassing for a white man to have to sleep in a bed after a Negro, he told the on-duty lieutenant. Petronelli left the beds where they were, and when Williams went to him to protest, the deputy chief pointed out that such arrangements worked very well in the Boston Fire Department.[20] In the end, even the fire commissioner conceded that Petronelli needed to be checked. The beds were ordered back to their usual places, but they remained assigned to the Negro firefighters. Williams understood what was happening. The segregationist forces in the fire department, seeing the Vulcans had survived the recent skirmishes over black firehouses and a Jim Crow medical plan, were bringing out the heavy artillery. They were going to take their best shot at mowing down the group's growing activism. Williams needed his young black smoke eaters to be ready for it. He needed to rile them up.

"Are we mice or are we men? Don't you think we need something to put us in a militant mood?" Williams roared to the Vulcans the night of the September 18 meeting about Engine 221.

"I am very surprised they did not put the beds into the toilet, or down into the cellar. The more we stand for without protesting, the more they will force down our throats. Why, even the Commissioner's aide, Chief Heaney, said that this is going too far. In plain words, it is alright to kick the Nigger in his ass but do not leave your shoe up there," the Chief said. "We are too complacent. No other racial or religious group in this Fire Department would stand for this bed treatment except we Negroes. You owe it to your children to fight this until we are successful."[21]

The men whistled and clapped wildly, but at the meeting's end the tense firefighters filed out feeling even more anxious and on edge. Williams had succeeded in riling them up, and now the Vulcan Society had decided on a course of action to force the FDNY to abandon black beds once and for all. He just hoped all his young Bravest would survive it.

CHAPTER 11

FDNY AFLAME

New York City
2005–2007

JANUARY 23, 2005, DAWNED GRAY AND FROZEN. AN EARLY MORNING CALL in the Bronx rousted firefighters in the Morris Heights neighborhood out of bed and into the frigid morning. The sun was just breaking through the winter sky as fire trucks, lights and sirens blaring, tore through the empty streets to an apartment building at 236 East 178th Street. A fast-moving fire was gobbling it up, bursting from the confines of the third floor and threatening to consume the rest of the building. Four firefighters from Ladder 27 and two others from Rescue 3 were sent to the fourth floor with orders to search for victims. The rest of the firefighters battled the core of the conflagration a floor below. On the ground outside, engine crews cursed the numbing cold as they raced to get pumpers connected to fire hydrants and bring their heavy water hoses to life. The icy water hissed and popped as it hit the searing flames.

The six firefighters told to trek up to the fourth floor entered a baffling maze of small, cramped apartments. The scant description they had on the building showed a fourth floor filled with airy, spacious units—not this warren of single rooms, blocked off by cheap partitions. They carefully navigated through the hazards, blind men feeling their way in the black, disorienting smoke. Out of nowhere, a volcano of fire erupted, a flashover that blocked the only exit, the fire escape behind an illegal wall. The six men moved backward, to the fourth-floor windows. Above them, on the roof, firefighters from the ladder companies cut holes with saws to vent the smoke and heat. All six men below gathered near the glass panes. At any moment they expected to hear the steamy sound of water hitting the flames that licked at their backs. But the welcome sound never came. The life-saving water flow had been interrupted, probably by a kink in the hose or a burst hose length. Cornered by a wall of fire, Lieutenant Curtis Meyran, 46, a married father of three, ordered his crew to exit the only way they could. Frantic shouts from both the roof and the ground rang out as one by one, the six smoke eaters took calculated leaps. Only one carried a rope, which broke as he tried to descend. Another clung to the small shred that remained, fighting to do anything to lessen his fall. Meyran and another senior firefighter, also married with a family, died at the scene. The rest survived, three with multiple critical injuries. The fourth—a probie just out of the academy—walked away with a punctured lung and messed-up ankle.

The trauma of the day was not over yet. Six hours later, firefighter Richard Sclafani died while battling a routine basement fire in East New York. The 37-year-old from Bayside, Queens, was following his senior officer up the stairs, but when the officer got outside, Sclafani couldn't be found. He'd gotten tangled somewhere in the debris-filled staircase and run out of air. By the time distraught firefighters found him, he'd succumbed to the smoke.

January 23, 2005, known as Black Sunday, was the biggest loss of life in one day that the FDNY had suffered since 9/11. The crushing grief, never far from the surface, came flooding back. On assignment in a Brooklyn firehouse, Paul Washington felt a familiar sick sensation as each of the line-of-duty deaths came over the radio. He'd worked alongside Curt Meyran earlier in his career. Washington knew that all the men fought like hell to try to stay with their families; every firefighter caught in a crisis did. He pulled out his phone. He had something big planned for the Vulcans for Tuesday, but that was going to have to wait now.

"Yeah, the press conference we had scheduled, we're gonna have to cancel that," he said to the firefighter who answered. "We'll reschedule it, it is gonna happen, I just don't know when yet. But now is not the time to bring this out."

The two talked a few minutes more, with Washington explaining the sad circumstances. Then he called the few Vulcans who knew about his secret.

"It's still important to keep the details quiet. I don't want anything to leak out," he told Michael Marshall and the others he confided in. "We'll just have to hold off on this for a while."

What Washington had up his sleeve was sure to infuriate the fire commissioner and Mayor Michael Bloomberg. But it was too inflammatory to reveal now as the fire department once more plunged into mourning. It involved a black firefighter and close friend of his, Lanaird Granger. The two had a long history together.

Granger joined the job off the 1992 exam, and was a staunch Vulcan member and recruiter up until 9/11. Although he was permanently assigned to Ladder 102 in Brooklyn, at that time he was detailed to a firehouse at the foot of the Brooklyn Bridge. He was off duty that terrible day, but when he heard the news he drove his car straight across the graceful span to join firefighters in Manhattan, staring in wordless horror at the belching smoke and flames from the Twin Towers. The lung damage and other injuries Granger sustained kept him on medical leave for nearly a year. When he finally returned to his permanent home in Ladder 102, a problem arose almost immediately. Granger, a practicing Muslim, called Washington to say he'd gotten into a tense situation with two firefighters who accused him of stealing some boots. The firefighters cornered him in the booth known as the house watch and harangued him over the supposed theft. Granger wound up calling FDNY headquarters to alert them. He also told the firehouse captain that he wanted to file a complaint with the fire department's equal employment opportunity office. The officer, against FDNY protocol, didn't follow through. When Granger told Washington what happened, the Vulcan president paid a visit to the firehouse that night. The captain got defensive, until Washington whipped off his jacket to show the other man that he was a captain too. Realizing he was talking to an officer of his own rank, the captain calmed down enough to listen. He agreed to make the complaint on Granger's behalf.

But Washington suspected that wouldn't end Granger's difficulties—and he was right. The black smoke eater was bounced to another firehouse and then moved again—against his wishes—to Engine 238 in the Polish neighborhood of Greenpoint in 2004.

Granger butted heads with some firefighters there when he over-head one of them telling another that if he'd been involved in the Amadou Diallo confrontation, there'd be no media circus because he would have made the kill in two shots. Granger, who'd protested the FDNY's hiring of McMellon in 2001, had been equally opposed to its subsequent hiring of another one of the Street Crime cops who shot Diallo. When he heard the firefighter in Engine 238 talk about two shots, Granger told him flat out he was wrong to say it. A thunderous argument followed, with tense shouting and yelling. Another time, after the Vulcans had a press conference on the steps of city hall, someone in Granger's house photocopied a picture and article that ran in a newspaper and drew an arrow to one of the black firefighters in it. It was left on the kitchen table for Granger to find. When he saw it, he stared quizzically. It wasn't actually him in the picture, but he realized the firefighters thought it was.

Tensions in Engine 238 came to an ugly head in early 2005, and on January 20—three days before Black Sunday—Granger sought Washington out at a City Council hearing on FDNY diversity.

"Hey man, how you doing? You all right?" Washington asked. He kept his voice low so as not to disturb people around them. Granger nodded, then opened the small bag he carried with him. He tilted it slightly so Washington could look at its contents. Washington peered down and saw a length of black rope coiled around itself to fashion a sinister loop.

"It's a noose," he said, staring at Granger in confusion. He didn't know why Granger had it, but he was disgusted just looking at it.

"Yeah. I found it by my gear a few days ago. Someone put it there," Granger said. Whispering so that they didn't disrupt the hearing, he told Washington the details. He'd been in Engine 238 going about his business, and he walked over to his gear to get ready for a fire run. He saw something draped partially over his boots, and when he stepped closer to examine it, he realized it was an 18-inch rope, placed alongside and atop his equipment. It took him several long seconds to process what he was seeing. It was a noose. He was too shocked to move. Finally he grabbed his gear and got on the fire truck. He didn't touch the noose at all. He just left it where it was. When he got back to the firehouse with the rest of his company a little later, it remained there. He still didn't touch it. Even though it was in the open, where everyone left their gear, nobody spoke about it. After a few hours, Granger said, he picked the noose up and put it in his car. That's where it stayed until he brought it to show Washington.

Washington knew right away what he wanted to do with the hateful symbol—but it all depended on what Granger was feeling. Washington had been searching for a way to get the fire department to take the Vulcans' claims more seriously, and this was the chance he'd been waiting for. Even after he filed his federal discrimination complaint with the Equal Employment Opportunity Commission (EEOC) in August 2002, the FDNY seemed inclined to ignore the Vulcans. City lawyers were cooperating—albeit slowly and in a piecemeal fashion—by producing documents requested by Electra Yourke, the chief investigator for the EEOC. But Bloomberg's people adamantly refused to sit down for conciliation talks. There was a way to resolve the problems easily, Washington felt. They weren't asking for much—maybe a recruitment van. But the Bloomberg administration refused to come to the table.

And the pressure wasn't just coming from the feds—the city's own Equal Employment Practices Commission had once again written a warning to the fire commissioner that his agency was at risk for a lawsuit. On December 10, 2002, the EEPC sent a letter to Nick Scoppetta telling him that an adverse impact study had to be done. It was ignored. Four days after it was sent, the city pushed ahead with firefighter exam 2043—with the usual bad results for blacks. Roughly 1,400 blacks took the test, about 200 fewer than applied in 1999. Eighty-four percent of the black test takers in 2002 surpassed the cutoff mark of 70 set by the city, but they were grouped on average 974 ranking places lower than whites. The city eventually hired 2,100 candidates from that list, but only 80 were black, approximately 3.7 percent.[1] Many black candidates who scored above a 70 were never called, among them 22-year-old Malcolm Flythe. He scored well, but his number never came up. Others, like Rich Santos, an ambitious 25-year-old from Queens, got knocked out partway through the process. Santos earned high marks on both tests, but was rejected because he was a few college credits shy of the minimum 30 required.

Mayor Bloomberg was put on notice too. The EEPC wrote him directly in April 2003 to tell him the FDNY's written exams posed a serious legal risk to the city. The agency urged him to compel Fire

Commissioner Scoppetta to conduct adverse impact studies and get the written firefighter test assessed by an outside expert to make sure it really measured job-related skills. Bloomberg took his time answering.

"I am satisfied that the Fire Department has adequately addressed the points raised in the EEPC's report," he finally wrote back in October 2003. In reality, the FDNY addressed none of the points raised by the EEPC. It was relying on the same type of exam that raised the EEPC's concerns back in 1994, when the agency wrote its first warning to then Commissioner Howard Safir.

Bloomberg and his current commissioner, Scoppetta, weren't interested in paying for expensive studies that would tell them what they already knew. The FDNY was racially skewed, terribly unbalanced, and something had to be done to rectify it. Scoppetta admitted as much from his earliest days in office, even testifying to it in front of the City Council. But the administration's approach differed significantly from the Vulcans' solutions. The Vulcans were determined to get better recruitment, more attention on the five residency points and lessen the number of background disqualifications. But they realized the main point of attack was the written test. It was the city's Achilles' heel, and practically assured the black firefighters a legal victory if Bloomberg truly wanted to take this to the courts. The FDNY could recruit 24/7, but until an entry-level written test was devised that didn't have an adverse impact on minorities, too many would continue to get washed out by that first, critical step. The FDNY disagreed. Their department could control the amount of resources and effort poured into recruitment. But, according to its top officials, the fire department was helpless to change the written exam.

"That's a DCAS issue," the agency insisted. The agency gave the same answer whether talking to reporters, the Vulcans or even answering questions before the City Council. The Vulcans heard that excuse through multiple mayoral administrations, and they were thoroughly sick of it. Both the Department of Citywide Administrative Services and the FDNY were equally obliged to follow city, state and federal employment laws. What was missing was someone in charge who would force them to do it.

Washington and Marshall had let City Hall know they were willing to meet. But they'd gotten no love from Bloomberg over the past three years. Even their powerful connection Charles Billups, of the Grand Council of Guardians, struck out when trying to get the mayor to make time for them again. The mayor was miffed by Washington's refusal to run the FDNY's most recent recruitment drive, and he was angered in general by their constant hammering at him in the press. Billups had spoken with the mayor about the Vulcans a few months after his first meeting with Washington and Marshall. Bloomberg had made his opinion quite clear even back then, and it wasn't a flattering one.

"The Vulcans are being asses," Bloomberg said in his candid conversation with Billups. The two men were having a private talk in a side room at Gracie Mansion ahead of a community event. "The Vulcan Society doesn't want to listen to anyone."

"Maybe you should try to listen to them," Billups said. "You're the new mayor here, you have an opportunity to make a real difference, to do something that will bring about real change."

Bloomberg shook his head. Billups could tell the talk was annoying him and he recognized the mayor's attitude. Bloomberg was in charge, after all. He felt the Vulcans should be trying to get along with him. "Listen, Charles, fuck that," the mayor said, with just a touch of heat. The two men let the subject drop.

Washington and Marshall didn't need Billups to spell the situation out for them. It was clear the mayor wasn't motivated then or now to really dig into DCAS's test prep—or lack thereof. He remained unfazed by the federal probe into DCAS's written tests, but he was bothered by the political pressure the Vulcans brought through the City Council and other black politicians. Commissioner Scoppetta, however, could read the proverbial handwriting on the wall. He saw the lawsuit coming, and tried to use it to goose his reluctant staff.

"Do you want to end up like we did with Sifton?" he asked. The mere mention of Charles Sifton, the federal judge who imposed a court mandate in the 1980s to bring more women on the job, sent an unpleasant ripple through the mostly male ranks at FDNY headquarters. Granger's noose, as awful as it was, fell into Washington's lap at just the right time. In early 2005 Bloomberg was preparing to run for a second term in office—and no politician is as pliable as one facing an election. The Vulcans needed to get themselves and their cause back on his radar. As soon as Washington heard Granger's story, he saw his chance.

"Listen, I want to hold a press conference about this noose. I want you to appear at it and we'll show everyone what you found. But I don't want to let the fire department know what we're doing, or tell them about the noose in advance. We'll file an official complaint after the press conference," he said.

Washington knew he was asking a lot. It was never easy to go public with a racial complaint in a firehouse—and Washington planned to do it in a big way. For one thing, it broke the omertà-like code of silence within the brotherhood. Granger would be in for a tough time even if he just quietly took his complaint to the FDNY personnel officials—but a press conference guaranteed a pissed-off rank and file. Not many firefighters had the courage to willingly make themselves the firehouse goat. But in the end, after thinking it over, Granger agreed. A happy Washington decided to call a select few of his Vulcan board members to fill them in. Some of them disagreed with his approach.

"We should take this to the fire commissioner, you know, a one-on-one meeting. Show him that we're reasonable people, and we want to work with him," said one dissenter.

That was the exact opposite of what Washington wanted. He swore everyone to secrecy and they kept their silence, even after the tragedy of Black Sunday interrupted their timetable. Washington delayed things into the first week of February. He was just two days away from his big reveal when he got a surprise phone call. It was Bloomberg's office. The mayor wanted to talk.

For a few seconds Washington was sure news of the noose had leaked out, but it soon became clear the mayor only had his reelection on his mind. Charles Billups had been working on him behind the scenes, and—perhaps remembering how important the black vote had been to him the first time around—Bloomberg suddenly found it desirable that he and the Vulcans talk.

"I know I haven't been really good on this issue," Bloomberg said to Washington in their brief phone conversation. Washington knew the mayor was also peeved by the constant criticism the Vulcan leader fed to the media. Shortly after he took over as Vulcan president, Washington decided to make it a practice to attend every FDNY graduation and hold a press conference to highlight the pitiful number of blacks in each class. Every time the department tried to grandstand to the press about its diversity efforts, Washington popped up like a bad penny to undercut the FDNY's message. It pissed off the top brass to no end, to Washington's delight. But it was a little too aggressive for some in the Vulcan Society. "You're making it too hot for our guys in the firehouses," some Vulcans grumbled. "It's not making us look good." However, the core membership, including Marshall, had no quarrel with it. Washington's press conference blitz was effective, and it got them and their cause in front of the cameras. A little extra irritation in the firehouses was just the price they had to pay. When Bloomberg finally did call, he invited the Vulcans back to City Hall and said his scheduler would be in touch in the next day or two. Washington hung up the phone with a deep surge of contentment. He knew that meeting would never take place—not after the mayor got hit by his surprise press conference—but he was willing to sacrifice their one-on-one to make a larger point.

The press conference, when it happened, was everything he'd hoped for and more. Granger showed up with the noose, backed by a row of stern-faced black firefighters. Teased and coiffed network reporters jostled for space against their less telegenic print and radio colleagues. The conference room inside the swanky downtown

Firefighter Lanaird Granger holds a noose he says he found on his gear in his Brooklyn firehouse, at a press conference held at the Center for Constitutional Rights in Lower Manhattan, February 10, 2005. Photo Credit: NY Daily News.

law office that the Center for Constitutional Rights borrowed for the event was standing room only. The rapid whir of cameras almost drowned out Granger's soft words when he held the black rope aloft. News soon trickled down to the Vulcans that the top brass was apoplectic that they hadn't been given a heads up.

"Good," Washington said, when he and the other Vulcans got the news that they were in serious hot water with the chiefs. "That's exactly what we were aiming for." He wanted to ring the mayor's bell, and ring it hard, like Muhammad Ali, his personal hero, tagging George Foreman.

"The next time we have something to say, they're going to listen," Washington vowed. But as he suspected, he never heard from Mayor Bloomberg's scheduler. The offer to visit City Hall had apparently been rescinded. The subtle feelers the FDNY put out about him running their upcoming recruitment drive were also retracted.

There was more bad news yet to come for the FDNY. Black Sunday and Granger's noose revelation were soon swallowed by a lurid sex scandal so tawdry that it coated the entire department in shame. Not three weeks after the Vulcans' press conference, the city's Department of Investigation released a 30-page report on the notorious "Animal House" incident. Three FDNY firefighters were accused of having sex while on duty with a mentally ill Staten Island woman with a fetish for smoke eaters. The sickening sexual liaisons occurred inside what one newspaper dubbed the FDNY's "icky sex grotto," the basement of Engine 75 in the Bronx, otherwise known as the Animal House.[2]

An abashed fire department put on a brave face as city newspapers gleefully chewed over the sleazy, vulgar details of the Staten Island woman's early morning trip to the Bronx firehouse—after calling 311 for directions when she lost her way. She was smuggled through a side door under the sleeping officer's nose, and down into the basement where three firefighters took turns performing a variety of sexual hijinks. The woman, who later claimed she had a mental breakdown after 9/11 and was bipolar, liked to sleep with firefighters because she felt sorry for them, she told investigators. Yet when she left the Animal House early that morning after multiple trysts, she called 911 and claimed she was raped. The DOI's 30-page report, which came out a few months after the incident, was devastatingly detailed and laid bare the frat-like atmosphere of the firehouse, including a picture of a naked woman in a cage that was posted on a wall.

Among the many crude and damning specifics, one fact in particular stood out: one of the firefighters caught up in the ignominy was Anthony Loscuito, the young man Tommy Von Essen had personally championed for the job. The new wrinkle added a fresh round of newspaper critiques of the FDNY, especially after it was revealed that Loscuito already had a criminal history when Von Essen gave him a waiver in 2001. Loscuito had even been arrested again in 2003 for marijuana possession, but still held on to his job. The FDNY put him on a 90-day suspension and a two-year probation with frequent, random drug testing.

The exposure of Loscuito's privileged path into the FDNY embarrassed the department but didn't come as much of a shock to the Vulcans—although it did make good fodder for their ongoing dialogue with sympathetic City Council members and federal discrimination investigators at the EEOC. The Vulcans argued for years that the FDNY's background checks favored white candidates over blacks, especially when it came to the shadowy, all-powerful Personnel Review Board that made the final cut in hiring, subject only to an override by the commissioner himself. Made up of FDNY top chiefs, a few human resources people and—when a tie-breaker was needed—the fire commissioner, the PRB got final say on which questionable candidates had a shot at the job and which were turned away. In the parlance of the fire department, some on-the-fence candidates would get stipulations, allowing them on the job if they promised to stay problem-free. Others would be "considered but not selected," which meant they were cut loose with no further explanation as to why.

The Vulcans had long suspected more blacks and Latinos got dropped by the PRB than whites, but they had no evidence beyond the anecdotal claims from minority candidates who came to them for help. The PRB was completely self-determined. It had no department guidelines to follow, there were no specific procedures for it to consider in making decisions and no minutes or memos were taken of its meetings—in fact, almost no paper trail existed. The only people who knew what went on inside its meetings were its high-ranking members—and they were tight-lipped.

The Vulcans got another chance to take a whack at the secretive PRB process in 2005, when a firefighter with a history of cocaine abuse tested positive in a routine drug check. But that wasn't all—his retired firefighter father, a union official, got arrested for trying to bribe the laboratory that took the career-ending samples.

Firefighter Christopher De Parma was hired by the FDNY in 2003 despite two misdemeanor convictions, including one in 1996 for possession of drug paraphernalia. He got a stip that said he agreed to periodic drug testing for 36 months. He came back clean on 15 such tests, but in May 2005 he tested positive for cocaine. He was suspended without pay and faced dismissal—but quit in midsummer. His story came to light in September after the arrest of his dad, who was charged with offering thousands of dollars in bribes to get employees at a Brooklyn medical lab to destroy his son's tainted urine samples.[3]

A weary fire department was forced once again to defend its use of stips, while admitting that in the past three years it issued 50 percent more such exceptions to new hires than in the past. Stipulations were approved by the PRB, in a process that was fair and above board, the department said. Still, Commissioner Scoppetta was willing to look at the procedures to see if "there is room for improvements," a fire department spokesman told the *New York Times*.[4]

Scoppetta, steeped as he was in the more courtly ways of white-collar management, was deeply offended by the rash of fire department excesses he'd been forced to defend over the past few years. Aside from the sex scandals and drug busts, there was an incident in which one firefighter smashed another in the face with a chair in a Staten Island firehouse. Scoppetta didn't know if the FDNY's bad streak was a product of the heightened emotions still spilling over from 9/11 or the massive brain drain caused by the multitude of retiring senior officers, but he wasn't one to overlook such reprehensible actions. His zero-tolerance stance on drug abuse outraged firefighters, who felt it broke the brotherhood code to air dirty laundry. They preferred the old-school way of solving those problems, which allowed a firefighter to seek treatment on his own while being mentored and monitored by senior officers. Scoppetta was done with that. Any firefighter who came forward voluntarily to admit to a substance abuse problem got full benefits and salary and a free stint in rehab. Any who got caught through random drug testing or other monitoring methods was out of a job, no questions asked.

It was a no-nonsense approach that won him few fans. The Vulcans could only wish he were as willing to flout tradition when it came to their diversity claims. Here was one more example of how the FDNY could change traditions when it really suited the department. In response to Granger's noose allegation, Scoppetta ordered a full investigation, wrote a department-wide letter reminding the troops that such acts were not to be tolerated and mandated that all firefighters watch a video on diversity awareness. The FDNY's equal employment opportunity office (EEO)—criticized by all firefighters for its toothless and interminable investigations—hauled 12 firefighters to MetroTech for interviews within two months of Granger's claim. There was enough witness evidence to substantiate Granger's story, the EEO said. But investigators couldn't pinpoint the guilty party.

"Nobody would come forward, and none of the firefighters who knew anything would talk," Scoppetta would say later of the incident. "It would have been a tremendous thing if one of them had."

The Vulcans saw the investigation as a total cop-out. The FDNY knew something occurred, but wasn't willing to dig deep enough to nail it all down.

"They could have called them all in, said 'Put your badges on the table, and anyone who doesn't cooperate has to go,'" Washington said to a fellow Vulcan when the nebulous results were released. A lawsuit and union blowback would have been sure to follow, but it would have sent a message, like Mayor Rudy Giuliani did with the shameful Broad Channel blackface float. Giuliani had been willing to take the First Amendment hit, and the Vulcans felt Scoppetta should have done the same over the noose.

Scoppetta also let the Giuliani- and Von Essen–era Fire Cadet program lapse, over the objections of the Vulcans and City Council members like Yvette Clarke, who as chair of the Fire and Criminal Justice Committee took an active role in probing FDNY diversity. The Vulcans lobbied hard to keep it, but Scoppetta had made up his mind. At a City Council hearing over the summer, the fire commissioner was asked if he would resume the program if the council allocated an extra $2.8 million for it.

"No," said Scoppetta. It was costly and an unnecessary dupli-cation of FDNY efforts to bring in more minorities. His response prompted a rather loud outburst from Washington, who was listen-ing from the audience benches. Washington shouted that Scoppetta wouldn't be happy until the FDNY was 99 percent white. A secu-rity guard came over and told the visibly agitated Vulcan to leave.

"My advice to Paul is that he become a part of the solution and not continue to be a part of the problem," Scoppetta told reporters after the hearing, noting again how the Vulcan head had rejected his offer to run FDNY recruitment.[5]

As 2005 came to an end, Scoppetta was focused on the pre-stages of the next FDNY exam, which would be given in 2006 or early 2007. He wanted to pull together a recruitment effort that would really make some inroads. Although DCAS, the mayor's of-fice and even the city's law department seemed inclined to ignore the rumblings from the Department of Justice, Scoppetta, as a law-yer, wasn't unaware of the danger his department was in.

The EEOC in 2004 found probable cause for the Vulcans' claims regarding test 7029 and probable cause in November 2005 for test 2043. It cited significant adverse impact in the city's written exams in its determination. Moreover, its D.C. testing expert found that DCAS's in-house validation study was inadequate and incom-plete. Three individual black candidates who took exam 2043 but were never hired also filed EEOC complaints mirroring the allega-tions of the Vulcans. Those were now being bundled together to go to the Department of Justice and its civil rights unit. Scoppetta knew enough about disparate impact to grasp that the FDNY hir-ing numbers spelled disaster. But given the Bloomberg administra-tion's refusal to consider any of the Vulcans' recommendations, that's where everything seemed headed. Scoppetta could see only one way out of trouble: dedicate every spare resource to a knockout recruitment drive. To do that, he had to mend some fences, starting with the Vulcans.

In August 2006, Scoppetta called up Washington and invited him to a Brooklyn firehouse. The FDNY was holding a press con-ference to announce its latest recruitment drive for upcoming exam 6019, and Scoppetta was eager to show the world what was com-ing. Washington—for once—was on his best behavior. He and the FDNY had their differences, but it was always boots on the ground during recruitment time. Besides, he had some fence-mending in mind himself. He wanted to get hold of Mayor Bloomberg. They hadn't spoken since Washington sucker punched him with the noose incident. He was hoping the mayor's temper had cooled enough that they could have their second meeting. Washington dutifully played his supporting role at the firehouse press conference, and when the mayor got in his proximity, Washington signaled he wanted a tête-à-tête. The mayor nodded and directed the Vulcan to his ever-present aide Ed Skyler to set something up.

A month later, Washington and Marshall found themselves back at City Hall, looking across a wide table into the no-nonsense stare of the mayor. With them this time was firefighter Duery Smith, a long-time Vulcan nearing the end of his active-duty career. His family had twice nearly died in house fires when he was a little boy growing up in Brooklyn. Even now, decades later, Smith could close his eyes and relive the sweet sensation of firefighters, all but invisible in the darkness, reaching out and grabbing him. The minute he felt their hands, he knew he was safe. When he got older, like many working-class kids in 1960s New York, Smith took every civil service exam the city had—including the test for the FDNY. But his first offer came from the Metropolitan Transportation Authority. By the early 1970s, Smith was a city bus driver, assigned to the route transit workers facetiously called the "Ho Chi Minh" line. It ran through parts of Brooklyn that were so drug-addled and crime-ridden the bus drivers joked it was as dangerous as being in Vietnam. When the FDNY contacted him two years later, Smith was more than ready to go.

"Running into fires has to be safer than what I'm doing," he cracked to his transit buddies. And for most of his career it was, until his luck ran out in 2003. A call came in for a commercial fire that quickly became a four-alarm conflagration in a Queens apartment building. Smith's Ladder 136 was among several units that raced to the blaze. It was one of those calls where everything that could go wrong did. Before Smith and his men knew it, they were on a rooftop staring at five-foot flames that shot into the sky.

Hurried orders started coming over the radio from officers. The engine company straining to spray water miscalculated the length of the building. It was far larger than they realized—stretching a whole block. The source of the flames wasn't 25 feet inside the cavernous space, as they incorrectly surmised. It was more like 100 feet back. The conditions were too dangerous to stay inside. Firefighters could easily get disoriented in the dark, windowless unknown of a massive commercial building. The officers pulled the company out so the firefighters could attack from the exterior. That left Smith and his men, on the rooftop of the adjacent building, at the mercy of the spiraling flames. The fire spread from the commercial building through the small crawl space that ran underneath the roof and the top floor. As the firefighters on the ground floor of the commercial building drew their quenching water hoses back, unchecked flames shot upward, causing the center of the roof to collapse. Heat and smoke exploded in all directions, blowing over Smith and his company on the roof next door, which was also on fire. Smith did a hasty head count. Too many firefighters were on the roof with only one exit ladder. He needed to get a secondary means of escape set up in case they had to bail in a hurry. Shouts and yells reached his ears from the chaos below as he carefully stepped through the smoke to the roof's edge. In one heartbeat to the next, he went from walking to falling. He stepped right into the 4-foot-wide air shaft that ran between apartments. In the chaos, nobody saw it. Smith plunged several stories and hit the ground. Fortunately, he landed on his feet. Unfortunately, his heel bones shattered. He crumpled upon impact.

When his head cleared, he took stock of his situation. He was in a brick box with no visible exit, smothering smoke curling around him, and he was splintered and tattered from the ankles down. Above him, he could make out a window in one of the residential building's apartments that faced the light shaft. That would be his way out. Smith managed to get an arm hooked on the ledge and hauled himself halfway up. With the other hand, he pulled off his air mask and banged at the glass. He swung as hard as he could, several times, until finally shards went flying. But the whole window fell out. It smashed over him and ripped the air mask from his hand.

I can't believe this, Smith thought as he rolled around on the broken glass, feeling desperately for his mask. *I survived this damn fall and now I'm going to die from the smoke.*

He likely would have, if another firefighter on the roof hadn't been looking in his direction in the split second Smith dropped out of sight, too startled to even shout. The firefighter sent out a mayday, and the crew succeeded in breaking into the ground-floor apartment and pulling Smith through the window before smoke overtook him. He wound up in Elmhurst Hospital with 11 rods in his left foot and 10 in his right. His injuries earned him a hospital visit from Mayor Bloomberg, who always found time for wounded cops and firefighters.

Sitting across from the mayor in City Hall two years later, a memory from that visit came back to Smith. The mayor had asked if there was anything he could do for the injured firefighter, and Smith, smiling in his hospital bed, made a reference to the some-what acrimonious contract talks going on with the Uniformed Fire-fighters Association at the time.

"Just give the guys a good raise," he said, and the mayor laughed.

Smith didn't expect that the mayor would remember their hos-pital chat, but to his surprise Bloomberg did. The two spoke for a few minutes about Smith's recovery until the real talk began.

Bloomberg, direct as always, got straight to the point. He knew there was a problem with FDNY diversity, he told the men. He just truly didn't know what the best solution was.

"We've got solutions for you," Marshall said. The Vulcans spent the next 20 minutes walking him through all their ideas for better recruitment and ways they thought the FDNY could lower the attrition rate for black candidates. It wasn't just a one-step fix, they told the mayor, but a series of things that could be tweaked to keep more blacks in the running.

But the key, as always, was doing something about that written test. It remained one of the biggest blockades to blacks getting on the job. Washington presented a letter that Congressman Charles Rangel—an ardent Vulcan supporter—sent to the mayor. It advo-cated changing the written to a pass/fail grading system, and in-creasing the importance of the physical exam.

"UFA president Steve Cassidy has agreed to this proposal," Washington noted. Cassidy had proven to be a tough and wily union president who often went toe-to-toe with the mayor, but Washington knew he had a decent relationship with Bloomberg underneath the bluster.

"Ask around among the FDNY chiefs and even they will say that the test doesn't tell you who is going to be a good firefighter, that's the kind of thing you start to figure out when you get the recruits into the training academy," Marshall added. "It's not fair to hire off a test that ranks people in order of a score when there's absolutely no proof that those who score higher make better firefighters. I scored an 86 on my test and I think I'm a really good firefighter."

Smith also chimed in. He'd done well on his test, but even his score had been considered potentially too low to get him on the job. "I scored a 92 on my test and I think that I'm a pretty good firefighter," he offered.

Bloomberg, who listened quietly to what the men said, turned to Smith. "You fell through a roof," the mayor deadpanned. "How good a firefighter could you be?"

The men couldn't help but laugh at Bloomberg's lighthearted teasing, as Smith joked back that he'd bring in all his medals to show Hizzoner. As the meeting ended, Bloomberg told the Vulcans that he would meet with DCAS to discuss some of the changes they proposed. He also informed them that the city had hired consultants to revise the written exam before DCAS administered 6019. Someone would get back to them about the issues they raised, the mayor said.

A few months later, the Vulcans were called in for a sit-down with Martha Hirst, the head of DCAS, the administrative agency that actually wrote and developed all the city's civil service exams. Washington and Marshall walked into the gathering to find Commissioner Scoppetta, Deputy Mayor Ed Skyler and another high-ranking Bloomberg official present. Washington and Marshall didn't expect to get everything they discussed with the mayor implemented in that one hiring cycle, but they did nurse hopes that at least some of their issues would be addressed. Instead, the opposite happened. Commissioner Hirst informed them that the physical tests were going to be changed from a ranked score to a pass/fail exam. Anyone who finished all the elements in the allotted times would be given a passing score. That meant a candidate's written score was more important than ever in determining who would get the job. That grade alone would determine an applicant's spot on the hiring list. An outside expert had revised the types of questions the written firefighter test posed to candidates. The passing grade was the usual 70. Only candidates who passed the written and the physical would be eligible to apply for the five-point residency bonus points. It was everything the Vulcans had not wanted, and more.

CHAPTER 12

BURNED

New York City
2007

TEST TAKERS FOR FIREFIGHTER EXAM 6019 BEGAN LINING UP HOURS BE-
fore the 9 a.m. kickoff for the morning session on January 20,
2007. The freezing temperatures hadn't eased by the time the afternoon candidates showed up for the four o'clock exam. Shivering
firefighter hopefuls queued for hours in lines that snaked around
the block. Several of the high schools where the tests were administered suffered inexplicable delays in opening the doors. Some didn't
open until 10:30 a.m., and even then testing didn't start for another
hour or so. The same problems happened at the 4 p.m. sessions.
Some who showed up never received the official admissions card
the Department of Citywide Administration Services was supposed
to mail applicants ahead of the exam. The first step in the official
hiring process to become a member of the Bravest was under way,
and it was a disaster.

   As shell-shocked candidates stumbled out after their tests, they
began to compare notes. Many told of delayed openings, confused
proctors who gave misleading or incorrect instructions and talked
throughout the proceedings, test takers who were allowed to bring
in cell phones and use them during the exams. Others reported
widespread cheating, with test takers copying off each other, taking extra time under the eyes of inattentive proctors or flipping

ahead to start on new portions of the exam before each timed segment began. Most disconcerting of all, the questions weren't the type the students had been told to expect by the FDNY tutorial sessions. Instead of traditional, logic-based, cognitive-style queries with multiple-choice answers, the test takers found hypothetical scenarios. In each situation, test takers were asked to imagine a series of events and choose how they would respond from a range of possible reactions. It was a bizarre, counterintuitive approach to those who expected the usual format of the firefighter exams used in the past. The applicants were furious—and worried. Many of them grew up fantasizing about the day they would become one of New York's Bravest; others had left promising careers after 9/11 to become a firefighter, which had become an even higher-than-usual calling. For many of them, the events of January 20 were a dream-ending curveball—and all because of a single standardized test that was supposed to be too easy to fail.

It didn't take long for some of the more outspoken candidates to organize themselves into a protest group: Fighting 6019. It was a small representation of the total test takers—about 490 people out of 22,000 who sat for the exam. But they were well connected and vocal. One of their leaders was the son of a high-ranking FDNY chief. Several members had family on the job. The protest group also had plenty of ammunition in some of the test's more ridiculous-sounding questions, which they leaked to the media.

"Fire Department Hopefuls Burned by Easy Test," blared a *New York Post* headline. "FDNY Exam Has 'em Fuming," screamed the *NY Daily News*. The papers had a field day with the wacky questions, which included one about the desirability of a senior officer calling firefighters "lazy couch potatoes" if they wanted to buy a TV for the firehouse instead of a workout bench. Then there was the most infamous question of all—what to do about spilled chili.

"As a rookie firefighter you are responsible for cleaning the kitchen. You arrive for the beginning of your shift to find the kitchen area is a mess. And there is a bowl of chili spilled on the floor from the firefighters from the previous shift. The reason the kitchen is such a mess is due to the previous crew having gone out on a call to a fire during their dinner, and they are still actively fighting the fire . . . What should you do with the following circumstances?"[1]

Candidates were told to use a range of "highly desirable" to "highly undesirable" to rate possible reactions to the chili mess. They were given five possible outcomes, like "Clean the mess up, but complain to anyone who will listen," or "Wait for everyone from the previous shift to return, yell at them that they should have cleaned up the mess." On the face of it, the question seemed ridiculous to those expecting the traditional approach.

DCAS rushed to defend its actions as the Fighting 6019 group called for a protest rally in Union Square. They wanted DCAS to toss out all the results and give them a do-over. The FDNY's highest-ranking uniformed officer, Chief of Department Salvatore Cassano, spoke out in defense of the test.

"That question is a legitimate firefighting question. You could substitute a thousand things for the chili. The question isn't about chili, it's about discipline and Fire Department procedures. Any probie that went through our training would know what to do," Cassano told the NY Daily News.[2]

The FDNY and DCAS put on a united front for the press and for Fighting 6019, but inside the marble halls of FDNY MetroTech, reactions ranged from anger and disgust to displeased frustration. A top FDNY official who'd been involved in parts of preparing for 6019 wrote a blistering memo to Deputy Commissioner Doug White about DCAS's disastrous bungling. The inept agency was so overwhelmed, it couldn't even get training questions over to the FDNY until after the department started giving its tutorial classes, the official said. "Inadequate sample questions in an extremely inadequate time frame. We were emailed sample questions on 12/4 and 12/21. The tutorial program started 11/27. We did not receive sample questions for all new categories and we obviously were not made aware the degree to which situational judgment questions would dominate the exam. We received 2 sample questions on situational judgment. Situational judgment questions accounted for roughly 50% of the exam. We could have saved ourselves a lot of grief if we had a better sense of what to cover in the Tutorial Sessions," the memo complained.[3]

And it didn't stop there. The problems carried over to the actual exam day itself, the memo said. Roughly 23 percent of registered test takers who never showed up told the FDNY it was because they never got the necessary admission card from DCAS that was required to enter test sites. Complaints of cheating, bad proctoring, delayed starts and locked schools were "consistent for sites in all boroughs." The FDNY was flooded with calls from "angry fathers" complaining about the test, the memo said. It concluded with a devastating assessment of DCAS's failings:

> I could go on and on about what went wrong on test day. I think it is imperative that Martha [Hirst, DCAS commissioner] hear these concerns . . . I am pretty sure her response will be that this happens in every test, every time. Nevertheless, with all the $$ spent on this effort and all the attention focused on it (the Feds, City Hall, etc.) makes no sense for them to drop the ball like this on test day.
>
> We directed a lot of complaints to DCAS . . . If they respond that they "investigated" and responded to every complaint, just know that several test-takers called me and read me their letters. They were maddening. They basically put all the blame back on the applicant . . . As we have said before, from beginning to end, DCAS was a disaster on this test. I know you can't tell Martha that.
>
> I know I am crazy to think that the City should set a higher bar for themselves on this. And I do know that on some level, this does happen every exam. No kidding—that is unacceptable. It will continue to happen until someone in a position of power decides it will no longer happen and actually makes change to ensure that. It can be done.
>
> And that is not even taking into account the actual, miserable exam.

For Fire Commissioner Nicholas Scoppetta, the botched rollout was devastating. The FDNY had hired a new head of recruitment, a skilled and effective woman with grassroots organizing and voter-drive experience. Thanks to a $1.2 million boost secured by city comptroller Bill Thompson, the FDNY doubled its recruitment budget to $2 million; did a targeted media outreach with radio, print and TV ads; assigned full-time recruiters to go to nearly 3,000 events; and paid overtime for others. Washington, hearing about the changes via the FDNY grapevine, was happy. At last the department was making a real effort. Scoppetta personally went to black churches and to the sprawling New York City Housing Authority projects to make his pitch. This time, instead of relying on the emotional pull of 9/11, he tailored his speeches to the incredible benefits offered by the FDNY, especially the handsome salaries and flexible schedules. He recorded robocalls to urge candidates to fill out their paperwork and show up. That effort paid off—to a degree anyway. Of the 22,000 test takers for 6019, more than 34 percent of the top 4,000 scorers were minorities—a huge leap from prior years. Blacks accounted for 11 percent, Latinos for 21 percent and Asians for 1.6 percent.[4]

To see all that progress get mired in what many perceived as DCAS's incompetency was maddening. Scoppetta, reading the newspapers' coverage, decided to take a look at test 6019 for himself. He was staggered when DCAS told him he couldn't have a copy.

"That's ridiculous, why not? I just want to see what some of the questions were," he protested. "Do you mean to tell me that the fire commissioner can't even see his own department's test? Look, I'll give you my home address, just mail it to me there. Nobody in MetroTech will even know I have it."

But DCAS officials were unmoved. There was supposed to be an unbreakable wall between the FDNY and DCAS regarding the test—a holdover from the days when Fiorello LaGuardia and others tried to move civil service out of Tammany Hall's corrupt reach. The development of the test was DCAS's purview, and it wasn't about to cede any territory to the fire commissioner. It was a ridiculous attitude, especially in the face of an incoming lawsuit. DCAS didn't even like the intrusion of Scoppetta's questions about the validity of its exams.

"The test is fine," he was told, whenever he inquired. In fact it was not, far from it, but both agencies let the matter drop. As the city's Equal Employment Practices Commission had said nearly a decade earlier, the incomplete validation process used by DCAS was by itself enough to leave the city legally exposed. But nobody stepped up to fix the problems.

The Vulcans were upset about 6019 too. They invested a lot in that exam and got bang-up results from their tutoring classes. As soon as they heard in 2006 that the city was adopting a new format, Paul Washington called up a testing expert who for years had been sending his flyers to Vulcan Hall. The city had a list of

17 qualities it was hoping to measure with 6019's new format, but none of it made sense to the Vulcans. How could qualities like teamwork, resilience, spatial and interpersonal relationships, and situational judgment be vetted through a written exam? Washington was skeptical about the expert soliciting them but willing to give him a try. His name was Brent Collins, a fire chief in Ohio. He ran a successful side business advising firefighter candidates across the country how to score well on different types of entrance exams. Washington doubted a working firefighter had the academic chops to demystify DCAS's format, but Collins proved him wrong. Within minutes of their first phone conversation, he sent Washington several examples of the types of questions he thought would likely appear on the FDNY test. For $10,000 he designed a tutorial booklet and study guide based on a mix of the traditional and new. The Vulcans had gotten the money from the City Council, which earmarked $1.2 million in its recent budget for the FDNY to use for its diversity efforts. The FDNY—likely the only agency to ever turn down money—declined it, saying it wasn't needed. So the council carved out a chunk for the Vulcans. They put $10,000 toward hiring Collins, and he was worth every cent. The 6019 candidates who sat in the Vulcans' tutorial classes got a good long look at the new format, with its subjective questions and range of answers. Those who only took the FDNY's tutorial classes—still based on the traditional multiple-choice set up—did not.

If he had still been the Vulcans' president, Washington would have shared the success with reporters. But he was term-limited out at the start of 2007. In his place, the Vulcans elected John Coombs, the hard-nosed firefighter from Brooklyn who worked in Engine 250. Coombs had asked Michael Marshall to stay on as his number two. Together with Washington and Duery Smith, the group was known as the Committed Four. By then, the Vulcans' lawsuit was already five years in the making. The city had refused—at every juncture—to sit down and talk. It wouldn't meet with the Vulcans, it wouldn't meet with the Equal Employment Opportunity Commission, and it wouldn't settle with the Department of Justice (DOJ). There was no end in sight.

The EEOC in 2002 took up Washington's original complaint and tried and failed many times to entice the city to the bargaining table. The Vulcans submitted charges to the EEOC as a group, but

FDNY firefighter John Coombs, recently retired Vulcan Society president, September 2014. Photo credit: Michel Friang.

later three new black test takers stepped up to add their names as individuals. The EEOC's final determination for both the Vulcans' discrimination claim and the three add-ons came in late 2005.

When the city's law department refused yet again that November to meet with the EEOC, the case was turned over to the DOJ's Civil Rights Division. During its subsequent, two-year investigation into the FDNY, there was at least one hush-hush exploratory meeting between federal lawyers and one female Bravest. The DOJ wanted to know if there was a case for gender discrimination too. But the women, as a group, didn't fit the Vulcans' disparate impact pattern, mainly because they didn't have a problem with the written test. However, DOJ experts did spot a pattern of disparate impact for Latino candidates that fell in line with what blacks were reporting. Latinos were folded into the DOJ probe, over the protests of the FDNY's Hispanic Society. The group's president didn't want anything to do with the Vulcans or their lawsuit. The United Women Firefighters Association had also declined to stand alongside the Vulcans at press conferences. The women had a tough enough time in the firehouses already, the group's president told Washington.

The city's law department also had some discussions with the DOJ. Mayor Michael Bloomberg wasn't willing to settle, but some city lawyers, stuck with a hard-to-win case, hoped to find a way out of the weeds. They agreed to some concessions with the DOJ—without running it past Bloomberg. When the time came to confess, law department head Michael Cardozo called a private meeting with Scoppetta, Mayor Bloomberg and Deputy Mayor Ed Skyler to tell them he had promised to drop the FDNY's 30-college-credit requirement. Bloomberg was aghast and strongly objected. Both the mayor and Scoppetta felt the FDNY should require more education, not less. But it was too late. A deal had been struck. To compensate, a reluctant Bloomberg and Scoppetta lengthened the Fire Academy training period from 13 to 23 weeks—the better to make sure no real slackers sneaked through.

That was as far as Bloomberg was willing to go in terms of concessions. It was indisputable that the FDNY was racially imbalanced, but it wasn't because the department tried to make it that way, as far as the mayor could tell. His attitude was closer to that of the majority of white firefighters: there was a civil service test, everyone took the same test and the best scoring candidates were hired. That's about as fair a shot in life as anyone got. It was a fine philosophy, but it didn't change the fact that the city wasn't complying with federal civil rights law.

The top chiefs inside the FDNY were also in deep denial about the seriousness of the legal challenge confronting them. Anytime the possibility of a lawsuit came up in a meeting, it was brushed away. "There is no way the Department of Justice is going to sue the New York City Fire Department while George Bush is president," was the rationale heard again and again among the white shirts in FDNY MetroTech as the federal investigation continued. To the fire chiefs who flourished inside the good-old-boy network of the FDNY, there was no doubt that President Bush—the biggest good-old-boy there was—would take care of them. Bush came to Ground Zero three days after 9/11 and, in an iconic moment, took a bullhorn to give an impromptu, patriotic speech while hugging a tearstained firefighter. He heaped honor on the wounded department and took swift vengeance against America's enemies, and if he didn't exactly use pinpoint precision in how he identified them, his War on Terror nonetheless won the loyalty of many Bravest.

When he ran for reelection in 2004, he did so with the FDNY's biggest union at his side. Steve Cassidy and Uniformed Firefighters Association members stumped for him in Ohio.

"We've got nothing to worry about. Bush will take care of it," was the common refrain among Scoppetta's chiefs. They were about to find out how very wrong they were. In May, just a few months into the tumult over test 6019, the DOJ dropped the legal bombshell the Vulcans and the Center for Constitutional Rights were waiting for: a discrimination lawsuit based on the violation of Title VII of the 1964 Civil Rights Act. The city and the FDNY gave written exams in 1999 and 2002 that were rigged against minorities, the suit claimed. Candidates of color passed both tests at lower rates than whites, but the exams "do not accurately determine whether an applicant will be able to perform the job of firefighter," the DOJ wrote.[5]

Predictably, the lawsuit set off Mayor Bloomberg's notoriously short fuse.

"The Justice Department is wrong, and we'll see 'em in court," Bloomberg told the press.[6] He was so livid when he got the news he reached out personally to U.S. Attorney General Alberto Gonzales, the head of the DOJ, to complain about the case.

Shayana Kadidal at CCR was stunned as well when he heard that the DOJ lost patience with the FDNY. He and the other lawyers hadn't given any credence to the possibility that President Bush would intervene on behalf of the fire department. But they had worried about rumors among civil rights attorneys that the Title VII cases the DOJ usually pursued were related to religious freedom, not race discrimination. Also, Kadidal and original CCR attorney Barbara Olshansky hadn't done much to endear themselves to anyone in the pro-Bush camp. In 2006 Olshansky coauthored "The Case for Impeachment," a legal guide on how to remove Bush from office. And when the DOJ finally announced its lawsuit, Kadidal was on the verge of handing off the Vulcan case to a new CCR lawyer so he could dedicate all his time to the Guantánamo Global Justice Division. Kadidal was on the West Coast in late December 2006 when CCR first got word that the DOJ was ready to sue. He called Washington in Brooklyn to tell him two very strange things were happening: it was raining in Los Angeles, the land of perpetual sunshine, and the Bush DOJ was going to sue the FDNY. It wasn't quite hell freezing over, but pretty damn close.

By the time the DOJ made its formal announcement in May 2007, Kadidal was transitioning the Vulcans' case over to Darius Charney, a San Francisco native who'd been a special needs teacher in New Orleans before moving to law. Kadidal was confident that Charney had the skills and the patience to take over the case. Now they just needed some money.

From the very earliest days of the Vulcans' complaint, CCR had estimated it would cost about $250,000 in up-front cash to pay for the testing experts who would analyze the city's development process and also its finished exam results. It wasn't an amount CCR was able to front, and Kadidal expended considerable time and energy meeting with other law firms he hoped would partner with them. Many were interested. But even after the DOJ's blockbuster announcement that it was going to sue the FDNY, none wanted to commit. Some of them legitimately had a conflict of interest because they did other business with the city. In others, Kadidal could tell the partners didn't have the stomach to sue the city's hometown heroes. Their best shot was a partnership with Levy Ratner, a firm with a long history of civil rights and union-related legal work. CCR's main point of contact, Richard Levy, was an experienced litigator who'd handled race discrimination lawsuits before, and he was connected to one of the city's most socially progressive and powerful unions, Service Employees International Union (SEIU) 1199. The two law firms had been in talks since November 2004, but even as the DOJ was filing its suit three years later, CCR and Levy Ratner were still lining up the necessary financing.

For the Vulcans, the main concern was blowback in the firehouses. The imminent lawsuit frayed tempers already stretched to the flashpoint. Lanaird Granger's noose incident continued to be a sore topic. There were those who accused Granger of planting the black rope himself—an accusation that flourished in part because the FDNY's inconclusive investigation was easily dismissed.

One of the noose naysayers was Paul Mannix, then a battalion chief and the future founder of Merit Matters. Mannix, lightly freckled with rusty brown hair and vivid blue eyes, had a sharp wit and an appetite for inflammatory dialogue. He delighted in putting both on display with lengthy, voluminous letters to the editor that were published in the *Chief-Leader*. The 100-year-old broadsheet—dedicated to covering City Hall, public-employee unions and the civil service system—was widely read among city workers. Mannix's fusillades—directed mostly at the department's diversity efforts—were popular among the rank and file. He went back and forth in the *Chief*'s pages with many of his detractors. Washington chose to ignore Mannix's missives—even though most called him out by name. He viewed the battalion chief as an ineffective nuisance. Plenty of others traded barbs with Mannix though. He filled the *Chief*'s pages at least once a month, and dissecting Granger's noose story was a recurring theme.

"Granger has stated he returned from a routine run and the noose was lying on his firefighting gear. This has me confused, because in the Fire Department I'm employed by, we usually bring our firefighting gear with us on runs in case we have to, say, fight a fire," Mannix observed in one tart letter in April 2006, titled "FDNY Noose Mystery."[7]

He unloaded several more sarcastic observations about Granger's "changing" story, before taking aim at the FDNY's equal employment opportunity (EEO) office and Assistant Commissioner Paulette Lundy, who investigated the noose complaint.

"Although no one has been disciplined and there has been no one identified as being directly involved in this matter, Ms. Lundy's report claims that Granger's complaint has been substantiated and, further, the noose was placed in retaliation for Granger's association with the Vulcan Society. That's quite a trick—Ms. Lundy has detected the motives of a person who doesn't exist," Mannix mocked.[8] In many firehouses around the city, Mannix's writings were cut out and posted on walls.

While Mannix fanned the flames of firehouse unrest, Washington was called upon to show up at many of the hot spots. One of those included a Brooklyn firehouse that had a Confederate flag on the wall. A black firefighter detailed there had seen it. Washington went to the firehouse with a fellow Vulcan to have a word with the commanding officer. The captain told Washington the flag had been stuck on a back wall, partially obscured, for many years, with nobody paying it any mind. Washington, satisfied with the response, let the incident die there once the flag was removed.

He was not as content with the reaction in another house in Brooklyn, where a young black firefighter was summoned to the kitchen one night to see a fellow Bravest in uniform, with a white KKK hood on his head. The firefighters said they were teasing the young man because he'd gotten angry earlier when a retired white firefighter called the firehouse and greeted him over the phone with a friendly salutation that included the n-word. Washington got wind of it through his older brother, Kevin Washington, who was an officer in the house. Kevin had taken the story to FDNY personnel. The FDNY deemed it a prank gone too far and mandated sensitivity training for the house. No further discipline was required, the department said. Paul Washington wanted the kid to go public with the story, but the younger black firefighter didn't want to lodge a formal complaint. Privately, many inside the FDNY accused the Vulcan leader of trying to arm-twist the younger man for his own agenda. Mannix went so far as to hint at it publicly.

Responding to a black firefighter who wrote to the *Chief* to criticize the FDNY's reaction to the Klan hood, Mannix argued that it hadn't been the young black firefighter who was offended by the sight of a racist symbol in his firehouse kitchen. "The black firefighter understood this as an attempt to help him and did not object; in fact, he did not want the incident reported and did not cooperate with the investigation," the battalion chief wrote. "Hard-edged humor, yes, but humor nonetheless and designed to help a brother firefighter."[9]

Mannix went on about the "over-reaction" to the KKK hood and suggested it was still an unhappy topic between the young firefighter and the officer who insisted on reporting it. Then he swung back to the FDNY EEO office, one of his favorite targets to lambast. He had no confidence in it or its investigations, Mannix wrote. But he had some "Constructive Suggestions" for those minorities—including women—wishing to join the FDNY. "Study for the written test, train for the physical test, take advantage of the equal opportunity afforded you by the Civil Service system and take personal responsibility for the results of your efforts, good or bad. Not everyone can become a firefighter (or a lawyer, baseball player, etc.), and standards must be upheld regardless of your race or gender," his letter concluded. It too was a fan favorite among his many FDNY followers.

Mannix's loud voice was just one of many clamoring against the Vulcans as the anger and heartbreak from test 6019 continued to simmer—even after the DOJ announced its intention to sue. John Coombs, finding his way into his new role as the Vulcan Society president, attended a Union Square rally in support of the 6019 protest group's demand for a do-over. So did Mannix, who took advantage of the chance meeting to introduce himself. The two shook hands and exchanged a few casual remarks. Coombs knew of Mannix through his stir-the-pot letters. Now that they'd met, Coombs could see he was the same in person as he was on the page: blunt, assertive and smart enough to argue around any holes in his facts.

The Vulcans also remained enemy number one to many of the firefighting families who'd seen their hopes for the next generation die with test 6019. Plenty of other families who wanted their kids to get a good middle-class job felt the same way. Rumors swirled that the test was "dumbed down" in the name of diversity, and whispers surfaced that the Vulcans cheated. Critics insisted they must have been given a copy of the exam in advance. Nobody was willing to consider the Vulcans simply did what the DCAS and the FDNY should have long ago: brought in an outside expert.

The FDNY met quietly with DCAS officials to go over the distressing occurrences around 6019. But despite all its acknowledged problems, the test results were certified and accepted. For all those who took the test expecting to score well and wound up below the 95th percentile—or out of the 90s entirely—it was a devastating blow. Many would be too old—over the cutoff age of 29—by the time the next firefighter exam rolled around.

As the year drew to a close, the Vulcans made some important decisions of their own. The Committed Four spent a long summer with lawyers Darius Charney of CCR and Richard Levy and Dana Lossia of Levy Ratner. The firefighters spent hours explaining how the FDNY hiring system worked and the various steps along the way where blacks got wiped out. The adverse impact case on the written exam was a slam dunk, but the Vulcans were thinking about going for more.

"How are we going to protect our guys in the firehouse when things start to get really hot? You know the department doesn't investigate a lot of complaints even now," said Coombs. "Why settle for the easy victory? Let's make them put it all on the table."

Coombs had worked many times inside MetroTech as part of the recruitment team. He knew a lot of the department's internal vulnerabilities and he wanted to go after them. Staffed with officials fond of repeating the agency's unofficial mantra—"200 years of tradition, unspoiled by change"—the FDNY never put much stock in managerial training or techniques. In fact, most upper staff were smoke eaters who climbed the civil service promotional ladder. Scoppetta, a perennial manager, was horrified when he took office and realized that most of his operational top staff worked two 24-hour days and then went home for the rest of the week. "But who's managing here if you're all coming and going?" he said at the time.

On the lower level, things weren't much better. The FDNY used what it called light-duty firefighters—those recovering from a minor injury—to handle most day-to-day clerical affairs. The bored smoke eaters, untrained and uninterested in handling paperwork, shuffled documents in almost all parts of MetroTech.

"We're already going after the department's recruitment effort. Let's go after its handling of complaints, and the personnel department that decides about firefighters' background, let's make them prove everything that they're doing," Coombs urged. "This is all stuff they've systematically let build up and it hurts us in a lot of ways."

The DOJ lawyers didn't see any reason to add more charges to their case or muddy their chances of an easy disparate impact victory. They let the trio of Vulcan lawyers know they wouldn't support any additional claims. Richard Levy and Lossia weren't 100 percent convinced themselves, but as they sifted through and absorbed the information, it all started to make sense.

"Trust me. It's there," Coombs insisted. Before long, they were all in. Over the DOJ's strenuous objections, the Vulcans filed a separate and additional claim of intentional discrimination against the city, the FDNY, Mayor Michael Bloomberg and Fire Commissioner Nicholas Scoppetta.

CHAPTER 13

UP IN SMOKE

New York City
2007–2010

IN OCTOBER 2010, FEDERAL JUDGE NICHOLAS G. GARAUFIS PREPARED TO render a decision on the fate of test takers who desperately hoped to join the FDNY off the entrance exam known as 6019. For three years, more than 21,000 possible FDNY candidates were held in limbo while the Vulcans' discrimination lawsuit wound its way through Brooklyn federal court. Technically, exam 6019 had nothing to do with the two firefighter tests from 1999 and 2002 being challenged by the Vulcans. But along the way, the young men and women who sat for 6019 became collateral damage.

The Vulcans' lawsuit had gone down a very fraught, contentious road in the time since the U.S. Department of Justice (DOJ) filed its civil rights claim against the City of New York and the FDNY in 2007. Several things impacted the suit's trajectory, not the least of which was the judge assigned to the case, Nicholas Garaufis. The 60-year-old was a double grad of Columbia University, having gotten his BA and law degree there while supporting himself by teaching at a public school. Nominated to a judgeship by President Bill Clinton in 2000, Garaufis replaced Charles Sifton, the judge who ruled in favor of Brenda Berkman's landmark sex discrimination case in 1982. That detail was not lost on many FDNY bigwigs, who were inclined to feel Sifton had it in for them then and now Garaufis did too. The judge also had a nephew who'd taken firefighter exam 6019 and whose career hung in the balance of his ruling. Garaufis disclosed the potential conflict of interest as soon as he was given the case, but it wasn't found to be improper enough to warrant his reassignment. That didn't stop various Vulcan opponents from later trying to leak the information to the press to push the story that Judge Garaufis was biased.

In the fire department, a change occurred at the uppermost echelon. Fire Commissioner Nicholas Scoppetta stepped down in 2010 and was replaced by his former chief of department, Salvatore Cassano, a Vietnam veteran who dedicated his life to the FDNY when he became a firefighter in the mid-1970s. He learned his craft in a different sort of city, one with a lower skyline and calmer streets. Although Cassano was the natural successor to Scoppetta, having been his number two for years, his appointment was not without discord. Many in the fire department harbored harsh feelings toward Mayor Michael Bloomberg and his top FDNY chiefs over the handling of the most controversial conflagration since 9/11: the Deutsche Bank fire.

The empty, 41-story Deutsche Bank skyscraper had been an eyesore in Lower Manhattan since the day of the terrorist attacks. The collapsing South Tower tore a 15-foot gash in its side, filling it with toxic debris and even some human remains. But it miraculously stayed upright, alongside the famous 10 House that also survived. For six years, tourists coming to pay homage at the tiny firehouse could also gawk at the huge, scarred monolith leaning over it. The skyscraper was finally cleared for destruction after a lengthy, fraught debate over the environmental impact of stirring up its dangerous dust, and workers began dismantling it floor by floor. When a seven-alarm fire broke out inside the Deutsche Bank building around 4 p.m. on Saturday, August 18, 2007, firefighters raced through the late afternoon sunshine. One of the key concerns was that demolition crews might still be inside. More than 100 firefighters trooped into the blazing building, which was wrapped in scaffolding and black netting to keep debris from falling on pedestrians. Inside, they found an empty death trap.

The blaze raged on the seventeenth floor in a pile of garbage left by careless workers, one of whom likely dropped a smoldering cigarette butt even though smoking on the site was prohibited. As was standard procedure, firefighters started attacking the flames from the floors below. It was the safest vantage point, since heat and smoke rise. But this fire roared with unusual intensity, and it was only later that officers realized there were 25 exhaust fans running on the thirteenth to the seventeenth floors. There had been workers in the structure, and when the fire broke out they ran, leaving the fans on high speed. The turbulence was like a mini twister, with a funnel that pushed and sucked all the heat and smoke down—directly onto the struggling firefighters. Many of them dove for cover inside the rickety building's stairwells, as they were taught to do when conditions got extreme. If the doors were closed, it was usually a slight refuge to catch some relief. But the firefighters who dodged into the Deutsche Bank stairwells got a crippling surprise. From the fourteenth floor up, they were wide open, with no doors at all. The staircases were like express lanes for the speeding flames, whipped into an unnatural downward frenzy by the fans.

Two firefighters on the fourteenth floor, Joseph Graffagnino, 34, and Robert Beddia, 53, were grappling with their hose. Graffagnino, usually assigned to Ladder 5, was detailed that day at Engine 24, Beddia's company. Outside, firefighters were struggling to get water flowing. Nothing was coming from the modern standpipe system, a network of vertical pipes that should have given firefighters a place to connect their hoses and draw water on every floor of the building. Instead, they had to rig fire ropes to lift hoses—hooked to hydrants on the street—up to the seventeenth floor. It was the only way to get water on the blaze. Fed by the fans and unchecked by water, the conflagration roared. With no stairwells to duck into, firefighters resorted to hanging off the construction scaffolding, dangling more than a dozen stories above the city. There was no other place to hide from the voracious flames. If the scaffolding hadn't been there, fire officers said later, the death toll would have been massive. Instead, it was two. The bodies of Graffagnino, a young father, and Beddia were discovered near the stairwell of the fourteenth floor, where they likely had been trying to escape. While all the stairwell doors above them had been cut off, for some reason the one to the thirteenth floor below, which might have led them to safety, was sealed shut.

In the wake of the disaster, when inspectors crawled over the debris, it was discovered that a 42-foot chunk of the basement standpipe had been cut out and removed—and nobody reported it to the FDNY. That was why the pipe system was unable to produce water the night of the fire. That was just one of many flagrant safety violations that emerged. Angry finger pointing erupted. Fire union officials accused the private contractors of hiding information to avoid costly demo delays; city officials faulted fire chiefs for failing to inspect the building; and developers tried to hush up as much as possible in light of the expected criminal probe. In the end, Mayor Bloomberg, Fire Commissioner Scoppetta and Chief of Department Cassano hung seven well-respected fire officers out to dry, making them scapegoats for all that went wrong. Some of their careers were over for good; others had to swallow being written up for errors they knew they didn't commit. A new term entered the firefighting lexicon. From that day onward, firefighters in trouble were no longer railroaded by management. They were "Deutsche Banked."

Scoppetta and Bloomberg—referred to unflatteringly as Bloomturd by many a firefighter—were the biggest targets of ire, but Cassano got his share too. By the time Bloomberg appointed Cassano as fire commissioner in 2010, the mayor had already set a new record for unpopularity just a year into his historic third term. Cassano was too close to both him and Scoppetta to be viewed as the big change firefighters wanted to see.

The Vulcans also were not thrilled with Bloomberg's choice. They'd been dealing with Cassano for years as the FDNY chief of department and they had the same opinion of him that they had of Bloomberg and Scoppetta—they only made changes happen for the things they wanted to get done. For everything else, it was excuses. Bloomberg could find a way to get around the city charter and strong-arm the City Council so he could run for a third term. But ask his administration to yank the Department of Citywide Administrative Services into the twenty-first century and develop a firefighter exam that didn't discriminate against blacks, and everybody threw up their hands like it was impossible. When the chance came for the Vulcans to petition Judge Garaufis to join the DOJ's disparate impact claim as plaintiff-intervenors, they jumped on it. To their delight, Garaufis approved it over objections from the city and the Uniformed Firefighters Association. That meant the Vulcans' lawyers got a lot of leeway to litigate alongside the DOJ. Even better, the group's claim of intentional discrimination against the city and FDNY got the green light too—even though the DOJ declined to be a party to it. The Vulcans also named Mayor Bloomberg and Nicholas Scoppetta as individual defendants, but Garaufis granted them immunity.

The firefighters' union also tried to intervene as a relevant party on behalf of the city and FDNY and was rebuffed by the court. But the UFA and the union for fire officers, the Uniformed Fire Officers Association, filed papers in support of the city's legal arguments.

Between the legal wrangling of motions, cross-motions and voluminous briefs in support of a dozen different arguments, one very important development that could have changed the outcome of everything came and went behind the scenes. In November 2008, Judge Garaufis ordered both sides to appear before the magistrate judge to negotiate a settlement. The Vulcans had tried since 2002 to wrangle the city into solving their issues without going to court. It was never about money—and until lawyers got involved there was no price tag included. But all of their approaches were declined.

"We'd have settled for a fire cadet program," Washington said of their early efforts.

The stakes were considerably higher in 2008, with the Center for Constitutional Rights and the DOJ both demanding some form of back pay for black and Hispanic candidates whom they argued could have gotten hired in 1999 and 2002 if the city's tests had been valid. All parties knew the FDNY was willing to do almost anything to avoid losing in court and having a judge impose some sort of hiring quota on them. Many thought that the city's lawyers, already weary from trying to prepare a defense for what many saw as an unwinnable disparate impact case, would be happy to find a solution that avoided a trial, even though Bloomberg declared the suit was "wrong." The UFA tried to interject at the last minute as a participant to the talks, only to be rejected by the courts. Still, things were progressing well enough that Vulcan lawyers drew up a 50-page settlement document.

The offer on the table was $10 million. For the first time in nearly eight years, after multiple efforts to settle out of court that the city shot down, a deal was imminent. Or so the Vulcans' lawyers thought. At the last minute, the settlement talks fell through, and the $10 million deal was cast aside. No reason was given, but the Vulcans were unperturbed by the news. If the city wanted to litigate what everyone felt certain was a fairly open-and-shut disparate impact case, the Vulcans were happy to oblige. The intentional discrimination claims were far less clear-cut, but that didn't deter Paul Washington and the others. Even if they lost, they'd likely learn something useful about the FDNY's internal hiring procedures in the process.

The lawsuit crept along, with both sides arguing that Judge Garaufis should make a summary judgment in favor of their case. The city said the claim of disparate impact against Latinos and blacks had no merit and should be tossed, along with the Vulcans' charge that the FDNY intentionally discriminated against blacks. The DOJ and Vulcan lawyers filed for summary judgment in favor of their cases, claiming the statistical and anecdotal evidence clearly supported their charges. Both sides met in front of the judge to make oral arguments for a rapid decision in their favor. The city submitted a mere three pages of data to support the validity of DCAS's tests; CCR and the DOJ filed hundreds of pages from their experts outlining the ways the tests were flawed. The best the city could do to rebut was argue that the experts relied on a sample size that was too big, and therefore drew erroneous conclusions. The city's law department also argued that its newest test, 6019, was developed by outside experts and wasn't discriminatory. In fact, city lawyers said, had they been using it in 1999 and 2002, more minorities would have been hired—a point that didn't exactly seem to help their case. Garaufis didn't need much time to reach a decision. On July 22, 2009, he released his verdict in favor of the DOJ and the Vulcans.

"From 1999 to 2007, the New York City Fire Department used written examinations with discriminatory effects and little relationship to the job of firefighter to select more than 5,300 candidates for admission to the New York City Fire Department," Garaufis wrote. "These examinations unfairly excluded hundreds of qualified people of color from the opportunity to serve as New York City firefighters. Today, the court holds that New York City's reliance on these examinations constitutes employment discrimination in violation of Title VII of the Civil Rights Act of 1964."[1]

Garaufis's disparate impact judgment hinged on the fact that the city couldn't prove that the tests it gave in 1999 and in 2002 were in any discernible way able to weed out candidates based on their potential firefighting abilities. Even though the city persisted in ranking the candidates based on the test grade, and hiring them in that order, it couldn't prove that the test scores meant anything in terms of how good a firefighter a person would be. At the same time, the court found that the city had known or should have known that blacks and Latinos were disproportionately the ones being knocked out by the essentially meaningless tests.

What Garaufis didn't say—and what the lawsuits never contended—was that the content of the exams, the questions themselves, were too challenging for minorities or specifically biased against minorities. It was a fine point of distinction that the Vulcans' main detractors never grasped, or chose not to. One of their favorite accusations was that the tests were "dumbed down" in the name of diversity to make them easier for minorities to pass. If the city had watered down the intellectual content of its exams over the years, it wasn't at the request of the Vulcans. They'd only asked the city to make valid, job-related tests—not easier ones.

In his decision, Garaufis also noted that the FDNY's hiring of blacks and Latinos was out of proportion to the number of age-eligible minority applicants in the city, a problem that the NYPD didn't seem to have. Since the 1970s the NYPD underwent significant diversification, from 8.9 percent black police officers and 3.8 percent Hispanic officers in 1978 to 18 percent black and 28.7 percent Hispanic as of 2009.[2] The NYPD had its diversity challenges, but it was far more successful at recruiting, hiring and retaining a workforce that matched the pool of eligible candidates in the city.

Garaufis's ruling hardly came as a shock to any of the lawyers involved in the case, but it spurred Paul Mannix, now an FDNY deputy chief, into action. Since meeting with John Coombs in 2007 at Union Square, Mannix had invested countless personal hours drumming up support for 6019 test takers. He churned out letters to the *Chief-Leader* at an unbelievable rate, urged both the UFA and the UFOA to get involved, and put as many reporters as he could on speed dial. After Garaufis's decision, he decided to make his cause official. He needed his own organization so others in the fire department who felt the way he did could combine their efforts and hopefully push back against the changes they now knew were coming. Mannix chose a name he felt reflected his group's main ethos: Merit Matters.

"It's about merit, not race," he told prospective members. "This is not the white guy's group."

By September 2009, Merit Matters was an official entity, dedicated to promoting the civil service system implemented by Tammany Hall a century earlier. It was driven by Mannix's deep opposition to what he called social engineering—i.e., special treatment handed out to some candidates based on race and gender. The ex-cop–turned-firefighter's own life was impacted by diversity challenges to city hiring. His promotion exam for sergeant in the 1980s was delayed so many times by discrimination challenges he finally got sick of waiting and transferred into the FDNY. Over the years he'd become thoroughly steeped in the ins and outs of civil service law and followed diversity challenges elsewhere around the country, like the 2003 discrimination suit by the New Haven 20 that wound up in the Supreme Court. That lawsuit was eventually concluded to Mannix's satisfaction. The Supreme Court ruled that the city of New Haven, Connecticut, erred in 2003 when it threw out the results of a promotional exam because too few minorities scored well on it. The city argued that it put them at jeopardy for a disparate impact claim—but 19 white firefighters and one Latino who should have been promoted from it filed their own discrimination claim. They won—after a long battle that put their case before Sonia Sotomayor, then a justice on the Second Circuit Court of Appeals.

That case was one of several on Mannix's mind in 2009 when he started calling Garaufis's chambers with background information and suggestions he thought would help enlighten the judge. He averaged about one phone call a month for six months until someone in the city's law department set him straight: he shouldn't be in contact with Garaufis, even if it was just through his law clerk. In case Mannix didn't get the message, a team of federal marshals went out to his Long Island house two weeks later. Someone felt that Mannix was taking an undue interest in Garaufis. Authorities wanted a better look at him. When Mannix realized federal marshals were at his house on a Saturday morning to make sure he wasn't mentally unhinged, he invited them in for coffee. He knew enough from his law enforcement days to recognize when he was being profiled. After they had an amicable talk, he handed the marshals his latest letter in the *Chief-Leader* and the Merit Matters mission statement and told them to take it back to their bosses.

"If this is an attempt to intimidate me into silence it's not going to work," he told the marshals, just as a friendly heads-up.

Once again, settlement talks between the Bloomberg administration and the DOJ and CCR were floated. The city had already lost on disparate impact, but it wasn't too late to make the Vulcans' intentional discrimination lawsuit go away. A speedy resolution would also clear up the 6019 mess so candidates could get hired in a timely fashion. The city again rejected the offer.

Five months later, on January 13, 2010, Garaufis issued a sweeping, 70-page ruling on the Vulcans' charge of intentional discrimination. His lengthy decision went back through the twists and turns of all the claims in the disparate impact case, and to the earlier lawsuits of the 1970s and '80s before coming to a simple conclusion: "The court holds that New York City's use of these examinations constitutes a pattern and practice of intentional discrimination against blacks, in violation of the Fourteenth Amendment to the United States Constitution, Title VII of the Civil Rights Act of 1964, and State and City Human Rights Laws."[3] It was not a "one-time mistake or the product of benign neglect. It was part of a pattern, practice and policy of intentional discrimination against black applicants that has deep historical antecedents and uniquely disabling effects," Garaufis added, calling it a "persistent stain on the Fire Department's record."

As far as CCR knew, it was the first time in history that a court found New York City guilty of intentionally discriminating against a large group of people in the workplace. As Coombs and Washington fielded calls from reporters, word spread through the Vulcan Society. The Committed Four were excited, but it was far too early to celebrate. For one thing, the city vowed to appeal the intentional discrimination ruling, and it was still unclear what actual remedies might come out of Garaufis's decisions. The Vulcans knew from the past that winning the lawsuit didn't guarantee change. They won in 1973 and watched their short-term gains disappear by the end of the decade.

As part of Garaufis's disparate impact ruling, the city was ordered to go back and find black and Hispanic candidates who took the firefighter exams in 1999 and 2002 but were never hired—applicants like Rohan Holt, Rich Santos, Jose Ortiz and Malcolm Flythe. They'd all given up on their firefighting dreams long ago. Some of them would be pushing 40 or even older, but if they were still interested in the job and able to pass the new written exam, along with the background check and the medical and physical fitness tests, they had to be hired—with back pay and seniority, Garaufis said. He held 186 future spots for blacks and 107 for Latinos, based on the DOJ expert's analysis of how many minorities would have been hired had the tests not been discriminatory. A special master, former federal prosecutor Mary Jo White, was appointed to help the city and FDNY devise a new firefighter entrance exam, to be given sometime in 2012, that would not discriminate against minorities.

The Vulcans were willing to celebrate those achievements—and one more that gave them tremendous personal satisfaction. Their lawyers succeeded in forcing Mayor Bloomberg to sit for a deposition under oath. Bloomberg and city lawyers had strongly resisted, arguing that the mayor was far removed from the nitty-gritty of developing tests and analyzing results. He was busy running the city, the lawyers said. The court, over objections from CCR and Levy Ratner, agreed. Bloomberg was off the hook—until his own mouth got him in trouble.

Appearing at a Senate Judiciary Committee meeting in D.C. in support of Judge Sonia Sotomayor's nomination to the Supreme Court, the mayor turned uncharacteristically chatty. He said he was a fan of Judge Sotomayor in general, but he disagreed with her ruling in the New Haven firefighter case when she was on the appeals court. She had upheld the city's decision to scrap the test because the results showed disparate impact. New York had a similar lawsuit, Bloomberg said, and in his digression he delved into the Vulcans' claims.

"I've chosen to fight this," Bloomberg told the panel, adding that the tests were business-related, in his opinion at least. The answer to diversity problems was more recruitment, like the FDNY had been doing, he said. "I really do believe that that's a better way to solve the diversity problem, rather than throwing out tests and thereby penalizing those who pass the test."[4]

When the Vulcans' lawyers saw his remarks in a newspaper the next day, they went straight to Garaufis. If the mayor had the time and understanding of the case to discuss it in a Senate hearing, then he had the time and knowledge of the case to come to a deposition, they argued. The judge agreed but, as a concession to the mayor's busy schedule, limited it to a single, three-hour session.

Bloomberg made his way to the city's law department, accompanied by city and personal counsel. Inside the room, another cadre of lawyers hovered, including some from the DOJ, Richard Levy and Dana Lossia from Levy Ratner, and Darius Charney and Anjana Samant from CCR. Also waiting for him were the Committed Four: Paul Washington, John Coombs, Michael Marshall and Duery Smith.

The mayor gave genial greetings to everyone, one of the few pleasant interactions in what turned out to be three strained hours. When asked directly, Bloomberg acknowledged the dismal racial breakdown of the FDNY, but said it all stemmed from the city's prior failures with minority recruitment. When asked what experts he consulted about the tests and who he asked about any possible testing bias, he said the fire commissioner, chiefs, officers, firefighters and even probies. None of them ever said the test was discriminatory or biased, Bloomberg insisted. Besides, he added, "tests can do anything you want them to." The mayor also said he couldn't recall his prior meetings with the Vulcans, but he did recall talking to Captain Paul Washington and asking him to help with recruitment. The city did not get the cooperation it needed from Washington, the mayor said pointedly.[5]

Quizzed about the multiple efforts from the Equal Employment Practices Commission to force an adverse impact study of the FDNY, Bloomberg said he only "vaguely" knew what the agency did. He didn't remember getting a letter in 2003 from the EEPC urging him to have Fire Commissioner Scoppetta do an adverse impact study of FDNY hiring. Attorney Richard Levy, who handled the questioning, asked Bloomberg if he was ultimately responsible for enforcing the city's equal employment opportunity laws.

"My understanding is that the Mayor has the responsibility to set policies, including EEO policies, and that the agencies, to the extent possible, should adhere to those policies," the mayor responded.

"So would you agree with me that if they don't, if policies are not set that are consistent with the law . . . that the Mayor is responsible?" Levy asked. After a flurry of objections from Bloomberg's lawyer and some back and forth, the mayor said he didn't know what "responsible" meant in the context of the question.

"I can't answer that question without knowing what the word *responsibility* means," he said.

Levy tried for an answer a different way. "Do you consider yourself responsible for seeing that EEO laws and policies are followed?"

"You just asked that question," a testy Bloomberg said. "I don't know what the word *responsibility* is and I can't answer your question."

"Well, do you consider yourself responsible in any sense?" Levy asked.

"I don't know what the word *responsible* is, counsel," Bloomberg said stubbornly.

"Do you think on equal employment practices of the city the buck stops with you?" Levy pressed.

The deposition went downhill from there. At the end of three hours, with an irritated Bloomberg exiting through a side door to avoid the reporters waiting out front, the lawyers were satisfied. There was no major *gotcha* moment with the mayor, but they hadn't really expected one. However, it was clear the mayor either didn't know or wouldn't admit to how serious a situation the city found itself in. By his own admission, Bloomberg was relying on feedback from those deep inside the FDNY, and what they were telling him came from their hearts, not their heads. If the fire department wanted to bring those kinds of arguments into the courtroom, things boded well for the Vulcans.

But first, Garaufis had to address the roughly 21,000 candidates whose lives were on hold waiting for a resolution to test 6019. The original protest group that formed immediately after the test in 2007 mainly consisted of those who were so surprised by the new format that they didn't score as well as they hoped—and therefore were unlikely to get hired if the test results stood. When their attempts to get the test tossed out failed, many drifted away. The new protest group was made up of young men and women—a fair amount of them minorities—who put other career plans on hold because they scored well enough to have a shot at the FDNY. They were anxious to know their fate. Test 6019 was not part of the Vulcan lawsuit, but Judge Garaufis had an obligation to make sure the city didn't use a discriminatory exam.

In the summer of 2008, the city had hired 216 people from exam 6019. The FDNY argued that the revamped format greatly improved the test's job-relatedness, and it now actually assessed candidates for abilities used in firefighting. Plus, it had the potential to bring a considerable number of minorities into the FDNY. Shortly after Garaufis made his finding of intentional discrimination in January 2010, the fire department signaled it was taking in another 6019 academy class. If it didn't get another 300 firefighters on the job by September, its overtime costs would soar, the FDNY said. The Vulcans' lawyers had a different analysis of the results.

"Exam 6019 is no success story. It is a continuation of the discrimination that occurred with Exam 7029 and 2043," attorney Richard Levy countered.[6] He accused the city of putting out "misleading" stats about the percentage of minorities up for possible hire by lumping in a group of test takers who'd come through the Emergency Medical Services promotional track. He also noted that only 14.1 percent of all the blacks who took the test got into the top 4,000, compared to 19.7 percent of all the whites. That gave the test an adverse impact ratio of .71, which was deemed "highly statistically significant" by exam experts. "The odds of this happening randomly are much less than one in ten-thousand," Levy noted.[7]

Over a two-day hearing in July, Garaufis listened to both sides and their experts about the validity of 6019. Although the city made significant alterations to the types of questions and the test format, it still insisted on ranking its candidates by score, down to just a few decimal points of difference. It was almost impossible for any test to justify such a ranking and still be compliant with Title VII law, yet the city adamantly refused to adopt a new method.

Two things happened during the hearing that turned out to be extremely damning for the city. The first was the discovery of a new box of evidence, which had been lost or misplaced in somebody's office in DCAS. The box contained evaluation forms filled out by FDNY firefighters and officers who were asked to take exam 6019 before it was given to the candidates and assess how good a test it was. If the documents had been turned over 18 months earlier during routine discovery, they might not have made such a splash. Coming as they did, unveiled as new documents, they caused quite an impact. The evaluations showed that the FDNY firefighters and lieutenants who reviewed 6019 before it was administered all agreed that large portions of the exam were no good.

"I feel all these questions are unfair. They have nothing to do with an entry-level exam," one firefighter wrote on the test feedback form.

"No good. These questions should be used to help in a psychological profile of the applicant. They should not be used for an entrance exam," said another.

"This should not be part of the test. It is subjective. Prior firehouse knowledge needed. Members/candidates with prior firehouse or fire ground knowledge will have a great unfair advantage compared to the general public," was another comment.[8] The city's test expert, Catherine Cline, who designed 6019, told the court that out of the 12 firefighters asked to assess the questions, 10 had rated the majority of them as "Don't use." Nine of the 12 reviewers wrote negative comments on the rating sheets.

Cline was the second unlucky happening for the city at the hearing. Through her testimony, mostly on cross-examination, she conceded that she essentially ignored the feedback because she didn't think the firefighters were qualified to judge the exam. She admitted the final analysis was done the day before the test was to go to the printer, when it was too late to make changes anyway. She acknowledged that the reading level of the test was never evaluated, and the cutoff passing grade of 70 was chosen arbitrarily. Nor could she provide data showing how the test was related to actual job skills.

Vulcan lawyers Richard Levy and Dana Lossia had actually taken test 6019, and there was one question that they were both certain they answered correctly. But according to the FDNY answer book, they got it wrong. When it was Levy's turn to cross-examine Cline, he asked her this question. She answered it the same way he and Lossia had. Levy showed her the answer book. Cline stared at it, and then admitted there was a mistake in exam 6019. The answer key showed the wrong answer as the right one.

"So, on a highly competitive test where every answer counts, where one wrong question can knock a candidate 500 places down the hiring list, there's a question that thousands probably got right but didn't get credit for, and maybe somebody got wrong but was given credit for," Levy said, just to make sure to drive his point home. The Vulcans were taking a beating in the press and in the court of public opinion about special treatment, when in reality the tests were so amateurishly designed they were bad for all candidates. Levy wondered if any of the thousands of whites who'd taken the test in past decades and not gotten hired had ever realized this.

During the two-day hearing, the city conceded to Garaufis that test 6019 was guilty of disparate impact, but argued that it was at least an improvement from the prior two tests. The city insisted Garaufis allow the FDNY to go ahead with hiring from the exam, claiming that a shortage of firefighters was driving up overtime costs and putting taxpaying citizens in possible peril. Garaufis was not swayed by the city's doomsday appeals. Before any more hiring occurred, he said, the city's lawyers had to explain to him why balancing its budget was more important than devising a test that was fair to everyone.

In August 2010, candidates from 6019 packed into the Brooklyn courtroom to hear the FDNY make its case for immediate hiring from their list. This was their last and best chance. They watched intently as FDNY Assistant Commissioner Stephen Rush told Garaufis that it was too costly to wait until the city, under the supervision of Special Master Mary Jo White, was done building a new test.

"The cost of a probie firefighter is far less than paying overtime," Rush said. The city would be 1,200 firefighters down by 2012 and paying $50 million a year in overtime if the FDNY didn't have new hires. It was also a public safety issue, said FDNY Chief of Operations Robert Sweeney: "In two years, we will have a safety issue. [Firefighters] will work with additional stress, there will be sloppiness and fatigue, and it's a safety issue for the firefighters if we are 1,200 men down."

The Vulcans told Garaufis they had no opposition to the city hiring, as long as the lucky 300 were picked in a nondiscriminatory way. The city said it was open to anything but a quota.

Outside the courtroom, Mannix kept up his media drumbeat and echoed official concerns. He made appearances on TV news shows to discuss the dangers of quotas, which had been used to correct racial imbalances in fire departments in other cities—to deleterious effect, Mannix argued. "We are against quotas. You're asking me to make my job more dangerous to satisfy a social engineering experiment," said Mannix.

The law firm that represented Merit Matters was also hosting a petition on behalf of 6019. The Merit Matters website showcased a 6019 video with a litany of young candidates—many of them minorities—pleading with the unseen powers-that-be to let them join the FDNY. "Man, I studied my ass off, that's what I did," one young black man told the camera. "I studied about two hours a day . . . I went to all the press courses so when I sat down to take that test it was a no-brainer, it was relatively easy."

Watching the men and women from 6019 tell the media how badly they wanted to get on the job was a bitter pill for the Vulcans, particularly when it came to the black applicants. The Vulcans wanted them on the job too, and it was within the city's power—and had been for quite some time—to put an end to the 6019 candidates' misery. After demanding a special hearing on the need for immediate hiring, the city was given five possible remedies that would allow them to take 300 candidates off the 6019 list. Garaufis carefully crafted choices that would allow the city to hire from 6019 without discriminating and without using quotas, which both he and the city opposed. Some of the 6019 candidates even went to Vulcan Hall to meet with President John Coombs to beg him to let the class move forward. One candidate, an African American ex-marine with combat experience, feared he would be too old to take the next test when it rolled around in 2012. The FDNY allowed military vets to take the test up to age 35—an exception from the usual cutoff of 29—but even though this man was only 30, he feared he would be timed out. Coombs regretfully told the ex-soldier that it was out of his hands.

"Now you're a casualty of this war," Coombs said in his hard-edged way.

Inside the FDNY, top chiefs gathered in September for a meeting to discuss the five possible solutions offered by Garaufis that would allow the city to hire at least some of the candidates from the tainted 6019 list. The judge's options were fairly straightforward, based on the standard civil rights theory of "applicant flow," a way of tracking the percentage of minorities who got jobs, in proportion to the pool of potential candidates. Most of them were similar to the solutions already proposed by the city.

When the judge's options were floated, the answer was swift and succinct: *No*. Not only were the top chiefs unwilling to even consider the options, they refused to send back any suggestions of their own. Around the wide conference table in MetroTech, FDNY brass vowed to fight all the way to the Supreme Court. The conversation with Garaufis, such as it was, ended.

"The city respectfully believes that using raced-based quotas to select firefighters is both illegal and unwise public policy," the city's head counsel, Michael Cardozo, wrote in a letter to the judge.[9]

Vulcan lawyer Richard Levy hit back. "Since Exam 6019 does not predict job performance in any way, hiring from higher or lower scores makes no difference in terms of hiring the most qualified firefighter candidates . . . The test has nothing to do with who would be the best firefighters," he said.[10]

Garaufis was out of options for test 6019. The only choice left was to trash the hiring list and start again. Garaufis nullified 6019's results once and for all in October 2010. His decision broke the hearts of hundreds of hopeful candidates, and threw away years of successful recruiting work from the fire department and the Vulcans.

With 6019 resolved—to nobody's satisfaction—the Vulcans on September 29, 2010, filed a motion for affirmative injunctive relief and compensatory damages in light of Garaufis's finding of intentional discrimination. The Vulcans asked the court to order the city to make significant changes to its firefighter hiring practices beyond the exam, arguing that major changes were needed to remedy the effects of 40 years of discrimination against black candidates.

Most of the Vulcans' demands were not new. As they had for decades, they asked for enhanced minority recruitment efforts, a more objective and transparent background investigation, reinstatement of the FDNY cadet program, and improvements to the way the FDNY investigated and resolved complaints of racial discrimination in the workplace. The Vulcans also asked for $14 million in compensatory damages for the thousands of black victims of the discriminatory 1999 and 2002 firefighter exams.

Paul Washington teaches a tutorial in Brooklyn, 2012. Copyright © NY Daily News.

For Coombs, Marshall, Smith and Washington, the last request was totally irrelevant, but something their lawyers said they should include. All the Committed Four cared about was getting in front of a judge. After nearly a decade of struggle, the Vulcans were finally going to get to spell out all the challenges their members faced.

CHAPTER 14

FIRE ESCAPE

New York City
September 1944

BATTALION CHIEF WESLEY WILLIAMS AND PREACHER-TURNED-POLITICIAN
Adam Clayton Powell Jr. had a plan. Shortly before Williams convened his group of fledgling Vulcans for his soul-stirring September
18 speech against black beds, the two men sat down to discuss the
best way to force the fire commissioner, the mayor and the Uniformed Firefighters Association to take their complaints seriously.
Together, the three entities formed a powerful triumvirate that was
nearly impossible to overcome. Williams and Powell saw only one
solution: they had to embarrass Mayor Fiorello LaGuardia into action. The commissioner and the UFA were fairly indifferent to public opinion, and impervious to any sense of shame about the black
beds. If anything, the Vulcans' allegations against them raised the
status of the FDNY and the union in the opinion of many. But La
Guardia—for all his slavish love of firefighting—was as sensitive to
the shifting political winds of the city as any other career bureaucrat. The Vulcans needed to smoke him out.

The attack was simple: gather hard data on the number of firehouses actively trying to Jim Crow blacks into exiled beds and to
keep them out of prestigious positions; convince a black newspaper to do a survey of the FDNY for the purpose of writing about
how well—or not—it was integrating its black firefighters; and then

have the black firefighters send a petition to the mayor against black beds, which would, of course, get leaked to the press. This attention would allow a few progressive City Council members close to Powell to put a resolution on the floor banning Jim Crow practices in the FDNY—and hopefully pass it. It was an ambitious scheme, and given Tammany Hall's stranglehold on the City Council, unlikely to succeed. Tammany was weaker than it had been in Boss Tweed's day, but still powerful enough to steamroll right over the nascent efforts in black communities to gain some political leverage.

Nonetheless, Williams rolled out the blueprint for his members after he concluded his battle cry. And for those who feared reprisals in the firehouses, he reminded them they should use any means necessary to ensure their safety.

"We should not feel too critical about this ignorant and criminal Negro who is quick with the knife and gun. If it wasn't for the fact that the average white man feels that he will run into that type of Negro, he would indiscriminately go around cuffing Negroes," Williams said. He wasn't above using force himself—very sparingly—on some of his firehouse visits to aid black firefighters in trouble. Williams could usually count on his diplomacy or his rank to convince the officer in charge to agree to at least treat the black firefighters decently, but there were a few who were too stubborn or stupid to wise up. In those cases, Williams didn't hesitate to haul the offender to a corner. "Let me tell you something, when you leave this firehouse, you have somebody in the back of you, and when you come to work, you have somebody with you, because I've got some people who will do a job on you," he'd growl. That usually got his message across.

Per Williams's instructions, a committee of five Vulcan members was formed. The goal was to get a definitive list of firehouses with black members, and which of those had black beds or other forms of racial discrimination.[1] There were three firehouses the Vulcans knew they could already cross off their list: Engine 55, naturally, was not a problem. Neither were Hook & Ladder 20 and Hook & Ladder 15. The white officers at both ran tight ships with no tomfoolery. There were also several firehouses the Vulcans already knew should be on their list, with the two biggest offenders being Engine 221 at 161 South Second Street, Brooklyn, under the command of Lieutenant Otto Claus, and Engine 17 at 185 Broome Street, not far from where Williams worked.

An anonymous letter was sent to Mayor LaGuardia in August warning him that Captain Paul Rush of Engine 17 was creating conditions that might bring about the type of racial strife just experienced by the Philadelphia Transportation Company.[2] White workers at Philadelphia transit walked off the job earlier that month to protest the company's decision to let black workers hold non-menial jobs. The company had only loosened racial restraints under heavy duress from the federal government, which was concerned about significant labor shortages. But that didn't stem the white outrage when eight black employees started training on August 1 to become motormen and conductors. A paralyzing six-day sick-out ensued.

Captain Rush, the letter warned, was equally determined to keep blacks segregated and out of contention for any of the more high-profile firehouse spots, such as the rig tillerman or chauffeur. "He is setting an example which weak or prejudiced officers of other companies in the Department might decide to follow and thereby start serious inter-racial trouble," the letter cautioned.[3]

There was no movement from the mayor's office in response.

A month later, Williams also wrote LaGuardia, telling him that because of the lack of action from the FDNY and higher-ups, Captain Rush had felt emboldened to impose his orders on the lieutenant of a neighboring house. "The Captain . . . has forced the Lieutenant in charge of Hook & Ladder 18 to adopt similar 'Jim Crow' tactics in regard to the beds. The Lieutenant, when appealed to, said that he could do nothing as those were the orders of his superior officer," Williams wrote.[4] But City Hall remained silent.

By then, the Vulcans had amassed enough empirical data about Jim Crow policies and black beds that they were ready to approach the FDNY. They found 35 firehouses with at least one black member. Within those, 20 practiced startlingly similar types of discrimination, predominantly with black beds. In a few houses, there were as many as three black firefighters—yet they were never assigned to the same shifts. By rotating them, the firehouse was able to ensure they all used the bed set aside for blacks. In some firehouses with only one black member, his name would be affixed to the bed, so everyone would know it was his.[5]

By early October, the Vulcans had begun pressing Fire Commissioner Paddy Walsh, UFA president Vincent Kane and—through the NAACP—LaGuardia for a sit-down to discuss the findings.[6] Their other complaint was that no promotions were being made from the lieutenant exam because several blacks scored well and were high on the list. But appointments for ranks where no blacks had applied, like captain, were going forward. A date for the meeting was set for October 30. Predictably, LaGuardia didn't show up—nor did he offer an excuse for his absence. That left the Vulcans and the NAACP staring across the table at the fire commissioner and the UFA president.

Walsh and his second-in-command, Fire Chief John J. McCarthy, listened to the Vulcans and carefully eyed their data, but insisted that "no rights of the Negro had been violated" in any of the cases presented.[7] The officers in the respective firehouses would have been brought up on charges if a violation occurred, Walsh said, then he sniped at the Vulcans that perhaps the best solution was "to remove all the beds."[8] However, Walsh did agree to let the Vulcans conduct more in-depth interviews of black firefighters and agreed to have some FDNY chiefs hear the accounts firsthand.

Williams was displeased overall with the campaign. LaGuardia was holding himself well out of the Vulcans' reach. Taking a leaf out of his father's book, Williams widened his point of attack. He called Hubert Delany, a black judge who'd recently been appointed in Manhattan. Not long after, on November 18, he followed up on that conversation with a letter. "We (Negro Firemen), are in hopes that you will find it possible to present our side of this situation (Jim Crow beds) to his honor the Mayor," Williams wrote. "It has been impossible for our group to personally contact His Honor . . . the opposition, apparently, has done everything within its power to prevent this meeting."[9]

The success of Commissioner Walsh and UFA president Kane in preventing the Vulcans from reaching LaGuardia had—as Williams predicted—empowered the race baiters within the FDNY to even more brazen acts, he wrote Delany. Since the October 30 meeting, two more firehouses had started segregating beds. To add insult to injury, one of them, Hook & Ladder 40, was a prominent company located at 6 Hancock Place, in the heart of Harlem.

"This condition is forced down our throats right in our own community. It is my opinion that no other racial or religious group, other than Negroes, would be so complacent about such treatment. Some of our more militant members (Vulcan Society) have suggested as a last resort picketing the fire houses that practice this discrimination and are located in Negro communities," Williams wrote. LaGuardia or the fire commissioner—or better yet both—had to take a stand to halt the insidious creep of Jim Crow. "We believe there is a well-organized group in the Fire Department that is determined to challenge any move we may make to remove the indignity and humiliation of 'Jim Crow' beds. The boldness and extent of the opposition from this group will only be governed or curbed entirely by the stand taken by our superiors," Williams concluded.

Judge Delany took up the fight on behalf of the Vulcans, informing LaGuardia that a picketing campaign against segregated firehouses loomed if he didn't act. LaGuardia shuddered at the thought of more racial upheaval in Harlem. He was still recovering from the Harlem riot that exploded a year earlier after a white cop shot and wounded an African American World War II soldier. The soldier, Robert Bandy, had tried to intervene in the arrest of a black woman for disorderly conduct, and in the melee he was shot leaving the scene, allegedly after punching the cop. Rumors spread that a white police officer killed a black soldier, and chaos descended. Over two days, Harlem raged. Six people died, 600 were arrested and the streets were ripped apart by looting and destruction. LaGuardia eventually restored order with the help of 2,000 police officers. He did not want the Vulcans to do anything that would spark the tinderbox of social unrest that was kindling in black communities.

And yet, LaGuardia was still not willing to sit down with the Vulcans or the NAACP for a face-to-face on Jim Crow. To placate them, he ordered Commissioner Walsh to remove Captain R. Denahan, the commander of Hook & Ladder 40 in Harlem. The mayor told Walsh to fix the problem to prevent "an ugly situation from developing."[10] Walsh complied. He also made sure that two of his fire officers were at a meeting November 18, when the Vulcans interviewed a black firefighter named Robert Cooper from Hook & Ladder 132. Cooper answered 21 straightforward questions from the Vulcans' discrimination survey. As with all the other blacks surveyed who worked in a Jim Crow house, Cooper said he was assigned to a specific bed whenever working the overnight tour. He was never detailed to another firehouse for the midnight to 6 a.m. tour, to prevent him from needing to use a bed there, and when another black was working in his firehouse, they were rotated so as not to have to use a whites-only bed.

At a summary at the end of the page, the Vulcans wrote: "Negro firemen are always assigned to [specific rotations], which is not practiced against any other Racial or Religious group. Though protest at this unfairness was made, the Captain refused to make any changes."[11]

The two fire officers sitting in at Walsh's behest reported back to him, but nothing changed. The Vulcans waited in vain for some kind of action from any quarter, but none came. It was time to bring in the press, Williams decided. Within days, articles began appearing in black newspapers about the Jim Crow FDNY. The publicity infuriated Walsh and upset LaGuardia, but it gave three Vulcan allies in the City Council a reason to call for a committee hearing on discrimination in the FDNY.

Tammany Hall held the bulk of the 25 City Council seats, but there were some rebels in the mix. There was Benjamin Davis, a black communist from Harlem with ties to Powell, who had recently become a congressman. Then there were Peter Cacchione, a white Italian communist sympathizer from Brooklyn, and Mike Quill, an Irishman from County Kerry who'd been elected in 1937 as part of a labor ticket. Quill, a staunch unionist and future founder of the Transport Workers Union Local 100, would decades later lead a contentious transit strike against the city, defying a judge's injunction against the walkout.

"The judge can drop dead in his black robes. I don't care if I rot in jail. I will not call off the strike," Quill famously said in 1966, not long before he succumbed to long-standing heart issues himself.[12]

In 1944, a black communist, a left-leaning Italian and a pro-labor Irishman formed the Vulcan Society's best hope of getting a resolution condemning the FDNY's black beds passed by the City Council. On November 28, Davis stepped up and put forth a motion to censure the FDNY for its Jim Crow policies.[13] The City Council had no power to actually punish the department, but Davis hoped at least to draw more attention to the matter. As expected, the Tammany Hall contingent—which blocked most of the motions made by Davis as a matter of course—killed the proposal on the floor.[14] But thanks to the coverage the topic was given in the black press, and through Davis's impassioned arguments, the council did agree to hold a special hearing to investigate the Vulcans' discrimination claims. The Tammany faction allowed it because they were sure none of the black firefighters would actually show up, out of fear of losing their jobs.[15]

On December 7, Battalion Chief Williams led a group of 40 black firefighters into City Hall for the special investigatory hearing on FDNY discrimination. The Vulcans were greeted by an unexpected sight: crafty Tammany Hall had summoned the fire commissioner himself to testify about the abundance of equality within the FDNY. He would speak first. Walsh brought a phalanx of FDNY chiefs with him, all prepared to echo his assertions. The surprise arrival of so many grim-faced officers stirred the infamous hornet's nest now known as Room 9—the City Hall press office. Hearing there was going to be a big show, reporters packed the chambers and even "hung from the rafters," according to Councilman Davis.[16]

"Chief Williams, you should be over here," one of the top officers snapped as the Vulcans filed into the tension-filled chamber and took seats across from the FDNY bosses.

"No, I am a Colored man. I belong over here," Williams answered. And with that, the show began. The Tammany council members gave a benign quiz to Walsh and his officers about daily firehouse practices. The commissioner and his second-in-command, McCarthy, set the tone, testifying that they'd never seen or heard evidence of discrimination. Councilman Davis was shouted down and censured by his Tammany colleagues whenever he tried to interject. But he got some surprisingly strong backing from Manhattan councilman Stanley Isaacs, a Republican. Isaacs's grandfather was a powerful rabbi and his father the publisher of the *Jewish Messenger,* the first English-language Jewish newspaper in the United States. Isaacs himself was a strong backer of social justice issues, and no fan of Tammany Hall.

When the FDNY chiefs had gotten their say, it was the Vulcans' turn. Williams took the lead. "It is needless for us to state, we believe, that you are fully aware of the tremendous courage it

Wesley Williams, promoted to captain in the FDNY, the only black officer in the department, assigned to Engine 55 at 363 Broome Street, June 1, 1934. Photo Credit: NY Daily News.

has taken, for us a minority group (approximately 80 colored firemen out of 7,000), to continue this fight until it has been brought to your attention. . . . We also believe, that the taxpayers of New York City, who are our employers, are not interested in the personal prejudices of an isolated city worker here or there," Williams began, after giving the council his thanks for holding the hearing.

"In my 25 years of service . . . never has an individual who may have been trapped in a building because of a fire, refused the help of my arms to aid him to escape just because I happen to be of a different color . . . every person who I aided remarked how their panic immediately vanished and that they confidently and calmly followed my instructions once I touched them. . . . As I recall it, all of them heartily thanked me after I had performed my duty," he said.

But the rest of a black firefighter's life was far from colorblind, especially in the firehouses, Williams noted. He detailed the results of the Vulcan Society's survey of firehouse Jim Crow practices. He brought up seven Vulcan members who worked in companies around the city. Each man described sleeping in the "Negro bed." Firefighter Herman Reed told the council that his commanding officer even made him bring in his own set of dishes for meals. When they finished, Chief Williams was asked if he'd seen any improvements in how blacks were treated over the course of his 25-year career. Williams replied that when he'd been a probie, his commanding officer tried to make him sleep in the cellar.

"He thought I would be more comfortable down there, but we didn't agree on that point so I was given a bed by the toilet," he told the room.

Councilman Davis, describing the highly charged scene later in his memoirs, praised the Vulcans' composure during the difficult hearing. "The Negro firemen, a militant and intelligent group, showed up with bells on. They were solid as a rock, and they burned with the kind of fire—the fire of the struggle for justice and dignity—that couldn't be put out. They jeopardized their jobs, their seniority and their tenure rather than be intimidated. They made a powerful and impressive appearance—surprising the Tammany majority on the committee," he wrote.[17]

When the Vulcans were finished, Councilman Quill fixed a forbidding glare on the row of FDNY officers and demanded their word that none of the blacks would face reprisals. Davis and Isaacs also jumped in, finally managing to put a question directly to Walsh, who, along with Kane, sat in stony silence as the Vulcans presented the results of their survey.

Asked by Davis if he thought assigning black beds was discriminatory, Walsh said, "No," and added that it was outside his jurisdiction. The firemen and officers should "iron it out themselves," he said. He blamed premature publicity in the black papers for causing the City Council hearing, which he said would only muddle up the department's own internal way of handling things. "It's up to the captains and the men in the companies," he insisted again. But Davis and Isaacs, working in tandem, got a grudging capitulation from him on the issue of punishment. If proper charges were brought against a captain about a black bed, he would do something about it, Walsh pledged.

In the immediate aftermath of the hearing, next to nothing was altered for the Vulcans. The council ultimately refused to push through Davis's resolution condemning discrimination in the FDNY, which put the black firefighters right back where they started. But the hearing—which was gleefully covered by the black press—also made the *New York Times*. That alone was enough to signal that some change was afoot. The old guard in the FDNY could no longer assume Mayor LaGuardia would continue to overlook the Vulcans' discrimination claims—not when mainstream newspapers started devoting ink to the topic. Also, Davis and Isaacs succeeded in extracting a second promise from Walsh: the fire commissioner agreed to meet with the Vulcans within the month to hear the final results of their Jim Crow investigation.

But Walsh had no intention of letting the Vulcans browbeat him into making a statement or taking any kind of a stand against the black beds. Nor was he going to agree to any policy that took the power of decision away from firehouse captains. Since LaGuardia could no longer be counted on, Walsh turned to union leader Kane.

The UFA head and the fire commissioner didn't often act in concert, but on this topic they shared the same views and desires. The two hatched a plot to stymie the Vulcans before December 21, the date Walsh had committed to meeting with them. Walsh and McCarthy secretly pulled Kane and his union cronies aside and urged them to have their members pass a new resolution that would permit the firefighters in each house to assign beds and shift rotations following a majority-rules vote.[18] Once the UFA membership voted in favor of the resolution, it would be presented at headquarters to Walsh. The fire commissioner would approve it and incorporate it into official FDNY procedure. That would end any discussion of race when assigning beds—and shut the Vulcans down. The UFA was more than willing to play along. It hastily convened its monthly union meeting for December 20—the night before the Vulcans were to see Walsh. There was only one crimp in the commissioner's plan that he hadn't foreseen: Wesley Williams already knew all about it.

On December 20, UFA president Kane called to order the sparse group that turned out for the hurried union meeting. Kane was prepared to drone on about innocuous matters until all but the most die-hard unionists remained. Then, one of his allies would propose the black bed resolution that Walsh wanted, and with little fanfare or fuss it would be voted through. Just as Kane lifted his head and cleared his throat to call the meeting to order, a commotion was heard outside the door. He watched, mouth agape, as a large group of white and black firefighters walked in. He had no idea how they heard about the semi-clandestine gathering, but they were union members. He couldn't prevent them from attending. Kane did a hasty head count. There were a lot of latecomers, but he could wait them out. Some of them would leave as the night wore on, and then he would make his move.

Outside, Williams was chuckling as he imagined Kane's reaction to the men streaming into what the union had intended to be a below-the-radar gathering. The union had no idea that the Vulcans had long ago embedded one of their own members into the group's upper echelon. Hidden in plain sight, the Vulcan was so light-skinned he easily passed as white, and nobody but Williams and his most trusted confidantes actually knew his identity. He was the Vulcans' most powerful weapon, a race man through and through. He fed them every piece of information and gossip that passed through that union. The Vulcans got wind of Walsh's scheme as soon as he cooked it up. And then they devised a way to turn it to their advantage.

Williams turned to one of his firefighting allies, a Jewish man who was part of the Ner Tamid fraternal group. Williams told the man's aide that he learned the UFA was plotting to enact some Jim Crow policies against the Jewish firefighters too. There wouldn't just be black beds in firehouses anymore, Williams warned. It wasn't true, but Williams told the fib with conviction. He urged the aide to take the secret to the officers at Ner Tamid, and tell them to contact him. It didn't take long to get the officers at both fraternal organizations together.

"Here's what we're gonna do," Williams said. "We get every one of our members who are part of the UFA to go to that meeting.

They are gonna show up, and they're gonna stay there all night if they have to. And when enough of the white guys leave so that we have the majority, we're gonna pass through our own resolution." The Jewish officers nodded. They and Williams also reached out to some white firefighters they knew could be trusted to help.

Inside the meeting, Kane was sweating. It had grown late, and many members were gone—save for the Jewish and black firefighters. His man was standing by, waiting to introduce the black bed resolution to the floor, but it was clear now that Kane wouldn't be able to get it approved. He didn't have the numbers to defeat the blacks and Jews if they voted together—and he saw that they would. It was time to end the meeting.

Before he could draw it to a close, a black firefighter stood up. He had a proposal for the floor, he said. It had been written by Vulcan Lindsay White, and it called on the UFA to denounce "any religious or racial discrimination in the department in any form."[19] It was essentially a reiteration of FDNY regulation 222, the one that prohibited inciting racial hatred. But getting the union to pass it meant it would enter the UFA's own bylaws. Then firefighters who backed discrimination in the firehouse would be breaking union *and* FDNY rules. The outnumbered Kane was powerless to stop the vote, and before he knew it, the resolution was rammed through by Williams's coalition.

When Chief Williams and the Vulcans traveled to FDNY headquarters the next day, they asked Commissioner Walsh again to enforce FDNY regulation 222 and outlaw black beds. The commissioner's eyebrows shot sky-high when he was informed by a smiling Williams that the UFA approved a similar measure in a near-unanimous vote the night before.

A stunned and crestfallen Walsh promised to do all in his power to combat discrimination. Not long after, the FDNY issued a department order warning firefighters that anyone who violated Section 222 would face official charges.[20]

While that wasn't the end of all the Vulcans' Jim Crow battles, the victory over the UFA and Commissioner Walsh signaled the death knell of the most overt forms of discrimination practiced against the black firefighters. The Vulcan Society Williams founded would grow and expand into a powerful progressive force in the city during the civil rights era, and the Chief, as he was called, was asked to consult on diversity issues in New York as well as in fire departments across the country. He retired in 1952 after 33 years on the job, but he remained a constant presence at FDNY headquarters, a diplomatic but determined advocate for improved treatment and equal opportunity for black firefighters.

In 1963, at an annual dinner held by the Vulcan Society for its members, Williams recounted for a younger generation of black firefighters how he'd stood outside the union hall that December night in 1944, waiting to hear Kane's reaction when the black and Jewish firefighters passed the proposal that Williams dubbed "The Freedom Resolution."

"I never saw so many Negro and Jewish firemen in my life," Williams chortled to the group, describing the excitement as the men poured out after the meeting.

Kane exited a defeated man, and, spotting Williams, approached him. "Wes, you beat me," the union leader said. "But tell me, will you, how did you know?"

Williams laughed, and promised the labor leader that he would clue him in someday.

It was one of the most fulfilling moments in Williams's career. But there was one other that was better still. It involved the Lieutenants' Association that snubbed him when he first became an officer in 1927. Williams never forgot the group's narrow-minded determination to slight him.

When the chance came, more than 15 years later, to form a new union for officers, Williams quietly threw his weight behind it. Some of the members of the Lieutenants' Association, fighting to keep their organization alive, visited him to ask for his help. This upstart new group, the Uniformed Fire Officers Association, would be their ruin, they cried to Williams. They needed him to back them up.

"You are 15 years too late," Williams responded. "And if you had been on the ball at all you would know that I was one of the first chief officers to help found the UFOA, and my main purpose was to destroy the old officers' associations. Fifteen years ago you needlessly insulted my race, and this is my revenge."

Reliving that moment again in 1963, Williams looked at the young black firefighters surrounding him and smiled.

"And believe me, it was sweet," he said.

CHAPTER 15

TRIAL BY FIRE

Brooklyn Federal Court,
The Honorable Judge Nicholas Garaufis Presiding
August 1, 2011

THE FIRST WITNESS TO TAKE THE STAND, SHORTLY AFTER 10 A.M. ON A humid August Monday inside the marble Brooklyn courthouse at Cadman Plaza, was the FDNY's director of the candidate investigation unit, Dean Tow. As he sat in the witness seat, he found himself facing a room full of reporters, firefighters, curious onlookers and more lawyers than most people see in a lifetime. The city law department sent Pat Miller, one of its toughest, most experienced litigators to handle the bench trial, and she brought a team with her. The plaintiffs had a trio of lawyers at their table: Dana Lossia and Richard Levy from Levy Ratner, plus Darius Charney from the Center for Constitutional Rights. Vulcans John Coombs, Michael Marshall and Duery Smith were also front and center. Behind them all sat a row of lawyers from the Department of Justice. They had no stake in this part of the case, having refused to get involved in the Vulcans' intentional discrimination claim. But they came to watch the proceedings nonetheless.

Levy started things off by giving Judge Garaufis a rapid précis of the points his team planned to attack over the next few days, starting with Tow and the alleged bias within the background checks used by the FDNY. Tow had been with the department since 1999, so he'd handled backgrounds on candidates for both test 7029 and 2043—and actually 6019 as well. Levy started out with some basic questions about what would disqualify a candidate right away: being too young or too old, not having a valid driver's license, getting a dishonorable discharge from the military or having a felony conviction. Any one of those things would halt the process immediately, Tow said. The only exception for a felony would be if a candidate got a certificate of good conduct through the state parole office. That candidate might get sent to the Personnel Review Board (PRB) to get a second look, Tow said. An applicant with a clean record was considered a certified candidate, and Tow's office would send out a packet of forms to fill out. The packet would include a date for the candidate to show up at FDNY headquarters for the next step in the intake process.

"And if the candidate didn't show up?" Levy asked.

"Our current process is if we get no response, the person doesn't show or the packet comes back as undeliverable, we then take a list of those people and we turn them over to our recruiting unit and they attempt to make further contact with the candidate to say, 'Please contact the CID and reschedule your interview,'" Tow testified.[1]

"Prior to that, and I think it was prior testimony of yours, at a deposition, you said that if you did not get a response, that was the end of the matter and the person was recorded as not reporting. Is that right?" Levy asked.

"Yes," Tow said. Asked if he was aware that black candidates proportionally didn't respond in larger numbers than whites, Tow said no.

"Why was there no follow up then?" Levy asked, about exams 7029 and 2043.

"We only receive from the Department of Citywide Administrative Services . . . the candidate's name and address and so on. When we mailed a packet to them, if in fact they didn't respond or didn't contact us and say, my address has changed for whatever reason, there was—because we don't go to the field, all my investigators work strictly from our office—there was no further information to check and verify and then reach out again," Tow explained.

Under further questioning from Levy, Tow said the process was the same for all candidates on the list, from the top to those grouped lower down. Generally, for every three applicants vetted, one got on the job. The investigators routinely called in about 1,000 applicants when they wanted to fill 300 spots, Tow said.

"Is it also the case that not infrequently people who are being called, particularly lower down on the list, may have actually taken the exam and filed their address at the time three or four or sometimes even five years before you send out your packet?" Levy asked. When Tow answered affirmatively, he repeated his earlier question. "Presumably these people have gone on to other jobs and other work and on with their lives. Why was no effort made to reach these folks knowing that such a long time may have elapsed?"

"If we had additional information, we could certainly reach out to them with that. But if we didn't have any additional information, there was nothing new to go on in terms of finding them," Tow said.

"But was any effort made to find additional information that you are aware of?"

"No," Tow said.

Levy went on to talk Tow through the investigation process, which included applicants bringing in filled-out forms on the specified date, paying $75 for fingerprinting, submitting employment history for independent verification and turning over any arrest records. As part of their character assessment, the candidates were allowed to write a brief description in their own words explaining any criminal record they might have. A criminal record might include an arrest that had not resulted in a conviction, Tow admitted. The packets then went to the PRB—composed of high-ranking FDNY officers and personnel—with a note from Tow called a consideration report. It either recommended the candidate be hired or that the person be passed over. Tow only wrote consideration reports for applicants with criminal histories, poor employer references, sometimes for a bad school record or a poor driving history. It was a subjective assessment, based on Tow seeing something in the candidate he "thought the department should be aware of." Candidates with clean records didn't get a consideration report sent to the PRB. Only those viewed as potentially problematic did. Tow would know the result of the PRB's vote when he got a report back to either hire the candidate or move to the next one on the list. He was never given a reason for the PRB's decision, he said, and rarely saw the vote breakdown among its members. Nobody knew how members got appointed to the PRB, Tow added. Its inner workings were largely opaque, with no written guidelines or procedures to follow. It kept no minutes of its meetings or records of its decisions. As far as anyone in the FDNY knew, its decisions were made on a case-by-case basis.

"A number of issues may have gone to the PRB. The letter you get back doesn't indicate on what basis they decided ultimately to reject an applicant?" Levy asked.

"That's correct," Tow replied.

"Does the applicant ever find out on what basis he or she was rejected by the PRB?" Levy followed up.

"No."

"Is that made available to any other agency of the department that you're aware of?"

"No."

"Is it made available to the Equal Employment unit in the Fire Department?" Levy asked.

"No."

"If someone is turned down by the PRB, the letter says what? Is there a form letter you could describe for us?" Levy said.

"We've used the considered/not selected designation which is part of the many choices an agency can avail themselves to use with regard to selecting or not selecting a candidate. So, they would get a letter from my office once we had passed the appointment date that would say you've been considered but not selected," Tow said.

His testimony wore on, with Judge Garaufis listening closely and even interjecting with his own questions when he needed something clarified. Then Levy handed a document to Tow and asked him to read it out loud, substituting "U1" for the candidate's name:

The candidate's file is before the review board because of his arrest record. On August 14th, 1993, U1 was arrested for unlawful possession of marijuana and having an altered license. He stated he was driving with a friend in the Hamptons and was pulled over by police. His friend had some marijuana and they were subsequently arrested. He pled guilty to disorderly conduct and paid a fine totaling $295. He was 19 years old. On August 12th, 2002, while going through a separation with his wife, U1 was arrested for criminal contempt violating an order of protection and menacing in the second degree. He stated he had returned to his apartment where his wife was still living and requested his clothes. An argument followed and he was arrested and charged. He pled guilty to harassment, second degree physical contact. He received a conditional discharge for one year and another order of protection was imposed. He was 29 years old. Although I am troubled by his arrest in 2002, there have been no further incidents since that arrest. Hopefully, he and his ex-wife worked out their differences. I recommend his appointment.

Levy called his attention to the candidate's attached arrest record: criminal contempt with a weapon, and harassment with physical contact. Under questioning, Tow admitted his investigators had not tried to find out what type of weapon was involved in the charge.

"Could you read the description of this individual?" Levy asked.

"The description says sex: male. Race: white. Ethnicity is blank. Skin tone is light. Eye color, blue. Hair color, blond. Height, 5-10. Weight, 152," Tow read.

Levy handed him a second document, another recommendation from Tow to the PRB board, and asked him to read it, substituting "U2" for the candidate's name this time.

"The candidate's file is before the review board due to his arrest record. On April 9th, 2000, U2 was involved in a verbal argument with his wife that escalated into a pushing match. Her father called the police and U2 was subsequently arrested and charged with assault in the third degree. The case was later returned in contemplation of dismissal. Although U2 was not convicted of this charge, incidents of domestic violence raise concerns of his ability to manage his temper and/or emotions. I do not recommend his appointment," Tow read.

"Can you tell the court why U2's domestic issue rose to the level of a non-appointment or recommendation of non-appointment while U1's, which apparently involved a weapon and a plea with physical contact merited a recommendation for appointment?" Levy asked.

Tow explained that the two reports had been more than a year apart.

"I did not have both these cases before me at the same time," he said.

Levy asked him to read the description of candidate U2.

"Sex: male. Race: unknown. Ethnicity: Hispanic. Skin tone: medium. Eye color: brown. Hair color: black. Height: 5-7. Weight: 165," Tow read.

Levy had one more document for him, this time for candidate "U3." He asked Tow again to read it into the record.

"In 1999, U3, acting as a police officer, was one of the officers involved in the shooting of Amadou Diallo in the Bronx while searching for a rape suspect. He was charged with murder in the second degree. He was acquitted of all charges in a jury trial. I recommend his appointment to the department," Tow intoned.

"When you consider arrests, do you consider the seriousness of charges?" Levy asked.

"Yes."

"I note that in the case of U2, one of your comments was your concern about his ability to manage his temper and/or emotions. Did you have any concerns about U3 who had shot an unarmed civilian, that perhaps his judgment, though not criminal, may have been faulty to the point where it would not be wise to hire him as a firefighter?" Levy pressed him.

"No," said Tow.

"Do you happen to know if U3 is white? Do you remember this case?"

"Yes, I do. Yes, he was white," Tow said.

Levy then introduced another document, prepared by Tow's predecessor but ultimately implemented by Tow's team of investigators. It involved a black candidate arrested twice on drug charges. Once in 1995, at 20 years old, and again in 1996 at 22 years old. Both times the charges were dismissed, Levy noted. He asked Tow to read the final recommendation.

"I gave [the candidate] the opportunity to clarify the above incidents during an interview. I didn't feel the candidate was being totally honest and forthright with his answers and had selective amnesia on occasion. I do not recommend his appointment," Tow read.

The Vulcans' lawyers would have liked to hold up more examples of the subjective nature of the background investigation, but it had taken Darius Charney hours and hours of hunting just to find these records. Anecdotally, there was ample evidence of double standards—the Vulcans had handled plenty of examples over the years. But finding written records was next to impossible because the PRB wrote almost nothing down. It had no human resource guidelines, no best practices to follow, not even a record of what was discussed in its meetings. Charney counted himself lucky to find what he did.

But Levy wasn't done with the PRB just yet. There was still the question of deposition testimony from Sherry Ann Kavaler, the FDNY's assistant commissioner for personnel in 2004. She'd been the one to write to DCAS before exam 2043 to ask who was going to validate the firefighter exam because questions were raised about its fairness. She had been Tow's boss in the background investigation unit until retiring in 2004, and she sat on the secretive PRB. In 2008, as part of the Vulcans' discrimination lawsuit, Kavaler was deposed by the group's counsel. What she said at the time astounded them. Levy saw no need to haul the retired woman back to the city to testify in the bench trial, not when he could put her deposition straight into the record. He asked Garaufis to start reading with him on a question that asked if PRB members recused themselves if a candidate up for review was someone they knew.

Kavaler said in her deposition that it would be a "positive thing" if someone on the PRB knew a candidate up for review because it would "bring insight into what was just on paper."

When Levy asked if that happened often, she said at almost every meeting there was a candidate who was known to someone on the PRB. Not so much a relative of someone on the PRB, she said, in response to a query from Levy, but likely a "relative of someone in the Fire Department that the PRB people knew." Asked if those candidates were given special consideration, Kavaler answered, "Yes," and added they would be more likely to be given a pass. Even though the PRB's doings were supposed to be confidential, Kavaler admitted, those with friends and family in high places always got tipped to which candidates were up for review—and did as much as they could to sway the results in the applicant's favor.

"Somehow or other, although I am very upset with my staff, it appears people knew who was going to PRB. It got leaked out of my [background investigation] area. No one would ever tell me who did or why," Kavaler said in her deposition.

> People knew what was going on and who was going to the PRB. You would have Lieutenants and Captains, whatever, Chief of Department, this is the son of so and so. This is the son of so and so. I lived next door to him for years. He's a good guy. He just had a fight in a disco. He got drunk. Someone made a pass at his girlfriend. He socked him. He did community service, something like that, whatever it was. He beat his wife but his wife took him back so he shouldn't be considered a wife beater. He still could be a good firefighter. These types of things would be brought to the table and people would say 'I know this guy. He's a good guy. His son has got to come on the job. I will vouch for him. I will bring him into my office tomorrow. I'll read him the riot act, say he's getting the chance of a lifetime and he better own up to it and make us proud.' And we would hire him.

Levy read the next question in the deposition to Judge Garaufis. He asked Kavaler if the PRB followed a checklist or guidelines while interviewing candidates.

"No, it wasn't a checklist or anything like that. You're dealing with a lot of Irishmen who are drunks and they get into bar fights and they get arrested and they get arrested again. They fight, they sock their girlfriends. [These are] the things that cause their records to pop up to us because they get arrested, because they fought with the police when they got arrested. This is boys being boys, that type of thing," Kavaler said.

The bench trial went on for nine days in total. Pat Miller, the city's attorney, did her best to point out that the Vulcans also used the friends-and-family network as often as possible, frequently calling FDNY deputy commissioner Doug White, an African American who sat on the PRB. They would ask him to intervene for black candidates, too, the city noted. And Kavaler, in her deposition, stated that nobody ever made race a factor in PRB decisions. City lawyer

Pat Miller's aggressive style at times put her at odds with Judge Garaufis. When Lanaird Granger was called to testify about the firehouse noose incident, the judge halted proceedings because Miller was objecting to answers before Granger finished speaking. A testy Judge Garaufis ordered her to stop harassing the witness and called a ten-minute break. Coombs also got his chance to talk about the FDNY's past recruitment efforts, which CCR said went from terrible to poor. Marshall took the stand to talk about the standards needed for the job, and Sheldon Wright put in an appearance to talk about the early efforts to build the Fire Cadet program. Paul Washington didn't speak until the very end of the trial to talk about his early days as a young firefighter in mostly white firehouses.

Paul Mannix and Merit Matters went on the attack as soon as the trial ended. Mannix wrote a lengthy letter to the *Chief-Leader* and accused Granger of perjuring himself under oath by fudging details about the noose.

Merit Matters was also outraged by Judge Garaufis's disparate impact decision, which said any black or Latino firefighter who scored as low as a 25 on the 1999 or 2002 firefighter entrance exams could reapply to take the tests again—the so-called second-chance hires. The standard set was dangerously low and would imperil the safety of firefighters and citizens, Mannix insisted.

On October 4, 2011, Judge Garaufis issued a searing decision that accused Mayor Michael Bloomberg of knowingly turning a blind eye to the racial disparities within the FDNY. "The evidence adduced in this case gives the court little hope that Mayor Michael R. Bloomberg or any of his senior leadership has any intention of stepping up to the task of ending discrimination at the FDNY," Judge Garaufis wrote. "Instead of facing hard facts and asking hard questions about the city's abysmal track record of hiring black and Hispanic firefighters, the Bloomberg administration dug in and fought back."

Garaufis berated the city for "blame-shifting" and "accountability-avoidance," writing that the administration "still doesn't get it." To avoid a repeat of more than a century of intransigence, a federal court monitor would be appointed to oversee a top-to-bottom overhaul of the FDNY's recruitment, testing, vetting and retaining of minority candidates, Garaufis wrote. The court monitor would be in place for ten years, he ruled.

"It is the court's view that nearly 40 years of discrimination will not be cured by a few simple tweaks to the city's policies and practices," Garaufis noted. But the blame didn't just fall on Bloomberg. "That this discrimination has been allowed to persist in New York City for so long is a shameful blight on the records of the six mayors of this city who failed to take responsibility for doing what was necessary to end it," he said.

Bloomberg did not take the verbal lashing with good grace.

"The judge was not elected to run the city, and you can rest assured that we'll be in court for a long time," the mayor said. The city filed an appeal on December 8, 2011, challenging Garaufis's decision to find the city liable for intentional discrimination.

Over at Vulcan Hall, the Committed Four cared not one iota about Bloomberg's appeal. The intentional discrimination ruling called for a federal monitor and special oversight of the FDNY—which were all good things, in their opinion. But it was the disparate impact ruling they really valued. That decision was not challenged by the city. Judge Garaufis's mandate that nearly 300 second-chance candidates could try again to get hired—plus the overhaul to the city's written exams—would stay in place. Change was going to come, regardless of the city's appeal of the intentional discrimination ruling.

The city was already advertising for exam 2000, to be given in early 2012. Unlike the three prior FDNY tests, this one was designed by an outside expert and with oversight from former U.S. attorney Mary Jo White, who made sure all the proper procedures were followed. As an added plus, exam 2000 required that a candidate actually live in the five boroughs for a year before taking the exam to qualify for the five bonus points. It was a long-awaited win for the Vulcans, who labored for years to get the residency credit tightened up. This effort came about after multiple meetings with City Council member Leroy Comrie and the Black, Latino and Asian Caucus. But it wasn't until Mayor Bloomberg and Commissioner Salvatore Cassano decided they wanted a one-time age exception for 6019 candidates that the Vulcans' chances improved. The fact that the FDNY wanted something opened the door for some behind-the-scenes aid from Council Speaker Christine Quinn. In the end, it came down to the usual political horse trading. The Vulcans got their stricter residency credit and the

City Council agreed to lift the age limit—just for exam 2000—to 35 so interested 6019 test takers could try again. Quinn and Comrie helped broker the deal. The trade only solidified Washington's cynical suspicion that the FDNY could find its way around any city rule when it was so inclined. It also didn't escape the Vulcans' notice that the city had traditionally insisted the residency credit was to give city dwellers city jobs—not necessarily to increase minority numbers. Only when the Vulcans filed an intentional discrimination lawsuit did the city claim the five points as evidence it tried to help black applicants all along.

"I feel bad for those kids, I really do," Washington said to Marshall about the 6019 furor. "But black kids have been getting knocked out for decades because of these tests and nobody cared. When white kids are affected, it's a big issue."

Giving the burned candidates from test 6019 a second chance to join the FDNY—much like the blacks and Latinos who'd been turned away a decade earlier—didn't appease Merit Matters, or other Vulcan detractors. Shortly after a federal monitor was finally selected by the judge, articles started popping up in daily tabloids about the excessive cost.

Federal monitor Mark Cohen's first bill of $310,758 for 53 days of work in March 2012 caused "howls of protest from the city," according to the *New York Post*.[2] Likewise, the Vulcans' tutorial classes in April and March 2012 caused headlines when white applicants, no doubt egged on by Merit Matters, decided to crash them. A week after the Vulcans had their blowout at a tutorial class in Jamaica, Queens, Judge Garaufis announced that the city would have to pay up to $128 million to the thousands of blacks and Latinos who were either not hired or got hired years later than they should have been because of discriminatory exams. The Vulcans also couldn't help but feel cynical about that too. Ten years of trying to get the city to settle for peanuts, and in the end the Bloomberg administration cost the taxpayers millions.

The rancor between Merit Matters and the Vulcans only increased as spring turned into summer. Mannix's vocal opposition rose to a fever pitch in July, when Judge Garaufis announced he would hold a fairness hearing. It would be for firefighters, applicants and others who wanted to object to his decision to compensate black and Latino firefighters. Mannix went into overdrive, sending out notices encouraging as many firefighters as possible to attend and lodge their objections. "I'm not very hopeful when it comes to Nick Garaufis, but they are providing this opportunity, and maybe somebody will pay attention. Maybe if enough people come out, they'll think, 'There's something going on there that we should look into,'" Mannix said in the *Chief*.[3]

He didn't hide his deep distaste for the part of Garaufis's ruling that gave as many as 293 black and Hispanic candidates a second chance to join the Bravest. They would be priority hires—meaning first on the job—if they met all the minimum hiring requirements and passed the upcoming written and physical exams.

"It's gonna affect the whole job. It really causes a lot of resentment. You're going to get seniority, you're going to get back pay, and just because I'm white or Asian or Native American, I don't get it? When you weren't out there putting your life on the line on the rig? How are you not going to resent that?" Mannix said.[4] He called Garaufis an "ideologue" and questioned how the entrance exams could be discriminatory when they were created by DCAS, an agency he claimed was staffed mostly by people of color.

Washington had his answer ready. If Garaufis was going to invite Merit Matters and others to share their opinions in Brooklyn court, the Vulcans would be there too.

"There's literally thousands of white firefighters on the job today who cheated to get the five residency points. Everybody knows it. Where's the stigma attached to them? Where's the resentment? That's white privilege, and it's out-and-out fraud. But black New Yorkers who've already been discriminated against on this job for 150 years—they gotta get ready to be resented," Washington said.[5]

The face-off came October 1, 2012, at a rally outside Judge Garaufis's Brooklyn courthouse. The judge invited firefighters to share their opinions about his ruling, but despite Mannix's intense beating of the bushes, only about 36 of the 180 opposing firefighters scheduled to speak that day actually showed up. Garaufis cleared four days of his calendar for the testimony, but the so-called fairness hearing was adjourned at 11 a.m. after all the speakers had their two minutes. Of the 770 who registered initially, only about 150 testified in total.

"Seniority was earned in the dead of night when these benefactors were home sleeping," railed one firefighter, speaking of the priority hires who were being given a second chance.[6]

"I am concerned about the future of the department. Standards must remain high," said a chief, second only to Mannix in rank.[7]

"I feel I'm being discriminated against because I'm Caucasian," said a firefighter. As Garaufis listened to the litany of concerns and complaints in his courtroom, a mass of about 100 white firefighters stood outside on one side of Cadman Plaza while a group of about 50 Vulcans stood on the other.

The Committed Four were in the group, along with Damon Alston, who almost didn't get on in 1999, and Regina Wilson, then the president of the United Women Firefighters Association. But it fell to Coombs, as the Vulcans' president, to give the sound bite of the day.

"Whether they're angry or not, we could care less," he said dismissively.

The dueling press conferences marked the zenith of Merit Matters' influence in the FDNY. A month later, the top brass finally took a swipe at the 150-year tradition of looking out for family and friends with a new directive that forbid employees from contacting the PRB, or from communicating with the board at all about its hiring decisions.

A week later Mark Cohen, the court-appointed FDNY watchdog, took the department's highest officers to task for failing to halt the dissemination of Merit Matters material to firehouses around the city from an FDNY headquarters fax machine. Cohen found that a fax machine at FDNY's MetroTech headquarters was used to send 11 press releases copied from the Merit Matters website, which was replete with Mannix's controversial writings.

"Future minority hires who are . . . 'incapable' of earning the position through the testing process . . . will not be able to perform the requirements of the job" compared to "firefighters who 'earned' the position through the testing process," said one.[8]

The FDNY said it found no evidence the faxes were widespread or that Mannix sent them out. Cohen faulted its probe by noting that the agency "did not conduct any interviews (with) Mannix (nor) any individual in the fire houses" that got one of the missives.[9]

Vulcan Society members (from left to right) Captain Paul Washington, retired firefighter Ella McNair, retired firefighter James Tempro, retired firefighter Duery Smith, (behind him) lawyers Darius Charney of CCR and Richard Levy of Levy Ratner, firefighter John Coombs (in bowtie), Lieutenant Michael Marshall and others face off with members of Merit Matters outside the federal court in Brooklyn. Members of Merit Matters were there to testify against remedies proposed by Judge Nicholas Garaufis in the landmark civil rights lawsuit brought by the Vulcans against the city and the FDNY, October 1, 2012. Photo credit: Michel Friang.

The city had, however, tried to block Cohen's involvement in the fax probe.

Garaufis had just about lost patience with the backward, re-calcitrant ways of some FDNY officials and some of its firefight-ers. In November 2012, he brushed aside his numerous critics and issued a final order granting back pay, priority hiring and retro-active seniority to affected blacks and Latinos. He said he found the emotional, angry responses of some firefighters "disturbing," and worried they would make life difficult for incoming minorities. "Unfortunately, the overwhelming majority of the objectors used the process to . . . malign the court for daring to interfere with the culture of the FDNY," he wrote. His rulings were "necessary to remedy the city's past discrimination . . . it is not a punishment to firefighters, nor is it a statement about the value of firefighters in society." He was particularly concerned by the anger exhibited by some FDNY officers. He quoted an FDNY lieutenant who testified that the priority hires "do not belong, and more importantly they do not deserve what they have not earned," and another officer who stated, "in my opinion, anyone who failed test 7029 and 2043 is a moron and their becoming a New York City firefighter by judicious decree is a joke."[10]

Such comments and the firefighters' outrage at being forced to let go of some of their cherished traditions was precisely the problem Title VII was enacted to address, Garaufis responded.

EPILOGUE

OUT OF THE ASHES

TEN YEARS AGO, WHEN THE VULCANS' LEGAL BATTLE AGAINST THE CITY and the FDNY first started to take shape, I had just started covering City Hall for the *Chief-Leader* newspaper. The *Chief,* a well-respected broadsheet, is dedicated to chronicling and analyzing the endless push and pull between City Hall, the various unions that represent city workers and the internal politics within the labor movement.

My editor Richard Steier sent me to a Vulcan Society press conference, and I wrote three names in my notebook: Paul Washington, Michael Marshall and Duery Smith. They are the Vulcans I met that day. It was the first I had ever heard of the Vulcan Society. I had no knowledge of their prior lawsuit against the city in the 1970s; I knew nothing about the history of similar racial strife in fire departments across the country and within the labor movement in general. Having grown up in rural New England, I was only just beginning to wrap my head around New York City's ponderous civil service system, which to me seemed almost charmingly anachronistic, a leftover memento from another age.

But I was thrilled to be reporting on a real New York story, especially one connected to the fire department. Of all the city agencies, it was the most famous, and one of the most exciting. Its members were also represented by two of the most raucous and outspoken unions in the five boroughs. I hadn't been at the *Chief* long, but I'd seen enough to know that covering the Uniformed Firefighters Association and the Uniformed Fire Officers Association was going to be highly entertaining and rewarding.

When it came time to take questions from reporters at the end of the Vulcans' press conference, I asked why they felt they would end up in court.

The Vulcans' answer surprised me. They were trying to settle, they said. The city didn't want to.

"Why not?" I asked. Michael Bloomberg had been in office a few years by then. He was not to everyone's taste, but he'd made a name for himself as a pragmatic, numbers-driven leader whose decisions were based on financial imperatives and fiscal realities. Even with my superficial understanding of the Vulcans' allegations, I could look at the fire department and see it had a problem. It was 93 percent white in one of the country's most diverse cities.

"Ask the mayor," the Vulcans replied.

So I did. And ten years later, I still have no clear answer. But I did learn that the FDNY's so-called diversity problem was far from unique among public safety agencies—nor was the department's fervent distaste for trying to figure out the root cause. As a nation, we like to think we are light-years away from the Jim Crow era that influenced the early careers of trailblazing public servants like Wesley Williams. Many—but not all—are eager to declare that we live in a postracial world. For them, the policies meant to correct the sins of the past—affirmative action, for example—are no longer necessary and even unfair in light of the level playing field many think we have achieved. There's far less interest in examining where America has stumbled in advancing its 1960s civil rights agenda, and what those failures have meant in terms of actual jobs, housing opportunities and education for people of color. It often takes extreme action, like a federal discrimination lawsuit, to force the problems to the surface.

A few months after Judge Nicholas Garaufis's momentous intentional discrimination finding in October 2011, the Bloomberg administration started its appeal. Lawyers filed papers claiming Garaufis had erred in granting a summary judgment in favor of intentional discrimination without holding an actual trial. The city asked an appeals panel to kick Garaufis's summary ruling back down to the lower court—and they wanted a different judge

appointed to hear it. Garaufis exhibited bias in favor of the plaintiffs, city lawyers claimed.

The Second Circuit Court of Appeals heard oral arguments
from both sides—the Vulcans and the city—on June 26, 2012.
The Lower Manhattan courtroom was packed. Among the crowd
were many Vulcans, but also many firefighters sporting shirts
from Merit Matters and also from MADD, Minorities Against
Dumbing Down. The MADD motto was written across the back
of the dark blue shirts in bright script: "Getting it the old-fashioned way—earning it." The atmosphere was tense. Because the
city chose not to appeal Garaufis's ruling on disparate impact, a
lot of the judge's reforms were already moving forward, and the
changes were making a lot of the rank and file very unhappy.
Emotions were at an all-time high when the Second Circuit held
its one-day hearing.

Predictably, when the answer came from the appeals panel in
May 2013, nobody was pleased. The judges agreed with the city's
argument that Garaufis overstepped by making a summary finding on the intentional discrimination. It also ordered that a new
judge oversee any future proceedings, should the Vulcans wish to
go ahead with a trial. But in an unusual move, the appeals panel
kept in place the bulk of Garaufis's corrective measures; conse-
quently, the federal oversight of FDNY hiring practices stayed in
place, over the city's objections. The city was under the yoke of
court-appointed monitors for the foreseeable future.

As it turned out, the Vulcans did want a trial on the intentional
discrimination claim, and the city was determined to beat them.
Both sides were aggressively gearing up for a courtroom showdown
in the last few months of the Bloomberg administration. Center for
Constitutional Rights lawyers let it be known they were prepared
to call Bloomberg, Nicholas Scoppetta, then–fire commissioner Salvatore Cassano and others to the stand. The city was busy prepping
Scoppetta and others on testimony. But then newly elected mayor
Bill de Blasio stepped into office, and within his first three months
at City Hall, he settled the Vulcans' lawsuit. It definitely saved the
taxpayers a lot of money, but there was a keen sense of loss among
some of the players on both sides of the argument. Each had been
eager to set the record straight—but as always, each had a different
idea of what it should reflect.

The FDNY, just like other public safety agencies around the country, had always deeply resented any implication that its uneven hiring patterns were part of a deliberate policy. In New York City, as in many large cities, a significant portion of fire and 911 calls originate within communities of color. Public safety agents over the course of their careers help or aid scores of minority victims, and risk their own lives in the process. That's part of the reason many cops and firefighters—and in particular the FDNY—reject so adamantly the possibility that their beloved traditions might be built on a foundation that was constructed with an intrinsic bias.

The civil service system that is the cornerstone of many public safety jobs was, by and large, developed across the country more than 100 years ago. When it was first implemented, race relations in the United States were markedly different than they are today. But what many cities have failed to do—New York City among

Left to right: Captain Paul Washington, former Vulcan Society president; Lieutenant Michael Marshall (behind); firefighter and Vulcan president John Coombs (in bowtie); firefighter Rusebell Wilson (behind); lawyers Richard Levy, Darius Charney and Dana Lossia at a press conference to discuss the settlement reached with New York City under Mayor Bill de Blasio. The city, which was taken to court over allegations of institutional bias against minority FDNY applicants, agreed to broad injunctive relief and back pay, March 18, 2014. Photo credit: James Keivom/NY Daily News.

them—is stay in front on new standards of testing. As in many other places, that resistance to change was packaged as a profound and intimate bond to the traditions of public service. There has been little institutional will to really wade into the topic of why some public safety departments are staffed mostly by white workers, even when protecting mainly communities of color. There's also little appetite for discussing why diversity matters, either from the point of view of improving community relations or from improving the community itself by allowing them equal access to sought-after, high-visibility and well-paying jobs.

In 2012, the FDNY finally devised a firefighter hiring exam that did not disproportionately weed out black and Latino candidates. Forty-two percent of the blacks and Hispanics who took it scored a 97 or higher, a big improvement over top-scoring minorities who took the 1999 exam (14 percent), the 2002 exam (16 percent) and the 2007 exam (34 percent). In July 2013, the first group of firefighters hired from exam 2000 started at the FDNY Fire Academy. In December 2013, the class graduated as the most racially diverse group in the history of the FDNY. Of the 242 firefighters, 24 percent were black, 36 percent Hispanic.[1] There were 76 so-called priority hires in the group, those who took the test in either 1999 or 2002 but didn't get called up for the job. Despite the numerous claims of detractors, the priority hires appointed by Garaufis's ruling have not brought havoc to the department or imperiled the public. In fact, one priority hire, Jordan Sullivan, was the subject of a lengthy *New York Times* article when he made a once-in-a-lifetime rescue in the spring of 2014. On his first real fire run, which came 96 days after he got on the job, Sullivan pulled a five-month-old baby boy out of a fifth-floor inferno in a Park Slope apartment building. Since 2013, the FDNY hired approximately 1,600 people; roughly 20 percent were black. After doing everything in their power to quash the Vulcans' activism and efforts, Mayor Bloomberg and then–fire commissioner Sal Cassano in their final months in office brazenly claimed the credit for the FDNY's increased diversity.

The Vulcans also underwent some changes in the final days of their historic legal battle. Lieutenant Michael Marshall was appointed the FDNY diversity officer. The position itself was mandated by the courts as part of the lawsuit terms, and Marshall

Regina Wilson marches in the African American Day Parade, September 2014. Copyright © Michel Friang.

was everybody's choice. The diversity officer is now a permanent position, to be filled every two years by a candidate selected by the Vulcan Society, the Hispanic Society and the United Women Firefighters.

Firefighter John Coombs was term-limited out of the Vulcan Society presidency at the end of 2014. His replacement, running unopposed, was Regina Wilson, the first female president in the Vulcans' 75-year history.

Captain Paul Washington, while eligible for retirement, still works at his Crown Heights, Brooklyn firehouse. He remains active in the Vulcans' efforts to increase black gains in the FDNY and continues to work on the other factors he feels were critical to the Vulcans' success beyond the lawsuit: political leverage and media outreach. In the two years before this book's publication, he dedicated much of his time training black and Hispanic priority hires for the FDNY physical and written exams. He continues to challenge the FDNY to address the deep-seated issues that have a negative effect on black hiring and is pushing for a Fire Cadet program to increase diversity. Since the Vulcans' federal lawsuit was filed nearly a decade ago, Washington has been disciplined by the FDNY numerous times for infractions that usually don't merit official attention. Washington, who famously likened Mayor Bloomberg's attitude about the FDNY to Alabama governor George Wallace's—"segregation now, segregation tomorrow, segregation forever"—says he is nonetheless thrilled and deeply satisfied to see more black recruits joining the city's Bravest, even as much more remains to be done.

Duery Smith and Kirk Coy, both retired Vulcans, continue to volunteer with the organization and promote the department as a whole.

As of press time, Paul Mannix remains president of Merit Matters although the organization is not as active as in the past. Some of the white applicants who appeared at Vulcan tutoring sessions in 2012 filed complaints with the city's Human Rights Commission, alleging their civil rights were violated because they didn't get in. Merit Matters lawyers represented them, but the claims were denied. The Human Rights Commission cited the complainants' own "discriminatory animus" toward the Vulcans that night in their decision. Over the course of the Vulcan tutorials in 2012, more than 3,000 blacks and a few hundred whites received specialized instruction through their study sessions.

Wesley Williams, aka the Chief, was forced to retire from the FDNY after more than 30 years following an injury. His goodbye dinner was a gala affair, covered widely in the black and mainstream press and attended by FDNY brass, community leaders and city and state elected officials. He continued to be a vocal advocate for blacks in the FDNY and was consulted by departments in other cities that were trying to integrate or increase black participation. During the civil rights era, when high-pressure fire hoses were turned on peaceful protestors marching in Alabama, Williams and the Vulcan Society, spearheaded by member Vincent Julius, pushed the city's labor unions—including the UFA and UFOA—to publicly denounce the city of Birmingham for its actions. Williams died on July 3, 1984, at 86 years old. A section of 135th Street in Harlem was renamed Wesley Williams Way in his honor, near a section also named for his contemporary in the NYPD, Sam Battle. There is a bust of Williams on display at the Harlem Y, where he continued his regimen of daily workouts well into his 80s. His entire collection of photographs and pictures is on display at the nearby Schomburg Center.

AUTHOR'S NOTE AND ACKNOWLEDGMENTS

WRITING THIS BOOK WAS AN EXTREME CHALLENGE FOR ME FOR A VARIETY of reasons, and there were many times I despaired of finding a way through. I struggled to determine the most linear way to lay out a complicated and confusing timeline that spanned 150 years (and could have gone even longer had I wanted it to). At the same time, I was trying to untangle the modern elements of the federal discrimination lawsuit. The juiciest bits were reported in the newspapers, but I was determined to present something meatier. Then there was the multitude of viewpoints to be considered. Over more than a decade of interviewing and reporting on the FDNY and talking with all kinds of firefighters for all kinds of stories, I knew it would be impossible to reduce this nuanced issue to a simple good-guys-vs.-bad-guys narrative. The truth was so much more compelling anyway—but my difficulty lay in translating it all to the page. I decided that my salvation would be my characters. If I could make the men and women who served in the FDNY come alive, and place their stories in the context of the city as it was when they worked in it, I hoped readers would overlook some of the chronological bumps in the road.

This led to hours of interviews with active-duty and retired firefighters, City Hall staffers past and present, current and former employees of the FDNY and leaders of many of the city's unions and law enforcement associations. Among the firefighters, the majority of my interviews were with Vulcan Society members, although I also spoke to some black Bravest who chose not to join the fraternal organization. I am deeply indebted to all those who spoke to me again and again and also reread portions of their stories to help me try to get every fact right.

I did not have that luxury as I tried to reconstruct the long-ago lives and careers of Wesley Williams and the black firefighters who came before him, William Nicholson and John Woodson. But in that I was aided by several people and institutions.

Wesley Williams was thankfully born in the age of written correspondence. He left behind an incredible trove of letters, speeches, news clippings and other private papers. His family wisely donated them to the Schomburg Center for Research in Black Culture in Harlem, part of the New York Public Library system. I spent weeks poring over them, pulling out the people, places and moments that had created his life and shaped his career. Luckily, Williams left behind several speeches that he delivered, and so I was able to cull his exact words from them. His grandson, Charles Williams, also aided things by setting down all his personal recollections of Williams in a self-published book, aptly titled *The Chief*. He generously gave me a copy to help me flesh out my understanding of the trailblazing firefighter. He also gave me permission to reuse the family photos on display in the Schomburg.

One of the most amazing discoveries came in the form of a recorded interview with Wesley Williams, done many decades ago by retired FDNY captain and Vulcan member John Ruffins. The unofficial historian of the Vulcan Society, Ruffins shared many of his documents and mementos with me over two days of lengthy interviews at his Queens home. Sadly, Ruffins died February 18, 2015, as this book went to press. Ruffins had written up many of his own findings about blacks in the FDNY and published it as part of a thesis for his master's degree. His early efforts at recording black struggles in the FDNY were invaluable and he was a tireless mentor and advocate for disaffected youth in the city. His thesis contained the excerpts of Woodson's letter to Williams. It also contained the entire passage of firefighter Walter Thomas's early recordings of life in the FDNY around the time of the black beds. Ruffins's thesis was an invaluable source of information, but the gem of his collection was a fragile cassette tape. It was labeled May 7, 1976—the date of his distant interview with Wesley Williams. Ruffins had paraphrased the bulk of it into his thesis, but I wanted to hear Williams's voice for myself. I wanted to hear the exact words he used when he described his first day at Engine 55, and his descriptions of other events. With the help of a sound engineer, I was able to extract Williams's interview and put it on a CD. From that, I was able to reconstruct some of the major events described in this book.

Once I was armed with partial names, dates and descriptions of fires, I turned to the City Hall Municipal Archives and compared the information provided by Williams in 1976 to old FDNY records. Most of the names he mentioned showed up on the department roster at Engine 55, just as he said. The dates of major conflagrations and other background details also matched his memories. The New York Public Library's research division also performed miracles by searching census records, employment records and old newspaper archives. Between all these sources, the big pieces of Williams's life—buttressed by his own words and letters—fell into place.

The only remaining challenge for me in building Williams's world was to fill in the context of black life in New York City in the 1900s and into the 1940s. There were many historical texts to lean on for the former, but I wasn't up to speed on the black political landscape of the 1940s during the black bed days. For that, I am greatly indebted to the work of historian David A. Goldberg, specifically his doctoral dissertation, *Courage Under Fire: African American Firefighters and the Struggle for Racial Equality.* Goldberg tapped many of the same original sources as I did in his thesis, but he also unearthed crucial new details about the involvement of the NAACP, the unions and the roles of early black political power brokers Charles Anderson and George Wibecan in Brooklyn. For the background on the FDNY and the role of Boss Tweed, I am greatly indebted to Terry Golway's moving and intimate look at the history of the FDNY, *So Others Might Live.* I also interviewed author Edward P. Kohn, who generously filled me in on the creation of the civil service, and I used his excellent book, *Heir to the Empire City: New York and the Making of Theodore Roosevelt,* to further my knowledge of Roosevelt's role in New York City. Thomas Kessner's *Fiorello H. La Guardia and the Making of Modern New York* was also a vital text that I relied on. I thank Robert Polner of the NYU press office for directing me toward both those sources.

Quite a few of the people I interviewed for this book requested anonymity because of ongoing work with either the FDNY or the city. Therefore, I can't name them here but they have my heartfelt thanks for sharing their insights and knowledge. My thanks also go to all the firefighters—men and women—who talked to me. The biggest contribution came from the Vulcan Society, and in particular Captain Paul Washington and his family, who gave me hours of their time and attention. I also relied heavily on Lieutenant Michael Marshall, John Coombs, Regina Wilson, John Ruffins, Sheldon Wright, Duery Smith, Kirk Coy and Charles Williams, who is not technically a Vulcan but is part of its legacy.

Despite repeated requests, former mayor Michael Bloomberg declined to be interviewed for this book, as did several high-ranking FDNY officials. However, several others lent invaluable assistance, including former commissioner Nicholas Scoppetta, former commissioner Tom Von Essen, former deputy commissioner Lynn Tierney and the FDNY press office. Without the help of Scoppetta, Von Essen and Tierney in particular, many of the gaps I had in my information would never have been filled. A special thank you must go to Tom Butler of Tom Butler Associates and to the head of the Uniformed Firefighters Association, Steve Cassidy, who gave me a lengthy interview and fact-checked several pieces of information for me. Former City Council speaker Christine Quinn shared her memories and insights, for which I am grateful. The leaders of Merit Matters and Paul Mannix went out of their way to help me find information, and I thank them too. Fantastic anecdotes and feedback were also provided by Electra Yourke of the EEOC and Charles Billups from the Grand Council of Guardians.

Of course, none of this would have been possible at all without the early support of literary agent Faith Childs, who guided my idea into fruition. I leaned heavily on her experience and wisdom throughout this process, and was never disappointed. Faith brought me to an amazing editor, Elisabeth Dyssegaard, who gave structure, focus and—what I needed most—encouragement and excitement to my scattered project. My earliest efforts were awkward, to say the least, and I'm very grateful to Elisabeth for her skill in pushing me forward without sinking my spirit. Her production team was also aces; Donna Cherry guided me through all the steps and copy editor Bill Warhop greatly improved my text with his thoughtful, careful read. A special shout-out must go to Levy Ratner lawyer Dana Lossia, who fact-checked all my legal descriptions and helped me make deadline, even though she had—just days before—given birth to her second child. Darius Charney and Shayana Kadidal from the Center for Constitutional Rights and Richard Levy from Levy Ratner also gave me interviews and shared insights. Lawyer Mike Skelly, FDNY historian Gary Urbanwiecz, Harlem historian Erik Washington, Brenda Berkman, Guy Cephas of the Smokestack Hardy Museum, Seth Bookey, D. DeRubbio and Semra Coskuntuna are all among the people who contributed in ways great and small toward this book. My writer friends Rebecca Morris and Eileen Sutton were my biggest cheerleaders and champions; author Susannah Cahalan graciously shared agent tips, proposal ideas and general advice; my buddy Angela Rubin guided me toward the best resources the NYPL has to offer; Paul McPolin brought his laser editing to shine up final drafts, as did Richie Steier; my dear friends Reuven and Sarah Blau provided emotional and material support in myriad ways that helped more than I can say; and my friends Michel Friang, Debbie Egan-Chin and Mariela Lombard generously donated their photography skills. My thanks also to the *NY Daily News* for generously lending me archival pictures, to managing editor Rob Moore for his support, to Bill Hutchinson for working my shifts while I was on book leave, to all my colleagues and editors for their help, and a big thank you to Ioana, Leti, Adamma, Laurencita and all my friends who asked about my project, listened, encouraged and showed me you care. And last but not least, thanks to my family—Michael H., Joy, Dave, Michael O., Trevor and everyone else—for enduring three months of writing-deadline hell. I owe you all one summer vacation!

NOTES

CHAPTER 1: INTO THE FLAMES

1. Bureau of Labor Statistics, Consumer Expenditure Survey, and U.S. Census Bureau, Statistical Abstract of the United States, 1918–1919.

CHAPTER 2: UN–CIVIL SERVICE

1. American FactFinder, United States Census Bureau. New York City Profile of General Demographic Characteristics.
2. *The Newest New Yorkers: Characteristics of the City's Foreign-born Population,* Population Division of the New York City Department of City Planning, 2013. Also, see U.S. Census Bureau data.
3. Jarrett Murphy, "The Whitest City Agencies," *City Limits,* May 2010, http://citylimits.org/2010/05/27/the-whitest-city-agencies.
4. Gilbert Osofsky, *Harlem: The Making of a Ghetto* (New York: Harper-Collins, 1963), 52.
5. Ibid., 55.
6. Ibid., 67.
7. Terry Golway, *So Others Might Live* (New York: Basic Books, 2002), 35.
8. Ibid., 35.
9. Ibid.
10. Ibid., 70.
11. Ibid.
12. David A. Goldberg, *Courage under Fire: African American Firefighters and the Struggle for Racial Equality* (Amherst: University of Massachusetts, 2006), 25.
13. Golway, *So Others Might Live,* 73
14. Ibid., 69.
15. Ibid., 76.
16. Leslie Harris, *In the Shadow of Slavery: African Americans in New York City, 1626–1863* (Chicago: University of Chicago Press, 2003), 279.
17. Noel Ignatiev, *How the Irish Became White* (New York: Routledge Classics, 1995), 9.
18. Ibid., 9.

19. Golway, *So Others Might Live,* 113.
20. Ibid., 113–14.
21. Harris, *In the Shadow of Slavery,* 284.
22. Golway, *So Others Might Live,* 120.
23. Ibid.
24. Ibid., 125.
25. Edward Kohn, *Heir to the Empire City* (New York: Basic Books, 2014), 131.
26. Ibid., 8.
27. Golway, *So Others Might Live,* 139.
28. Ibid., 141.
29. Ibid., 142.
30. Goldberg, *Courage under Fire,* 32.
31. Ibid.
32. Kohn, *Heir to the Empire City,* 151.
33. Golway, *So Others Might Live,* 144.

CHAPTER 3: WE SHALL OVERCOME

1. C. J. Sullivan, "Fanning Racial Fires," *New York Post,* March 1, 2012.
2. Lou Young, "White Applicants Blast FDNY After Being Denied Entry To Preparation Class," CBS Local 2, New York, March 1, 2012.
3. Marcia Chambers, "2 Ex-Firefighters Await Job Ruling," *New York Times,* October 23, 1983.

CHAPTER 4: NEW BEGINNINGS

1. *United States, et al. v City of New York*, No. 1:07-cv-02067, Lexis doc. 345 (U.S. Eastern District of New York).
2. Ibid.
3. Nicholas Katsarelas, "Nationwide Study Shows Urban Poor Becoming More Concentrated," Associated Press, February 15, 1987.
4. David Pitt, "Jogger's Attackers Terrorized at Least 9 in 2 Hours," *New York Times,* April 22, 1989.

CHAPTER 6: GET OUT OF THE KITCHEN

1. Illinois Fire Service Institute, firefighter record on David Kenyon, Capt. of Engine Co. 21 in Chicago, death and service record, http://www.fsi.illinois.edu.
2. David A. Goldberg, *Courage under Fire: African American Firefighters and the Struggle for Racial Equality* (Amherst: University of Massachusetts, 2006), 26.
3. Ibid., 43.
4. Victor Collymore, "Series: Negro Firefighter," *New York Amsterdam News,* June 26, 1976.
5. Ibid.
6. Goldberg, *Courage under Fire,* 45.
7. Ibid.
8. Ibid.

9.   "Doings of the Race," *The Gazette* (Cleveland, Ohio), October 24, 1914.
10. "New York Notes: Colored Fireman Commended," *The Bee* (Washington, D.C.), July 14, 1917.
11. Ibid., 47.
12. Wesley Williams Collection, 1919-1984, Series: Negro Firefighter, Box 3, Correspondence, Archives: Schomburg Center, NYPL.
13. Ibid.

CHAPTER 7: THE CAN MAN

1.   *United States, et al. v City of New York,* No. 1:07-cv-02067, Lexis doc. 345 (U.S. Eastern District of New York).
2.   Ibid.
3.   Ibid., 345-2, pg. 19.
4.   Ibid., 345-2, pg. 20.
5.   Ibid. 345-2, pg. 22.
6.   Ibid., 345-2, pg. 24.
7.   Ibid., 345-2, pg. 24.
8.   Committee Files, LaGuardia and Wagner Archives, City University of New York, Box 050046, Series 3, Misc., April–May 1995.
9.   David Chen, "Officers and Firemen Wore Blackface on Float, Officials Say," *New York Times*, September 11, 1998.

CHAPTER 8: BLOWBACK

1.   *United States, et al. v City of New York,* No. 1:07-cv-02067, Lexis doc. 345 (U.S. Eastern District of New York).
2.   Ibid., 125.
3.   Michael White, "The New York City Police Department, Its Crime-Control Strategies and Organizational Changes, 1970–2009," *Justice Quarterly* vol. 31, no. 1 (2014): 74–95.
4.   Robert F. Moore, "FDNY Test Woes: Low Scores for Blacks Sparks Ire," *NY Daily News,* December 25, 2005.
5.   Dave Saltonstall, "Bravest Hard on Minorities; More Candidates Rejected On Character, Health Issues," *NY Daily News,* September 26, 1999.
6.   Thomas Von Essen, "New York City Fire Department Testimony," City Council Committee on Fire and Criminal Justice Services, September 28, 1999.
7.   Frank Lombardi, "Rudy: Job Breaks OK for Kin of FDNY Brass," *NY Daily News,* November 17, 2000.
8.   *United States, et al. v City of New York,* Lexis doc. 125-12, pg. 31.
9.   Ibid., pg. 36.
10. Ibid., pg. 10.
11. Ibid.
12. Frankie Edozien, "Furor over FDNY Plan to Hire Diallo Cop," *NY Post,* April 15, 2001.
13. Ibid.
14. *United States, et al. v City of New York,* Lexis doc. 345-1, pg. 4.

CHAPTER 9: AMID THE EMBERS

1. Michelle McPhee, "Petition: Stop Fire Statue: FDNY Faction Says Design Alters Sept. 11 History," *NY Daily News,* January 15, 2002.
2. *United States, et al. v City of New York,* No. 1:07-cv-02067, Lexis doc. 345-2 (U.S. Eastern District of New York), pg. 80.
3. Ibid., pg. 82.

CHAPTER 10: FIGHTING THE FIRE WITHIN

1. "Fireman Wins Promotion to Lieutenancy: Rated Among Best on Fire Force," *The Chicago Defender,* September 24, 1927.
2. "Wesley Williams, 'Smoke Easter,' Marks First Year as Fire Company Lieutenant; Only Negro Officer Directs White Company in Protecting Foreign Downtown District," *New York Amsterdam News,* September 26, 1928.
3. David A. Goldberg, *Courage under Fire: African American Firefighters and the Struggle for Racial Equality* (Amherst, NH: University of Massachusetts, 2006), 65.
4. "Only Four Negro Firefighters in New York," *New York Amsterdam News,* January 3, 1934.
5. Thomas Kessner, *Fiorello LaGuardia and the Making of Modern New York* (New York: McGraw-Hill, 1989), 237.
6. Goldberg, *Courage under Fire,* 69.
7. Ibid., 70.
8. Ibid.
9. Ibid., 70–72.
10. John Ruffins' Urban Studies thesis on black FDNY firefighters, unpublished, 35.
11. Ibid.
12. Ibid.
13. Goldberg, *Courage under Fire,* 72.
14. Wesley Williams Collection, 1919–1984, Series: Negro Firefighter, Box: 3, Correspondence, Archives: Schomburg Center, NYPL.
15. Ruffins, Urban Studies thesis.
16. Goldberg, *Courage under Fire,* 86.
17. Letter from Wesley Williams to Al "Smokestack" Hardy, October 28, 1941, provided to the author by Hardy's heirs.
18. Goldberg, *Courage under Fire,* 90.
19. Ibid., 92.
20. Ibid., 93.
21. Wesley Williams Collection, Schomburg Center, NYPL.

CHAPTER 11: FDNY AFLAME

1. *United States, et al. v City of New York,* No. 1:07-cv-02067, Lexis doc. 125 (U.S. Eastern District of New York).
2. Jennifer Fermino, "Scene of the Grime," *New York Post,* February 26, 2005.
3. Murray Weiss, "FDNY Vet in Bribe Rap," *New York Post,* September 1, 2005.

4. Kareem Fahim, "Fire Dept. Defends Policy on Hiring," *New York Times,* September 2, 2005.
5. Frank Lombardi, "Minority Project Doused; FDNY Boss Takes Heat for Refusing It," *NY Daily News,* June 2, 2005.

CHAPTER 12: BURNED

1. Jimmy Vielkind, "FDNY Exam Has 'em Fuming," *NY Daily News,* March 25, 2007.
2. Ibid.
3. *United States, et al. v City of New York,* No. 1:07-cv-02067, Lexis Plaintiff Exhibit I (U.S. Eastern District of New York).
4. 6019 test results, FDNY, Office of Recruitment.
5. Department of Justice press release, "Justice Department Sues New York City for Discriminating Against Black and Hispanic Firefighter Applicants," May 21, 2007, http://www.justice.gov/archive/opa/pr/2007/May/07_crt_375.html.
6. Michael Saul and Jonathan Lemire, "Mike Fumes as Feds Sue FDNY on Bias," *NY Daily News,* May 22, 2007.
7. Paul Mannix, Letter to the Editor, "FDNY Noose Mystery," *Chief-Leader,* April 7, 2006.
8. Ibid.
9. Paul Mannix, Letter to the Editor, "About the Klan Hood," *Chief-Leader,* August 4, 2006.

CHAPTER 13: UP IN SMOKE

1. U.S. Department of Justice Press Release, "*United States v. City of New York* FDNY Employment Discrimination Case," Liability-Phase Rulings, July 22, 2009, http://www.justice.gov/crt/spec_topics/fdny/overview.php.
2. *United States, et al. v City of New York,* no. 1:07-cv-02067, Lexis doc. 125 (U.S. Eastern District of New York).
3. Ibid., Lexis doc. 385.
4. David W. Chen, "Bloomberg Must Testify on Lawsuit in Bias Case," *New York Times,* August 5, 2009.
5. *United States, et al. v City of New York,* Lexis Bloomberg Deposition.
6. Ibid.
7. Ibid.
8. Ibid., Lexis doc. 505.
9. John Marzulli, "City Rejects Judge's Plan for New FDNY Hires; Charges Proposals Enforce Racial Quotas," *NY Daily News,* September 17, 2010.
10. Center for Constitutional Rights press release, "FDNY Refuses to Hire New Firefighters," CCR, September 17, 2010, http://www.ccrjustice.org/newsroom/press-releases/fdny-refuses-hire-new-firefighters.

CHAPTER 14: FIRE ESCAPE

1. David A. Goldberg, *Courage under Fire: African American Firefighters and the Struggle for Racial Equality* (Amherst, NH: University of Massachusetts, 2006), 95.

2. Ibid.
3. Wesley Williams Collection, 1919–1984, Series: Negro Firefighter, Box 3, Correspondence, Archives: Schomburg Center, NYPL.
4. Ibid.
5. Goldberg, *Courage under Fire,* 95.
6. Ibid.
7. Ibid., 55.
8. Ibid., 96.
9. Wesley Williams Collection, Box 2.
10. Goldberg, *Courage under Fire,* 97.
11. Wesley Williams Collection, Box 3.
12. Vivian Heller, *The City Beneath Us* (New York: NY Transit Museum, 2004).
13. Goldberg, *Courage under Fire,* 99.
14. Ibid.
15. Ibid.
16. Ibid., 100.
17. Ibid.
18. Ibid., 101.
19. Ibid., 102.
20. Ibid., 103.

CHAPTER 15: TRIAL BY FIRE

1. *United States, et al. v City of New York,* No. 1:07-cv-02067, Lexis doc. 70-3 (U.S. Eastern District of New York).
2. David Seifman, "City Rages at FDNY Bias Bill," *New York Post,* March 28, 2012.
3. Sarah Dorsey, "Fire-Test Judge's Order: Score 25, Get Back Pay," *Chief-Leader,* July 31, 2012.
4. Ibid.
5. Ibid.
6. John Marzulli, "White Firefighters Rally at Brooklyn Federal Court Over FDNY Hiring," *NY Daily News,* Oct. 21, 2012.
7. Ibid.
8. John Marzulli, "FDNY Too Lax In Fax Race Probe," *NY Daily News,* September 18, 2012.
9. Ibid.
10. *United States, et al. v City of New York,* Lexis doc. 1011.

EPILOGUE: OUT OF THE ASHES

1. Michael Schwirtz, "Minority-Dominated Class Graduates from New York Fire Academy," *New York Times,* December 5, 2013.

INDEX